CakePHP 2 Application Cookbook

Over 60 useful recipes for rapid application development with the CakePHP framework

Jorge González

James Watts

[PACKT] open source *
PUBLISHING   community experience distilled

BIRMINGHAM - MUMBAI

CakePHP 2 Application Cookbook

First published: August 2014

Production reference: 1040814

Published by Packt Publishing Ltd.
Livery Place
35 Livery Street
Birmingham B3 2PB, UK.

ISBN 978-1-78216-008-3

www.packtpub.com

Cover image by Larry Masters, taken at CakeFest, the annual CakePHP conference

Credits

Authors
Jorge González
James Watts

Reviewer
Lubomír Štork

Acquisition Editor
Owen Roberts

Content Development Editors
Joanne Fitzpatrick
Owen Roberts

Technical Editors
Tanvi Bhatt
Faisal Siddiqui

Copy Editors
Roshni Banerjee
Sayanee Mukherjee
Karuna Narayanan

Project Coordinator
Danuta Jones

Proofreaders
Simran Bhogal
Sandra Hopper
Amy Johnson

Indexer
Priya Subramani

Production Coordinator
Nitesh Thakur

Cover Work
Nitesh Thakur

Foreword

It's been almost 10 years now since I first worked on what would be known as CakePHP, one of the most popular PHP frameworks available today. Over the years, I've been involved and have also seen through other developers how it's evolved and advanced with contributions from the amazing community that's grown up around the project. I'm so proud of all the work that has gone into the framework; this work has helped make it such a powerful contender when it comes to choosing an open source solution.

As the latest version of the framework, 2.5 represents the best of CakePHP to date, and truly reflects the goals we had right from the very beginning: to make building web applications simpler, faster, and require less code. I believe we've done a lot to keep this promise in making CakePHP a framework that really is an "out-of-the-box" solution, while also maintaining a strong backward compatibility, which allows developers to keep using it without worrying about us totally abandoning legacy or significantly changing the code base they know best and love.

We've also been very serious about maintaining a migration path so that our community can move between versions of the framework, providing not only a clear outline of the new features and updates expected between versions, but also a migration shell, which handles most of the work for you. This has always been a trademark of CakePHP that I've been consistent in supporting, as it sends a clear message to our community that we have no intentions of leaving anyone behind and think about them every step of the way.

There's no doubt that the community drive behind CakePHP is what makes it such a popular option in the PHP framework's space, and it has been the principal factor in determining its success. If you're looking to build a great web application in record time that supports industry standards and common integrations through thousands of plugins, while also being backed by extensive documentation and a thorough API reference as well as a huge community for support and discussion, then look no further than CakePHP.

This book will help you jump right in and get a clear idea of how the framework can solve those typical issues you'll encounter when building an application. It provides a great head-first dive into CakePHP and will advance your knowledge of the framework by approaching the problems that will likely matter most early on.

Larry Masters
Founder of CakePHP

About the Authors

Jorge González has a degree in Computer Science and Engineering as well as extensive experience in different positions from development to consulting and management, allowing him to quickly understand problems and provide effective solutions. He started using CakePHP many years ago and has never looked back since, applying the framework to several projects and domains, specifically, the hospitality and tourism sector, where he has worked for over 8 years before joining the Cake Development Corporation (CakeDC). He also runs the official CakePHP standard training course for the Cake Software Foundation and the basic workshop at CakeFest since 2013.

This book is dedicated to the girls in my life: my mother, Ana, and my wife, Kathrin. Thank you for your endless love and support.

I'd also like to thank Larry Masters and José Lorenzo for giving me the opportunity to start working in CakeDC, the best team and the best people I've ever met.

James Watts is an experienced enterprise PHP architect, with a long track record in open source development. He is a core member of CakePHP and also handles community efforts, such as organizing CakeFest, the annual conference dedicated to the framework. He has also authored various technical specifications such as the Extended Hypertext Transfer Protocol (XHTTP) and the Documentation Markup Language (DocML). Professionally, he is the acting director of the Cake Development Corporation (CakeDC), the commercial entity behind the framework, where he works alongside Larry Masters, the founder of CakePHP.

It's impossible to not thank the CakePHP community around the world for making the project what it is today. I would also like to thank Larry Masters, Mark Story, Jose Lorenzo, Andy Dawson, Mark Scherer, Adnan Sarela, Marc Ypes, Jose Gonzalez, Christian Winther, Rachman Chavik, Juan Basso, Renan Gonçalves, Pierre Martin, Marc Würth, Bryan Crowe, and the rest of the core team and amazing people who have come and gone, and dedicated their time and passion to the framework; you guys are truly awesome.

I also want to thank my beautiful wife, Laura, for supporting me at every step of the way, and also our baby (work in progress), who, when born, will become the most important project in my life.

About the Reviewer

Lubomír Štork is an experienced software and database architect at the Cake Development Corporation (CakeDC) and has been actively using CakePHP since 2005. He is an author of TranslateBehavior in Version 1.2 of the framework and has also contributed to several other software libraries as well as provided help in open source community support channels.

www.PacktPub.com

Support files, eBooks, discount offers and more

You might want to visit www.PacktPub.com for support files and downloads related to your book.

Did you know that Packt offers eBook versions of every book published, with PDF and ePub files available? You can upgrade to the eBook version at www.PacktPub.com and as a print book customer, you are entitled to a discount on the eBook copy. Get in touch with us at service@packtpub.com for more details.

At www.PacktPub.com, you can also read a collection of free technical articles, sign up for a range of free newsletters, and receive exclusive discounts and offers on Packt books and eBooks.

http://PacktLib.PacktPub.com

Do you need instant solutions to your IT questions? PacktLib is Packt's online digital book library. Here, you can access, read and search across Packt's entire library of books.

Why Subscribe?

- Fully searchable across every book published by Packt
- Copy and paste, print, and bookmark content
- On demand and accessible via a web browser

Free Access for Packt account holders

If you have an account with Packt at www.PacktPub.com, you can use this to access PacktLib today and view nine entirely free books. Simply use your login credentials for immediate access.

Table of Contents

Preface   **1**

Chapter 1: Lightning Introduction   **7**

Introduction   7
Listing and viewing records   8
Adding and editing records   17
Deleting records   23
Adding a login   26
Including a plugin   32

Chapter 2: Advanced Routing   **41**

Introduction   41
Adding a prefix   41
Handling languages   51
Custom route class   53
Dispatch filter   59

Chapter 3: HTTP Negotiation   **65**

Introduction   65
Parsing extensions   65
Processing Ajax requests   68
Building a response   72
Uploading a file   74
Using a detector   80
Working with cookies   82
Cache control   87
Error handling   90

Chapter 4: API Strategies   95

Introduction	95
RESTful resources	95
Exposing a web service	99
Consuming a service	104
Authentication API	108
API versioning	114

Chapter 5: Using Authentication   121

Introduction	121
The HTTP authentication	121
Custom authorize class	127
Facebook authentication	134
Custom RBAC	141
Working with ACL	146

Chapter 6: Model Layer   163

Introduction	163
Has and belongs to many (HABTM)	163
Joining through	169
Containing models	171
Custom finders	176
On-the-fly associations	180
Using transactions	184

Chapter 7: Search and Pagination   187

Introduction	187
Pagination	187
Basic search and filter	193
The Search plugin	198
Advanced search	205

Chapter 8: Events System   213

Introduction	213
Listeners and subscribers	213
Event-driven process	217
Event stacking	225
Managing event priorities	234

Chapter 9: Creating Shells   241

Introduction   241
Console API   241
Import parser   246
Running cron shells   251
Using the I18n shell   255

Chapter 10: View Templates   263

Introduction   263
Using blocks   263
Building an XML view   266
Generating a PDF   268
Writing some PDF content to a file   271
Translations   272
View caching   275
The AssetCompress plugin   279

Chapter 11: Unit Tests   283

Introduction   283
Dependency Injection   283
Creating a fixture   286
Mock objects   291
Stub method configuration   294
Model unit testing   297

Chapter 12: Migrations   305

Introduction   305
Schema handling   306
Syncing changes   310
The Migrations plugin   312
Injecting data   316

Index   323

Preface

With this book, we've aimed to cover and resolve the typically common tasks when working with CakePHP. To do this, we collected the most popular questions from support websites around the Web on how to use certain features or perform common actions with the framework, and ranked them in order of frequency. We then proposed a solution for each of these; once this was done, we put together what we considered to be a comprehensive guide to how to get the job done fast, and right, in each scenario.

While we've done our best to approach each topic with a sound solution, we have been aware of the possibly uneven level of technical knowledge each reader may have. So, where possible, we've tried to keep our examples in line with simple or reasonably understandable parameters so as to reduce any additional knowledge that would potentially be required in each case.

We've dedicated many hours to reviewing each case and hope that you find something useful throughout the scenarios we've outlined. Where it's been obvious, we've relied on basic knowledge of the framework so as to not overburden each tutorial with additional instructions. However, for anyone completely new to the framework, after completing the blog tutorial included in the CakePHP documentation (`http://book.cakephp.org`), you should feel quite comfortable with the assumptions we've made along the way.

What this book covers

Chapter 1, Lightning Introduction, is a set of quick-start recipes to dive head first into using the framework and build out a simple CRUD around product management.

Chapter 2, Advanced Routing, looks at a couple of routing solutions and how to achieve them with the framework.

Chapter 3, HTTP Negotiation, looks at various scenarios where working with HTTP is greatly simplified by CakePHP.

Chapter 4, API Strategies, looks at a couple of ways to expose an API using CakePHP, so you can then decide which fits best with your application.

Chapter 5, Using Authentication, looks at various ways of handling authentication and access control when using the framework.

Chapter 6, Model Layer, looks at the various aspects of models and tells us how to wield their power.

Chapter 7, Search and Pagination, revises some recipes to help you get familiar with Search and Pagination in the framework.

Chapter 8, Events System, looks at the fundamentals of the events system, with a couple of recipes to get you handling events.

Chapter 9, Creating Shells, outlines some common use cases when using shell tasks as well as some built-in shell commands that come with the framework.

Chapter 10, View Templates, looks at various aspects of the view layer in CakePHP and tells us how to get the most out of templates, code reuse, translations, caching, and more.

Chapter 11, Unit Tests, looks at how CakePHP leverages the PHPUnit library to provide a solid base for unit testing, including handling dependencies, fixtures, as well as using the bake shell for testing.

Chapter 12, Migrations, looks at how simple it is to build and maintain your database while keeping your schema changes up to date with your code base.

What you need for this book

You should have comprehensive knowledge of PHP, understanding of the object-oriented nature of the language, as well as the base syntax and language constructs. You will also need a basic understanding of the CakePHP framework, which, for this book, should be enough after having set up and configured the framework to work on a local server (we use a Linux environment throughout the content of the book). You should also have completed at least the blog tutorial included in the CakePHP documentation (`http://book.cakephp.org`).

Who this book is for

We'd expect you to have some experience as a PHP developer and some level of knowledge of CakePHP, the solutions it provides, and the features it offers. If you have experience working in other frameworks that follow the MVC architecture, you should also find the content of this book accessible.

Conventions

In this book, you will find a number of styles of text that distinguish between different kinds of information. Here are some examples of these styles, and an explanation of their meaning.

Code words in text are shown as follows: "Now, create a directory named `Products/` in `app/View/`. Then, in this directory, create one file named `index.ctp` and another named `view.ctp`."

A block of code is set as follows:

```
CREATE TABLE products (
  id VARCHAR(36) NOT NULL,
  name VARCHAR(100),
  details TEXT,
  available TINYINT(1) UNSIGNED DEFAULT 1,
  created DATETIME,
  modified DATETIME,
  PRIMARY KEY(id)
);
```

When we wish to draw your attention to a particular part of a code block, the relevant lines or items are set in bold:

```
public function index() {
  $this->Category->recursive = 0;
  $this->Prg->commonProcess(null, array(
    'paramType' => 'querystring'
  ));
  $this->Paginator->settings = array(
    'Category' => array(
      'paramType' => 'querystring',
      'conditions' => $this->Category->parseCriteria($this->Prg->parsedParams())
    )
  );
  $this->set('categories', $this->Paginator->paginate());
}
```

Any command-line input or output is written as follows:

```
$ Console/cake bake all Gift
$ Console/cake bake all Recipient
```

New terms and **important words** are shown in bold. Words that you see on the screen, in menus or dialog boxes for example, appear in the text like this: "If we fill the search box with the example text and then hit the **Submit** button."

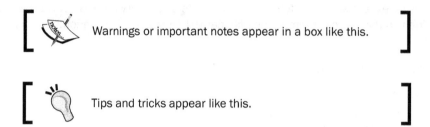

Warnings or important notes appear in a box like this.

Tips and tricks appear like this.

Reader feedback

Feedback from our readers is always welcome. Let us know what you think about this book—what you liked or may have disliked. Reader feedback is important for us to develop titles that you really get the most out of.

To send us general feedback, simply send an e-mail to `feedback@packtpub.com`, and mention the book title in the subject of your message.

If there is a topic that you have expertise in and you are interested in either writing or contributing to a book, see our author guide on `www.packtpub.com/authors`.

Customer support

Now that you are the proud owner of a Packt book, we have a number of things to help you to get the most from your purchase.

Downloading the example code

You can download the example code files for all Packt books you have purchased from your account at `http://www.packtpub.com`. If you purchased this book elsewhere, you can visit `http://www.packtpub.com/support` and register to have the files e-mailed directly to you.

Errata

Although we have taken every care to ensure the accuracy of our content, mistakes do happen. If you find a mistake in one of our books—maybe a mistake in the text or the code—we would be grateful if you would report this to us. By doing so, you can save other readers from frustration and help us improve subsequent versions of this book. If you find any errata, please report them by visiting `http://www.packtpub.com/support`, selecting your book, clicking on the **errata submission form** link, and entering the details of your errata. Once your errata are verified, your submission will be accepted and the errata will be uploaded to our website, or added to any list of existing errata, under the Errata section of that title.

Piracy

Piracy of copyright material on the Internet is an ongoing problem across all media. At Packt, we take the protection of our copyright and licenses very seriously. If you come across any illegal copies of our works, in any form, on the Internet, please provide us with the location address or website name immediately so that we can pursue a remedy.

Please contact us at `copyright@packtpub.com` with a link to the suspected pirated material.

We appreciate your help in protecting our authors, and our ability to bring you valuable content.

Questions

You can contact us at `questions@packtpub.com` if you are having a problem with any aspect of the book, and we will do our best to address it.

1
Lightning Introduction

In this chapter, we will cover the following recipes:

- ▶ Listing and viewing records
- ▶ Adding and editing records
- ▶ Deleting records
- ▶ Adding a login
- ▶ Including a plugin

Introduction

CakePHP is a web framework for **rapid application development** (**RAD**), which admittedly covers a wide range of areas and possibilities. However, at its core, it provides a solid architecture for the **CRUD** (**create/read/update/delete**) interface.

This chapter is a set of quick-start recipes to dive head first into using the framework and build out a simple CRUD around product management.

If you want to try the code examples on your own, make sure that you have CakePHP 2.5.2 installed and configured to use a database—you should see something like this:

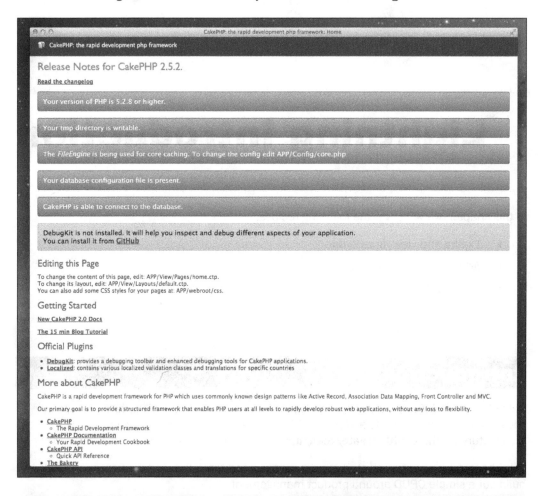

Listing and viewing records

To begin, we'll need a way to view the products available and also allow the option to select and view any one of those products.

In this recipe, we'll create a listing of products as well as a page where we can view the details of a single product.

Getting ready

To go through this recipe, we'll first need a table of data to work with. So, create a table named `products` using the following SQL statement:

```sql
CREATE TABLE products (
  id VARCHAR(36) NOT NULL,
  name VARCHAR(100),
  details TEXT,
  available TINYINT(1) UNSIGNED DEFAULT 1,
  created DATETIME,
  modified DATETIME,
  PRIMARY KEY(id)
);
```

We'll then need some sample data to test with, so now run this SQL statement to insert some products:

```sql
INSERT INTO products (id, name, details, available, created, modified)
VALUES
('535c460a-f230-4565-8378-7cae01314e03', 'Cake', 'Yummy and sweet', 1,
NOW(), NOW()),
('535c4638-c708-4171-985a-743901314e03', 'Cookie', 'Browsers love
cookies', 1, NOW(), NOW()),
('535c49d9-917c-4eab-854f-743801314e03', 'Helper', 'Helping you all
the way', 1, NOW(), NOW());
```

Before we begin, we'll also need to create `ProductsController`. To do so, create a file named `ProductsController.php` in `app/Controller/` and add the following content:

```php
<?php
App::uses('AppController', 'Controller');

class ProductsController extends AppController {

  public $helpers = array('Html', 'Form');

  public $components = array('Session', 'Paginator');

}
```

Now, create a directory named `Products/` in `app/View/`. Then, in this directory, create one file named `index.ctp` and another named `view.ctp`.

How to do it...

Perform the following steps:

1. Define the pagination settings to sort the products by adding the following property to the `ProductsController` class:

```
public $paginate = array(
   'limit' => 10
);
```

2. Add the following `index()` method in the `ProductsController` class:

```
public function index() {
   $this->Product->recursive = -1;
   $this->set('products', $this->paginate());
}
```

3. Introduce the following content in the `index.ctp` file that we created:

```
<h2><?php echo __('Products'); ?></h2>
<table>
   <tr>
     <th><?php echo $this->Paginator->sort('id'); ?></th>
     <th><?php echo $this->Paginator->sort('name'); ?></th>
     <th><?php echo $this->Paginator->sort('created'); ?></th>
   </tr>
   <?php foreach ($products as $product): ?>
     <tr>
       <td><?php echo $product['Product']['id']; ?></td>
       <td>
         <?php
         echo $this->Html->link($product['Product']['name'],
array('controller' => 'products', 'action' => 'view',
$product['Product']['id']));
         ?>
       </td>
       <td><?php echo $this->Time->nice($product['Product']
['created']); ?></td>
     </tr>
   <?php endforeach; ?>
</table>
<div>
```

```
<?php echo $this->Paginator->counter(array('format' => __('Page
{:page} of {:pages}, showing {:current} records out of {:count}
total, starting on record {:start}, ending on {:end}'))); ?>
</div>
<div>
  <?php
  echo $this->Paginator->prev(__('< previous'), array(), null,
array('class' => 'prev disabled'));
  echo $this->Paginator->numbers(array('separator' => ''));
  echo $this->Paginator->next(__('next >'), array(), null,
array('class' => 'next disabled'));
  ?>
</div>
```

4. Returning to the `ProductsController` class, add the following `view()` method to it:

```php
public function view($id) {
    if (!($product = $this->Product->findById($id))) {
        throw new NotFoundException(__('Product not found'));
    }
    $this->set(compact('product'));
}
```

5. Introduce the following content in the `view.ctp` file:

```php
<h2><?php echo h($product['Product']['name']); ?></h2>
<p>
  <?php echo h($product['Product']['details']); ?>
</p>
<dl>
  <dt><?php echo __('Available'); ?></dt>
  <dd><?php echo __((bool)$product['Product']['available'] ? 'Yes'
: 'No'); ?></dd>
  <dt><?php echo __('Created'); ?></dt>
  <dd><?php echo $this->Time->nice($product['Product']
['created']); ?></dd>
  <dt><?php echo __('Modified'); ?></dt>
  <dd><?php echo $this->Time->nice($product['Product']
['modified']); ?></dd>
</dl>
```

6. Now, navigating to /products in your web browser will display a listing of the products, as shown in the following screenshot:

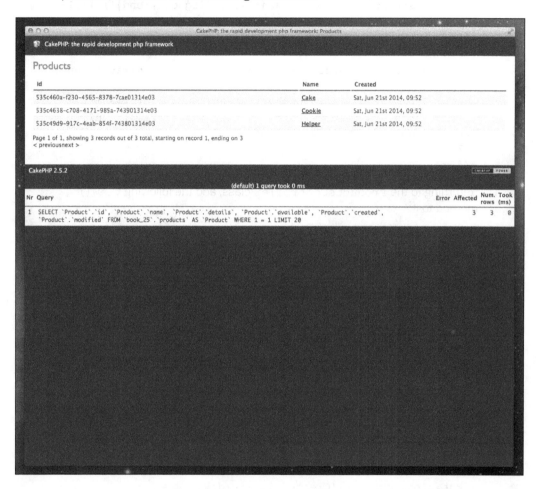

7. Clicking on one of the product names in the listing will redirect you to a detailed view of the product, as shown in the following screenshot:

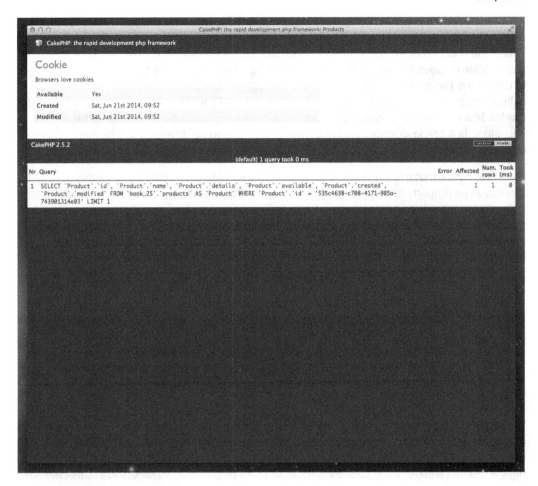

How it works...

We started by defining the pagination setting in our `ProductsController` class, which defines how the results are treated when returning them via the `Paginator` component (previously defined in the `$components` property of the controller). Pagination is a powerful feature of CakePHP, which extends well beyond simply defining the number of results or sort order.

We then added an `index()` method to our `ProductsController` class, which returns the listing of products. You'll first notice that we accessed a `$Product` property on the controller. This is the model that we are acting against to read from our table in the database. We didn't create a file or class for this model, as we're taking full advantage of the framework's ability to determine the aspects of our application through convention. Here, as our controller is called `ProductsController` (in plural), it automatically assumes a `Product` (in singular) model. Then, in turn, this `Product` model assumes a `products` table in our database. This alone is a prime example of how CakePHP can speed up development by making use of these conventions.

You'll also notice that in our `ProductsController::index()` method, we set the `$recursive` property of the `Product` model to `-1`. This is to tell our model that we're not interested in resolving any associations on it. Associations are other models that are related to this one. This is another powerful aspect of CakePHP. It allows you to determine how models are related to each other, allowing the framework to dynamically generate those links so that you can return results with the relations already mapped out for you. We then called the `paginate()` method to handle the resolving of the results via the `Paginator` component.

It's common practice to set the `$recursive` property of all models to `-1` by default. This saves heavy queries where associations are resolved to return the related models, when it may not be necessary for the query at hand. This can be done via the `AppModel` class, which all models extend, or via an intermediate class that you may be using in your application.

We had also defined a `view($id)` method, which is used to resolve a single product and display its details. First, you probably noticed that our method receives an `$id` argument. By default, CakePHP treats the arguments in methods for actions as parts of the URL. So, if we have a product with an ID of 123, the URL would be `/products/view/123`. In this case, as our argument doesn't have a default value, in its absence from the URL, the framework would return an error page, which states that an argument was required. You will also notice that our IDs in the `products` table aren't sequential numbers in this case. This is because we defined our `id` field as `VARCHAR(36)`. When doing this, CakePHP will use a **Universally Unique Identifier (UUID)** instead of an `auto_increment` value.

To use a UUID instead of a sequential ID, you can use either `CHAR(36)` or `BINARY(36)`. Here, we used `VARCHAR(36)`, but note that it can be less performant than `BINARY(36)` due to collation.

The use of UUID versus a sequential ID is usually preferred due to obfuscation, where it's harder to guess a string of 36 characters, but also more importantly, if you use database partitioning, replication, or any other means of distributing or clustering your data.

We then used the `findById()` method on the `Product` model to return a product by it's ID (the one passed to the action). This method is actually a magic method. Just as you can return a record by its ID, by changing the method to `findByAvailable()`. For example, you would be able to get all records that have the given value for the `available` field in the table. These methods are very useful to easily perform queries on the associated table without having to define the methods in question.

We also threw `NotFoundException` for the cases in which a product isn't found for the given ID. This exception is HTTP aware, so it results in an error page if thrown from an action.

Finally, we used the `set()` method to assign the result to a variable in the view. Here we're using the `compact()` function in PHP, which converts the given variable names into an associative array, where the key is the variable name, and the value is the variable's value. In this case, this provides a `$product` variable with the results array in the view. You'll find this function useful to rapidly assign variables for your views.

We also created our views using HTML, making use of the `Paginator`, `Html`, and `Time` helpers. You may have noticed that the usage of `TimeHelper` was not declared in the `$helpers` property of our `ProductsController`. This is because CakePHP is able to find and instantiate helpers from the core or the application automatically, when it's used in the view for the first time. Then, the `sort()` method on the `Paginator` helper helps you create links, which, when clicked on, toggle the sorting of the results by that field. Likewise, the `counter()`, `prev()`, `numbers()`, and `next()` methods create the paging controls for the table of products.

You will also notice the structure of the array that we assigned from our controller. This is the common structure of results returned by a model. This can vary slightly, depending on the type of `find()` performed (in this case, `all`), but the typical structure would be as follows (using the real data from our `products` table here):

```
Array
(
  [0] => Array
  (
    [Product] => Array
    (
      [id] => 535c460a-f230-4565-8378-7cae01314e03
      [name] => Cake
      [details] => Yummy and sweet
      [available] => true
      [created] => 2014-06-12 15:55:32
      [modified] => 2014-06-12 15:55:32
    )
  )
  [1] => Array
```

```
(
    [Product] => Array
    (
        [id] => 535c4638-c708-4171-985a-743901314e03
        [name] => Cookie
        [details] => Browsers love cookies
        [available] => true
        [created] => 2014-06-12 15:55:33
        [modified] => 2014-06-12 15:55:33
    )
)
[2] => Array
(
    [Product] => Array
    (
        [id] => 535c49d9-917c-4eab-854f-743801314e03
        [name] => Helper
        [details] => Helping you all the way
        [available] => true
        [created] => 2014-06-12 15:55:34
        [modified] => 2014-06-12 15:55:34
    )
)
)
)
```

We also used the link() method on the Html helper, which provides us with the ability to perform reverse routing to generate the link to the desired controller and action, with arguments if applicable. Here, the absence of a controller assumes the current controller, in this case, products.

Finally, you may have seen that we used the __() function when writing text in our views. This function is used to handle translations and internationalization of your application. When using this function, if you were to provide your application in various languages, you would only need to handle the translation of your content and would have no need to revise and modify the code in your views.

There are other variations of this function, such as __d() and __n(), which allow you to enhance how you handle the translations. Even if you have no initial intention of providing your application in multiple languages, it's always recommended that you use these functions. You never know, using CakePHP might enable you to create a world class application, which is offered to millions of users around the globe!

See also

▸ A complete detail of the conventions in CakePHP can be found at `http://book.cakephp.org/2.0/en/getting-started/cakephp-conventions.html`

▸ A complete overview of the pagination options available can be found at `http://book.cakephp.org/2.0/en/core-libraries/components/pagination.html`

> Note that multiple components can be defined in a controller by simply defining them in the array of the `$components` property. More information on Components in CakePHP can be found here: `http://book.cakephp.org/2.0/en/controllers/components.html`

▸ Additional information on reading data from Models can be found at `http://book.cakephp.org/2.0/en/models/retrieving-your-data.html`

▸ For more details on Helpers in CakePHP, see the documentation at `http://book.cakephp.org/2.0/en/views/helpers.html`

▸ The *Translations* recipe from *Chapter 10, View Templates*

Adding and editing records

While listing and viewing records is handy, the ability to create and edit records allows you to build up and maintain your data.

In this recipe, we'll create actions to both add new products and edit the existing ones in our database.

Getting ready

For this recipe, we'll continue using the `products` table from the previous recipe. We'll also extend the `ProductsController` that was created.

For the views, we'll add `add.ctp` and `edit.ctp` files to our `app/View/Products/` directory, and also a `form.ctp` file in the `Products/` directory that we'll create in `app/View/Elements/`.

How to do it...

Perform the following steps:

1. Add the following `add()` method to the `ProductsController` class:

```php
public function add() {
  if ($this->request->is('post')) {
    $this->Product->create();
    if ($this->Product->save($this->request->data)) {
      $this->Session->setFlash(__('New product created'));
      return $this->redirect(array('action' => 'index'));
    }
    $this->Session->setFlash(__('Could not create product'));
  }
}
```

2. Just below the `add()` method, also add an `edit()` method:

```php
public function edit($id) {
  $product = $this->Product->findById($id);
  if (!$product) {
    throw new NotFoundException(__('Product not found'));
  }
  if ($this->request->is('post')) {
    $this->Product->id = $id;
    if ($this->Product->save($this->request->data)) {
      $this->Session->setFlash(__('Product updated'));
      return $this->redirect(array('action' => 'index'));
    }
    $this->Session->setFlash(__('Could not update product'));
  } else {
    $this->request->data = $product;
  }
}
```

3. Introduce the following content in the `form.ctp` element file:

```php
<?php
echo $this->Form->create('Product');
echo $this->Form->inputs();
echo $this->Form->end(__('Submit'));
```

4. Introduce the following content in the `add.ctp` file:

```php
<?php echo $this->element('Products/form'); ?>
```

5. The `edit.ctp` file will also take the same content, but the header text will be changed to the following code:

```php
<?php echo $this->element('Products/form'); ?>
```

6. Return to the `index.ctp` file, and change it's content to the following:

```php
<h2><?php echo __('Products'); ?></h2>
<div>
  <?php echo $this->Html->link(__('Add new product'),
array('action' => 'add')); ?>
</div>
<table>
  <tr>
    <th><?php echo $this->Paginator->sort('id'); ?></th>
    <th><?php echo $this->Paginator->sort('name'); ?></th>
    <th><?php echo $this->Paginator->sort('created'); ?></th>
    <th><?php echo __('Actions'); ?></th>
  </tr>
  <?php foreach ($products as $product): ?>
    <tr>
      <td><?php echo $product['Product']['id']; ?></td>
      <td><?php echo $this->Html->link($product['Product']
['name'], array('action' => 'view', $product['Product']['id']));
?></td>
      <td><?php echo $this->Time->nice($product['Product']
['created']); ?></td>
      <td><?php echo $this->Html->link(__('Edit'), array('action'
=> 'edit', $product['Product']['id'])); ?></td>
    </tr>
  <?php endforeach; ?>
</table>
<div>
  <?php echo $this->Paginator->counter(array('format' => __('Page
{:page} of {:pages}, showing {:current} records out of {:count}
total, starting on record {:start}, ending on {:end}'))); ?>
</div>
<div>
  <?php
  echo $this->Paginator->prev(__('< previous'), array(), null,
array('class' => 'prev disabled'));
  echo $this->Paginator->numbers(array('separator' => ''));
  echo $this->Paginator->next(__('next >'), array(), null,
array('class' => 'next disabled'));
  ?>
</div>
```

7. Navigate to /products in your web browser, and click one of the **Edit** links to modify a product. The following screenshot shows the screen that will appear:

8. Return to /products, and click on the **Add new product** link to create a new product. The following screenshot shows the screen that will appear:

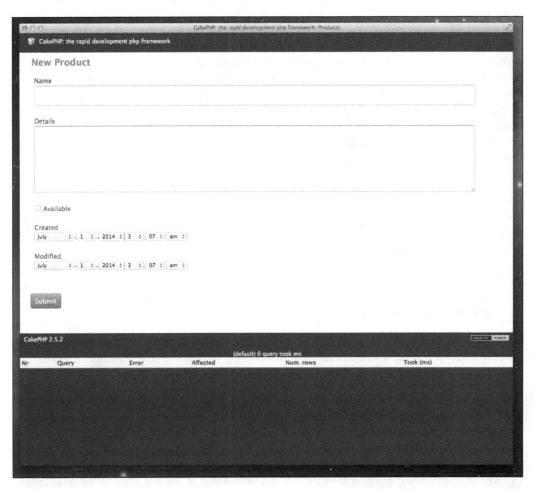

How it works...

Here, we extended our previous recipe by adding some extra methods to create new products and edit the existing ones. The add() method first checks whether the current request has been made using the HTTP POST method. If that's the case, we call the create() method on the Product model. This doesn't create a new record yet, but instead it prepares our model object for a new record to be created. We then call the save() method, passing the data provided in the request to it. The framework handles this internally through the Form helper, which we'll see in a moment. The condition checks whether the save is successful (here, a new record is created), and if so, it calls the setFlash() method on our Session component to register a success message to be displayed on the page that follows. We do the same in the event that the record could not be saved, and it provided a failure message. We then wrap up the method by redirecting the request to our index() action.

For the edit() method, we first check that the product for the given ID actually exists using the findById() method on the Product model. See the previous recipe, *Listing and viewing records*, for details on finding records. If the product doesn't exist, a NotFoundException is thrown; this is rendered as an error page. As with the add() method, we first check that the request was made via POST. However, instead of calling the create() method on our Product model, we set the $id property with the $id argument passed to our action. We then follow the same process of calling the save() method with the request data, as well as setting the result messages for the view and redirecting the request.

We finalize our edit action by populating the request data if it does not exist so that when you visit the form for editing, it's populated with the existing values from the products table.

For our views, we've taken the initiative to use an element. These are reusable sections of our views, which allow us to segment and organize our visual interface and cut down on duplicate code. Here, we've done this to avoid declaring the same form twice and reuse the same one instead. The framework is able to distinguish between the two (adding a record and editing a record) by the presence of an ID. In which case, it assumes that we're editing a record instead of creating one. In this file, we use the Form helper to generate a new form using the create() method and passing the name of the model to it, it will act against. We also called the inputs() method to create the required inputs based on the table schema and then called the end() method to complete the form.

For our add.ctp and edit.ctp view files, we included our element using the element() method, passing it the location of our form.ctp file. You'll notice that we created our element in the Products/ directory, as the form is intended for a product. We could change the contents of our element to receive the model name via an element parameter, making it more dynamic and, therefore, reusable even further. Finally, we updated the index.ctp view to include an **Edit** option using the link() method from the Html helper.

You'll also see that we passed the ID of each product to this method in our `foreach()` statement, thus generating a link for each product with its unique ID as part of the URL. We also added a link to "add a new product", which redirects you to the new `add()` action to create a new record in the `products` table.

See also

▶ You can read more on working with the session in CakePHP at `http://book.cakephp.org/2.0/en/core-libraries/components/sessions.html`

▶ More details on saving data in Models can be found at `http://book.cakephp.org/2.0/en/models/saving-your-data.html`

▶ For a complete overview of the Form helper in CakePHP, go to `http://book.cakephp.org/2.0/en/core-libraries/helpers/form.html`

▶ The `Html` helper in CakePHP will become a common tool used in all of your views; read more about it at `http://book.cakephp.org/2.0/en/core-libraries/helpers/html.html`

▶ The *Listing and viewing records* recipe

Deleting records

Just as we can list and view records, as well as edit and create new ones, you'll also want to be familiar with how to delete records using CakePHP.

In this recipe, we'll create an action that allows us to delete records from our table.

Getting ready

As with the previous recipe, we'll continue using the `products` table and also extend the `ProductsController` that we created.

How to do it...

Perform the following steps:

1. Add the following `delete()` method to the `ProductsController` class:

```
public function delete($id) {
  if (!$this->request->is('post')) {
    throw new MethodNotAllowedException();
  }
  if ($this->Product->delete($id)) {
```

```php
        $this->Session->setFlash(__('Product removed: %s', $id));
        return $this->redirect(array('action' => 'index'));
    }
    $this->Session->setFlash(__('Could not remove product'));
    return $this->redirect($this->referer());
}
```

2. Change the content of the index.ctp file to the following:

```php
<h2><?php echo __('Products'); ?></h2>
<div>
    <?php echo $this->Html->link(__('Add new product'),
array('action' => 'add')); ?>
</div>
<table>
  <tr>
    <th><?php echo $this->Paginator->sort('id'); ?></th>
    <th><?php echo $this->Paginator->sort('name'); ?></th>
    <th><?php echo $this->Paginator->sort('created'); ?></th>
    <th><?php echo __('Actions'); ?></th>
  </tr>
    <?php foreach ($products as $product): ?>
    <tr>
        <td><?php echo $product['Product']['id']; ?></td>
        <td><?php echo $this->Html->link($product['Product']
['name'], array('action' => 'view', $product['Product']['id']));
?></td>
        <td><?php echo $this->Time->nice($product['Product']
['created']); ?></td>
        <td>
          <?php
          echo $this->Html->link(__('Edit'), array('action' =>
'edit', $product['Product']['id']));
          echo $this->Form->postLink(__('Delete'), array('action' =>
'delete', $product['Product']['id']), array('confirm' => 'Delete
this product?'));
          ?>
        </td>
    </tr>
    <?php endforeach; ?>
</table>
<div>
    <?php echo $this->Paginator->counter(array('format' => __('Page
{:page} of {:pages}, showing {:current} records out of {:count}
total, starting on record {:start}, ending on {:end}'))); ?>
```

```
</div>
<div>
  <?php
  echo $this->Paginator->prev(__('< previous'), array(), null,
array('class' => 'prev disabled'));
    echo $this->Paginator->numbers(array('separator' => ''));
echo $this->Paginator->next(__('next >'), array(), null,
array('class' => 'next disabled'));
  ?>
</div>
```

How it works...

In this recipe, we added a `delete()` method to our `ProductsController` class. This first checks whether the HTTP method used to call the action was POST. In the event it wasn't, we throw a `MethodNotAllowedException` exception, which is presented as an error page when it is thrown from an action. This is to protect our application against attempts to delete data via a simple URL. If the HTTP method is correct, we proceed to call the `delete()` method on the `Product` model, passing to it the ID of the record to delete. If it is successful, we call the `setFlash()` method on our `Session` component with a message confirming the removal or with a failure message if the `delete()` method fails. Finally, we redirect the request to the `index()` action if the record was deleted successfully—if not, then we are redirecting the user back to the URL where the `delete()` method was called from. It may also be worth mentioning that the `delete()` action itself doesn't have a view associated with it, as nothing is displayed to the user as part of the request.

We then returned to the `index.ctp` view to add an option to delete a product using the `postLink()` method of the `Form` helper. This creates a form with a link that allows us to use POST when clicking on the link which submits the form. You will notice that this takes a third argument, which is an array with a `confirm` key. This prompts the user to confirm the action before submitting the request to delete the record. This is always recommended when dealing with actions that delete records, in case of a mistake on the user's behalf.

See also

  ▸ More details on deleting data in your Models can be found at
     `http://book.cakephp.org/2.0/en/models/deleting-data.html`

  ▸ The *Adding and editing records* recipe

Adding a login

It's not going to be long before you need to control access to certain areas of your application.

In this recipe, we'll look at adding a basic authentication layer to our existing products section, with a login view to enter your credentials.

Getting ready

For this recipe, we'll need a table for our users. Create a table named `users`, using the following SQL statement:

```sql
CREATE TABLE users (
    id VARCHAR(36) NOT NULL,
    username VARCHAR(20),
    password VARCHAR(100),
    created DATETIME,
    modified DATETIME,
    PRIMARY KEY(id)
);
```

We'll then create a `User.php` file in `app/Model/`, which will have the following content:

```php
<?php
App::uses('AppModel', 'Model');
App::uses('SimplePasswordHasher', 'Controller/Component/Auth');

class User extends AppModel {
}
```

We'll also need a `UsersController.php` file in `app/Controller/` with the following content:

```php
<?php
App::uses('AppController', 'Controller');

class UsersController extends AppController {
}
```

Finally, also create a `Users` directory in `app/View/`, and create `register.ctp` and `login.ctp` files in the new directory.

How to do it...

Perform the following steps:

1. Add the validation rules to the `User` model in `app/Model/User.php` with the following `$validate` property:

```php
public $validate = array(
  'username' => array(
    'required' => array(
      'rule' => 'notEmpty',
      'message' => 'Please enter a username'
    )
  ),
  'password' => array(
    'required' => array(
      'rule' => 'notEmpty',
      'message' => 'Please enter a password'
    )
  )
);
```

2. In the same class, add this `beforeSave()` method:

```php
public function beforeSave($options = array()) {
  if (!parent::beforeSave($options)) {
    return false;
  }
  if (isset($this->data[$this->alias]['password'])) {
    $hasher = new SimplePasswordHasher();
    $this->data[$this->alias]['password'] = $hasher->hash($this->data[$this->alias]['password']);
  }
  return true;
}
```

3. Locate the `AppController.php` file in `app/Controller/`, and add the following `$components` property to the same class:

```php
public $components = array(
  'Session',
  'Auth' => array(
    'loginRedirect' => array('controller' => 'products'),
    'logoutRedirect' => array(
      'controller' => 'users',
      'action' => 'login'
    )
  )
);
```

4. Open the `UsersController.php` file and add the following methods:

```php
public function beforeFilter() {
  parent::beforeFilter();
  $this->Auth->allow();
}

public function register() {
  if ($this->request->is('post')) {
    $this->User->create();
    if ($this->User->save($this->request->data)) {
      $this->Session->setFlash(__('New user registered'));
      return $this->redirect(array('action' => 'login'));
    }
    $this->Session->setFlash(__('Could not register user'));
  }
}

public function login() {
  if ($this->request->is('post')) {
    if ($this->Auth->login()) {
      return $this->redirect($this->Auth->redirectUrl());
    }
    $this->Session->setFlash(__('Incorrect username or
password'));
  }
}

public function logout() {
  return $this->redirect($this->Auth->logout());
}
```

5. Locate the `register.ctp` file in `app/View/Users/` and introduce the following content:

```php
<h2><?php echo __('Register'); ?></h2>
<?php
echo $this->Form->create('User');
echo $this->Form->inputs();
echo $this->Form->end(__('Register'));
```

6. In the same directory, open the `login.ctp` file, and add the following content:

```php
<h2><?php echo __('Login'); ?></h2>
<?php
echo $this->Session->flash('auth');
```

```
echo $this->Form->create('User');
echo $this->Form->inputs(array(
  'username',
  'password',
  'legend' => __('Login, please')
));
echo $this->Form->end(__('Sign In'));
```

How it works...

For this recipe, we first included a `$validate` property in our `User` model. This array is used to define the validation rules applied when creating or modifying records. Here, we simply defined the `username` and `password` fields as required, not allowing an *empty* value and specifying some custom messages to be returned by the model if the fields fail to validate correctly. There are plenty more validation rules such as `alphaNumeric`, `minLength`, `between`, `date`, and `email`. You can also create your own rules for custom validation.

After setting up our validation, we also added a `beforeSave()` method. This is one of the callback methods available on all models, to hook into a certain point of the process. These are `beforeFind()`, `afterFind()`, `beforeSave()`, `afterSave()`, `beforeDelete()`, `afterDelete()`, `beforeValidate()`, `afterValidate()`, and `onError()`. In our method, we added some logic to process the password and generated a hash value before saving it to our `users` table. This way, we store a representation of the password, instead of the password itself. This is very important as you don't want anyone viewing the actual passwords in your database.

The `SimplePasswordHasher` class helps us here by providing an easy API to quickly generate hashes of any value. You will also notice our use of `$this->alias`. This is the recommended method of referring to the model, to allow for extensions or aliasing of a model without impacting the internal logic.

We then added the `Auth` component to the `$components` array of `AppController`, with some global settings. This controller acts as a base controller for your application, so behavior or functionality that needs to be propagated to your entire application should be added in this class. Here, we defined the `loginRedirect` and `logoutRedirect` settings, which define the controller and action to redirect to in each case (after login or after logout). Where the action is not defined, `index` will be assumed by default.

After that, we proceeded to add some methods to our `UsersController`. The first of these is the `beforeFilter()` method. This is one of the callback methods available on all controllers, which include `beforeFilter()`, `afterFilter()`, `beforeRender()`, and `beforeRedirect()`. Here, we first called `parent::beforeFilter()` to make sure that we included any logic that has been defined by `AppController`. We then called the `allow()` method on the `Auth` component to allow access to the methods in the controller. Here, you could also pass some method names to only allow certain action, or also use the `deny()` method to explicitly deny some actions and require login.

After that, we added a `register()` method, using the same logic to create a record as we did in the `ProductsController` from a previous recipe, in order to allow the creation of new users. Here, we've only used a simple example, without contemplating any postregistration checks, such as a token via e-mail for confirmation. You can easily include this and many more features using a plugin, such as the CakeDC Users plugin, found at `https://github.com/CakeDC/users`.

We also included both the `login()` and `logout()` methods, which use the API exposed by the `Auth` component to process the user login. As we're following convention by creating a `users` table with the `username` and `password` fields, we take advantage of the framework's ability to configure most of the sign-in process for us. In our login action, we first called the `login()` method on the `Auth` component, which internally checks the data passed in the request. If this is successful, we redirect the user using the `redirect()` method from the `Auth` component, which takes the target we previously defined in the `loginRedirect` setting. If the process were to fail, we stay in the same action but use the `setFlash()` method from the `Session` component to display a message to the user that the sign in was unsuccessful. The `logout()` method is even easier, simply calling the `logout()` method on the `Auth` component and redirecting the user to that location. Here, as with the `login()` method, we use the `logoutRedirect` setting we had previously defined. As you can see so far, authentication in CakePHP is really a piece of cake.

We then went on to create our views to register a new user and sign in. In our first view, `register.ctp`, we used the `create()` method of the `Form` helper to create a form for the `User` model. We then used the `inputs()` methods to render the required inputs and finally called `end()`, passing our text for the submit button. In our `login.ctp` view, we did almost the same; except here, we also enlisted required inputs, added custom form legend, and called the `flash()` method on the `Session` helper, passing `auth` as the argument to it. This renders a location to collect the flash messages sent from the `Auth` component, such as the message we display when the login fails. The use of the `auth` value allows you to easily manage the messages being collected, in case you'd like them to be displayed differently or in different locations of your view.

If you go to `/products` in your browser now, you will be automatically redirected to the login page, and the default message for unauthorized access will be displayed, as shown in the following screenshot:

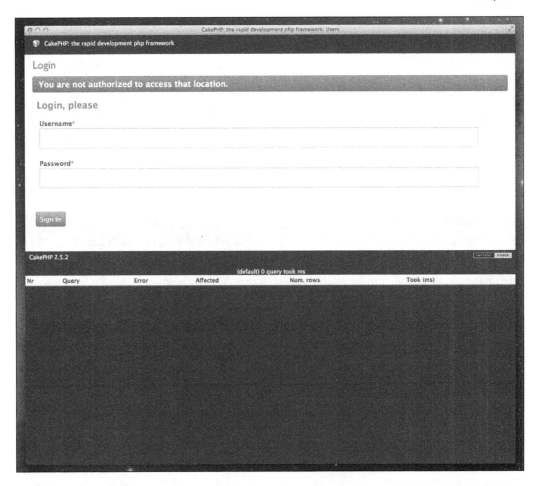

Of course, to log in, you'll have to register a new user account first by going to the `/users/register` URL in your browser.

See also

▶ Read more on data validation in CakePHP at `http://book.cakephp.org/2.0/en/models/data-validation.html`

▶ More details on callback methods in Models can be found at `http://book.cakephp.org/2.0/en/models/callback-methods.html`

▶ More settings available for the Auth component can be found at `http://book.cakephp.org/2.0/en/core-libraries/components/authentication.html`

▶ The *Authentication API* recipe in *Chapter 4, API Strategies*

▶ *Chapter 5, Using Authentication*

Including a plugin

One of the greatest benefits of using CakePHP is its extensibility. Using plugins, you can extend and enhance the core functionality, which provides you with even more cake than you bargained for!

In this recipe, we'll look at loading a plugin using DebugKit, the official development and debugging tool for the framework, as an example.

Getting ready

We'll need to have DebugKit included in the application file structure before we begin. There are a couple of ways to do this.

Git clone or submodule

If you use Git, you can create a clone of the code by executing the following command from your `app/` directory on the command line:

```
$ git clone https://github.com/cakephp/debug_kit.git Plugin/DebugKit
```

If you already have your application under version control using Git, you can also add it as a submodule. Assuming that the base of your repository is the `app/` folder, you would run the following command:

```
$ git submodule add https://github.com/cakephp/debug_kit.git app/Plugin/DebugKit
```

Using Composer

If you're using Composer as your dependency manager, you can simply include DebugKit as a plugin by adding the following code to your `composer.json` file:

```
{
  "require": {
    "cakephp/debug_kit": "2.2.*"
  }
}
```

After updating your `composer.json` file, simply update your application's dependencies using Composer.

Downloading files

An alternative method is to simply download the files and include them manually in your application from the following location:

```
https://github.com/cakephp/debug_kit/archive/master.zip
```

How to do it...

Perform the following steps:

1. Add the following code to your `bootstrap.php` file, found in `app/Config/`:

   ```
   CakePlugin::load('DebugKit');
   ```

2. Add the following code to your `AppController` in `app/Controller/`:

   ```
   public $components = array(
       'Session',
       'Auth',
       'DebugKit.Toolbar'
   );
   ```

3. Open your `core.php` file in `app/Config/`, and check if the following configuration value is set to a value higher than 0:

   ```
   Configure::write('debug', 2);
   ```

4. Now, load your application in your browser, and you'll find an icon in the top right-hand corner of the screen, as shown in the following screenshot:

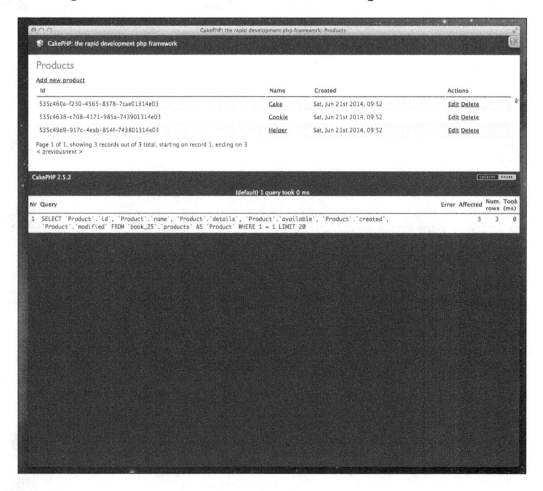

5. Click on the icon to see various panels (shown in the following screenshots) with data related to the current request:

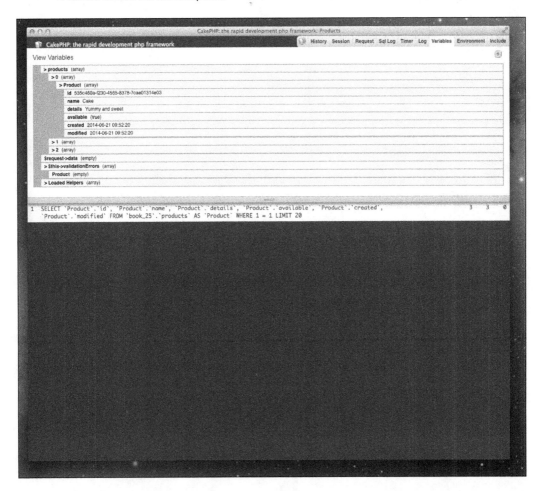

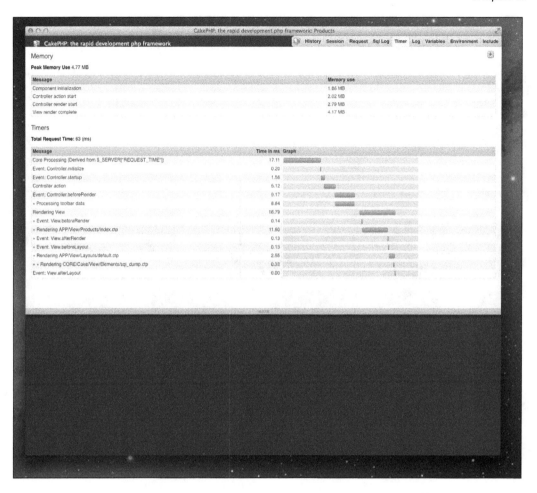

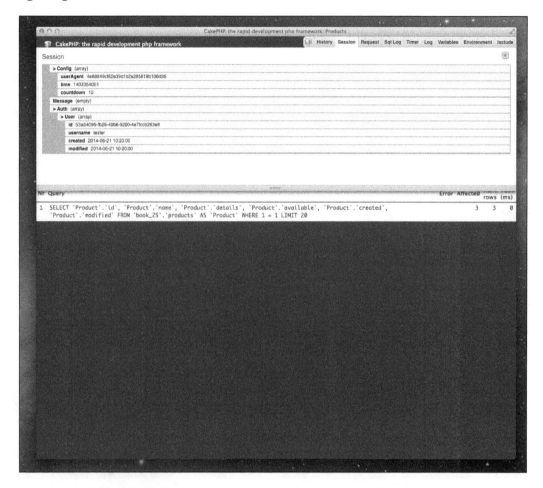

How it works...

When we call `CakePlugin::load()`, we request the framework to load the plugin by the given name, which also accepts an optional second argument, which is the configuration array for the plugin. We had already included the `DebugKit/` directory in `app/Plugin/`, which is where plugins are located. You can change the location of where the plugins are loaded from using the `path` option in the plugin configuration array.

After loading the plugin, we included the `Toolbar` component in our `AppController` so it's available in all applications. This is a component included with the DebugKit plugin, which allows us to display a toolbar in the browser, thus providing a range of panels to introspect the application, the current request, SQL queries, and more. You'll notice that we included both the `Session` and `Auth` components here as well to propagate them in our application. The plugin itself is also extensible, allowing additional panels to be added. Once our plugin was loaded and the `Toolbar` component available, we made sure that the debug mode was enabled in our `core.php` file; we then navigated to the application in the browser to view the loaded toolbar.

Plugins may also load their own `bootstrap.php` and `routes.php` files to set up configurations and define routing settings. However, when a plugin is loaded, you must specify to load these configurations and settings. For example, if you had a `Reports` plugin that used these, you would load the plugin using the plugin configuration array as follows:

```
CakePlugin::load('Reports', array(
  'bootstrap' => true,
  'routes' => true
));
```

You can also load all plugins in your `app/Plugin/` directory at once by calling `CakePlugin::loadAll()`.

See also

▸ For a complete overview of plugins in CakePHP, go to
  `http://book.cakephp.org/2.0/en/plugins.html`

▸ The *The Search plugin* recipe in *Chapter 7, Search and Pagination*

▸ The *Generating a PDF* and *The AssetCompress plugin* recipes in
  Chapter 10, View Templates

2
Advanced Routing

In this chapter, we will cover:

- ▶ Adding a prefix
- ▶ Handling languages
- ▶ Custom route class
- ▶ Dispatch filter

Introduction

By convention, URLs in CakePHP are formed by the controller name, followed by the action, and then any parameters passed to the action. Routing allows you to customize this by defining exactly how a certain controller or action is called via the URL.

In this chapter, we'll look at a couple of routing solutions and how to achieve them with the framework.

Adding a prefix

Prefixes are additional values prepended to the URL, which allow you to clearly separate collections of actions in your controllers. This is typically used to rapidly create an admin area for an application.

In this recipe, we'll create an inventory management area to a `books` controller, where the standard actions will simply display details of books and the inventory area will be used to manage our books.

Getting ready

For this recipe, we'll need a table for our books, so create a table named `books` by using the following SQL statement:

```sql
CREATE TABLE books (
    id VARCHAR(36) NOT NULL,
    name VARCHAR(100),
    stock INT(4),
    created DATETIME,
    modified DATETIME,
    PRIMARY KEY(id)
);
```

We'll then need some sample data, so run the following SQL statement to insert some books:

```sql
INSERT INTO books (id, name, stock, created, modified)
VALUES
('635c460a-f230-4565-8378-7cae01314e03', 'CakePHP Application', 2,
NOW(), NOW()),
('635c4638-c708-4171-985a-743901314e03', 'PHP for Beginners', 3,
NOW(), NOW()),
('635c49d9-917c-4eab-854f-743801314e03', 'Server Administration', 0,
NOW(), NOW());
```

We'll also need to create a `BooksController`. So, create a file named `BooksController.php` in `app/Controller/` with the following content:

```php
<?php
App::uses('AppController', 'Controller');

class BooksController extends AppController {

    public $helpers = array('Html', 'Form');

}
```

Then create a directory named `Books/` in `app/View/`, and create the following files in that directory: `index.ctp`, `view.ctp`, `inventory_stock.ctp`, and `inventory_edit.ctp`.

How to do it...

Perform the following steps:

1. First, open your `core.php` file in `app/Config/` and make sure the following line is uncommented and has the following value:

```
Configure::write('Routing.prefixes', array('inventory'));
```

2. Create the following `index()` and `view()` methods in your `BooksController`:

```php
public function index() {
    $this->set('books', $this->Book->find('all', array(
        'conditions' => array(
            'Book.stock >' => 0
        )
    )));
}

public function view($id) {
    if (!($book = $this->Book->findById($id))) {
        throw new NotFoundException(__('Book not found'));
    }
    if ($book['Book']['stock'] < 1) {
        throw new CakeException(__('Book not in stock'));
    }
    $this->set(compact('book'));
}
```

3. In the `BooksController` class, add the following `inventory_stock()` and `inventory_edit()` methods:

```php
public function inventory_stock() {
    $this->set('books', $this->Book->find('all'));
}

public function inventory_edit($id) {
    $book = $this->Book->findById($id);
    if (!$book) {
        throw new NotFoundException(__('Book not found'));
    }
    if ($this->request->is('post')) {
        $this->Book->id = $id;
```

```
        if ($this->Book->save($this->request->data)) {
          $this->Session->setFlash(__('Book stock updated'));
          return $this->redirect(array(
            'prefix' => 'inventory',
            'action' => 'stock'
          ));
        }
        $this->Session->setFlash(__('Could not update book stock'));
      } else {
        $this->request->data = $book;
      }
    }
```

4. Introduce the following content into your `app/View/Books/index.ctp` file:

```
<h2><?php echo __('Books'); ?></h2>
<table>
  <tr>
    <th><?php echo __('Name'); ?></th>
    <th><?php echo __('Created'); ?></th>
    <th><?php echo __('Modified'); ?></th>
  </tr>
  <?php foreach ($books as $book): ?>
    <tr>
      <td>
        <?php
        echo $this->Html->link($book['Book']['name'],
array('controller' => 'books', 'action' => 'view', $book['Book']
['id']));
        ?>
      </td>
      <td>
        <?php
        echo $this->Time->nice($book['Book']['created']);
        ?>
      </td>
      <td>
        <?php
        echo $this->Time->nice($book['Book']['modified']);
        ?>
      </td>
    </tr>
  <?php endforeach; ?>
</table>
```

5. Add the following content to your `app/View/Books/view.ctp` file:

```
<h2><?php echo h($book['Book']['name']); ?></h2>
<dl>
   <dt><?php echo __('Stock'); ?></dt>
   <dd><?php echo $book['Book']['stock']; ?></dd>
   <dt><?php echo __('Created'); ?></dt>
   <dd><?php echo $this->Time->nice($book['Book']['created']); ?></
dd>
   <dt><?php echo __('Modified'); ?></dt>
   <dd><?php echo $this->Time->nice($book['Book']['modified']);
?></dd>
</dl>
```

6. Introduce the following content into your `app/View/Books/inventory_stock.ctp` file:

```
<h2><?php echo __('Books Stock'); ?></h2>
<table>
   <tr>
      <th><?php echo __('Name'); ?></th>
      <th><?php echo __('Stock'); ?></th>
      <th><?php echo __('Created'); ?></th>
   </tr>
   <?php foreach ($books as $book): ?>
      <tr>
        <td>
          <?php
          echo $this->Html->link($book['Book']['name'],
array('prefix' => 'inventory', 'controller' => 'books', 'action'
=> 'edit', $book['Book']['id']));
          ?>
        </td>
        <td>
          <?php echo $book['Book']['stock']); ?>
        </td>
        <td>
          <?php
          echo $this->Time->nice($book['Book']['created']);
          ?>
        </td>
      </tr>
   <?php endforeach; ?>
</table>
```

7. Once more, with the following content into your app/View/Books/inventory_ edit.ctp file.

```
<h2><?php echo __('Edit Stock'); ?></h2>
<p>
  <?php echo __('Book') . ':' . h($this->request->data('Book.
name')); ?>
</p>
<?php
echo $this->Form->create('Book');
echo $this->Form->input('id');
echo $this->Form->input('stock');
echo $this->Form->end(__('Submit'));
?>
```

8. Now when we enabled the inventory routing prefix, we have to adjust the settings for AuthComponent so that it correctly redirects to the non-prefixed methods of UsersController even from any prefixed method. Open the file named app/Controller/AppController.php and adjust settings for AuthComponent like this:

```
public $components = array(
    ...
   'Auth' => array(
     'loginRedirect' => array(
       'inventory' => false,
       'controller' => 'products'
     ),
     'logoutRedirect' => array(
       'inventory' => false,
       'controller' => 'users',
       'action' => 'login'
     ),
     'loginAction' => array(
       'inventory' => false,
       'controller' => 'users',
       'action' => 'login'
     )
   ),
   ...
);
```

Note that we added `inventory` to all settings related to URLs and added the `loginAction` setting, as we're no longer going to use a default nonprefixed URL.

9. Finally, navigate to `/books/index`, `/books/view/635c460a-f230-4565-8378-7cae01314e03`, `/inventory/books/stock`, or `/inventory/books/edit/635c460a-f230-4565-8378-7cae01314e03` in your browser. The respective screenshots are shown as follows:

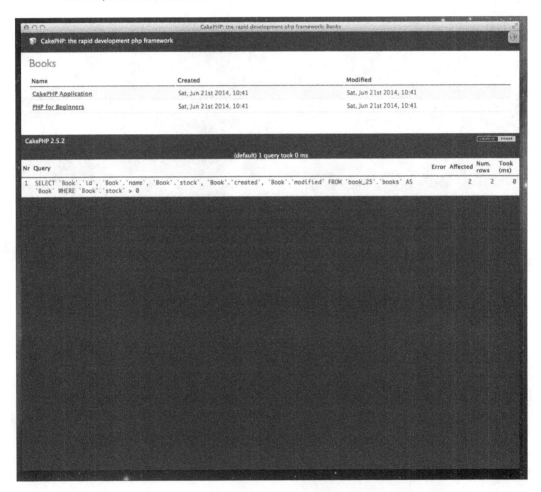

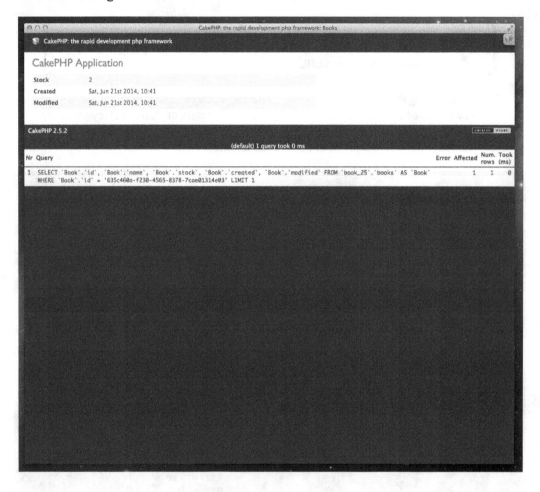

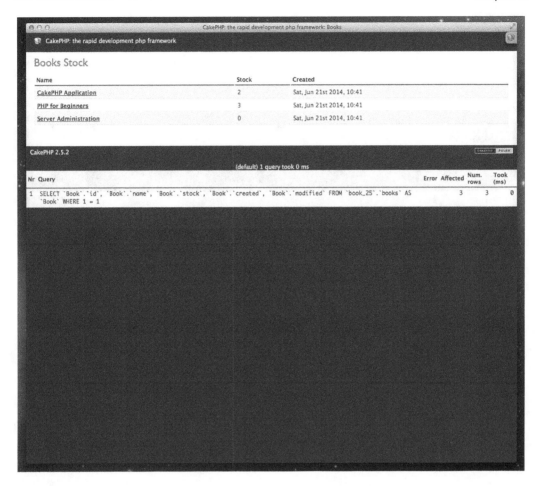

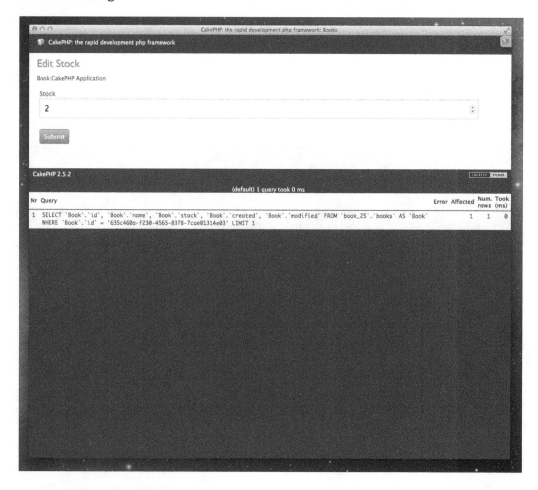

How it works...

In this recipe, we first set up the prefix settings for our routing. Specifically, we created a prefix named `inventory`. In this case, you could also define more prefixes by simply adding more values to the array of the `Routing.prefixes` configuration value.

We then created some `index()` and `view()` actions in our `BooksController`. These simply read the books available and show the details of a book, although the `find('all')` call of our `index()` method filters the results via the `conditions` option to not include any books with stock at `0` (out of stock). We also defined some `inventory_stock()` and `inventory_edit()` methods. You'll notice that these are prefixed with `inventory_`. This was intentional, as this is how the framework maps the router prefix with the action by convention. So, when calling any action of a controller prefixed with `/inventory/` in the URL, the router will search for the requested action where the prefix is prepended with `inventory_`.

You probably also saw that while generating the URL for our links in our inventory management area, we included the prefix option in our call to the link() method on the Html helper. This tells the router to create a link using that prefix. Without it, the router would simply create a URL to a normal action on the controller.

Here, we simply prefixed some actions. However, you could easily extend this controller now so that it requires some special attribute of the currently logged-in user account in order to use the inventory actions.

Handling languages

When building a multi-language application, you may want to allow your users to change the language of the content they're viewing through the URL.

In this recipe, we'll look at how you can use routing to deliver content in different languages.

Getting ready

First, we'll need a controller to work with, so create an ExampleController.php file in app/Controller/ with the following content:

```php
<?php
App::uses('AppController', 'Controller');

class ExampleController extends AppController {
}
```

We'll then need a view, so create a file named language.ctp in app/View/Example/.

How to do it...

Perform the following steps:

1. Open the routes.php file in app/Config/ and add the following lines to it:

   ```php
   Router::connect('/:language/:controller/:action/*', array(),
   array(
       'language' => '[a-zA-Z]{3}',
       'persist' => array('language')
   ));
   ```

2. Open your AppController.php file in app/Controller/ and add the following beforeFilter() method:

   ```php
   public function beforeFilter() {
       parent::beforeFilter();
   ```

```php
    if (!empty($this->request->params['language'])) {
        Configure::write('Config.language', $this->request-
>params['language']);
    }
}
```

3. Edit the `ExampleController.php` file in `app/Controller/` and add the following `language()` method to it:

```php
public function language() {
    $this->set('language', Configure::read('Config.language'));
}
```

4. Edit the `language.ctp` file in `app/View/Example/` and introduce the following content:

```php
<h2><?php echo __('Language Setting'); ?></h2>
<p>
    <?php echo __('The current language is: %s', $language); ?>
</p>
```

5. Finally, navigate to `/eng/example/language` and then navigate to `/esp/example/language` to see the website change language. This can be seen in the following screenshot:

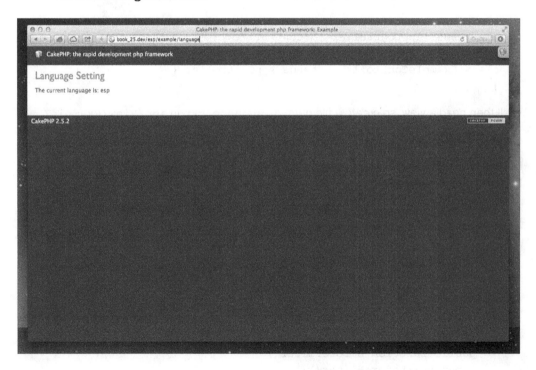

How it works...

Here, we first defined a route to handle our language setting via the URL. For this we used the `Router::connect()` method to register a new route. The first argument is the route template. You'll notice that we defined parts of the URL starting with a `:`. This character delimits a named element, which we'll want to capture. The second argument was left as an empty array, as we're not specifying any default route parameters. Finally, the third argument had two keys. The first, `language`, defines the regular expression for our `language` route element. Here, we're simply stating that it must be a three character string, which matches with the locale codes in the framework. The second key, `persist`, tells CakePHP that we want all URLs to have this element included. This helps keep our application consistent for all links.

We then added a `beforeFilter()` method to our `AppController` class, which reads the `CakeRequest::$params` array to get the value of `language` passed via the URL. This is then set to the `Config.language` configuration option, which sets the default language for the application.

To test the functionality that we added, we created a `language()` method on our `ExampleController`. This method reads the value of the `Config.language` configuration option and sets it to a view variable named `$language`. Then, in our view, we output some translated strings, as well as the `$language` variable. When changing the value of the language in your URL, you'll see how it updates the default setting in the framework. Then, if you create some translations of your strings for the given URLs, you would see the view change language.

To further extend the functionality of the language setting, you could add a list of default languages that your applications support. Bear in mind that when a translation is not found, the strings using `__()` or any other various translation functions will simply default to the given string.

See also

▶ The *Using the I18n shell* recipe from *Chapter 9, Creating Shells*.

▶ The *Translations* recipe from *Chapter 10, View Templates*.

Custom route class

Although the base routing system provided with CakePHP will cover almost all cases, there may be times when you need to handle things which are slightly more complex. For this reason, the framework provides the option to define a custom route class, which processes more complicated scenarios.

In this recipe, we'll create a custom route class to handle news headlines for given year and month.

Getting ready

For this recipe, we'll need to create a custom route class to use in our routing. Therefore, create a file named `HeadlineRoute.php` in `app/Routing/Route/` with the following content:

```php
<?php
App::uses('CakeRoute', 'Routing/Route');
App::uses('ClassRegistry', 'Utility');

class HeadlineRoute extends CakeRoute {
}
```

We'll then need some data to work with. So, create a table named `headlines` using the following SQL statement:

```sql
CREATE TABLE headlines (
    id INT NOT NULL AUTO_INCREMENT,
    title VARCHAR(50),
    year SMALLINT(2) UNSIGNED NOT NULL,
    month SMALLINT(2) UNSIGNED NOT NULL,
    PRIMARY KEY(id)
);
```

After creating the table, run the following SQL statement to insert some headlines:

```sql
INSERT INTO headlines (title, year, month)
VALUES
('CakePHP on top', '2013', '11'),
('CakeFest 2014', '2014', '08'),
('CakePHP going strong', '2014', '08');
```

We'll also need to create a file named `HeadlinesController.php` in `app/Controller/` and add the following content to it:

```php
<?php
App::uses('AppController', 'Controller');

class HeadlinesController extends AppController {
}
```

Finally, create a `listing.ctp` file in `app/View/Headlines/` for our view.

How to do it...

Perform the following steps:

1. Add the following code to the `routes.php` file in `app/Config/`:

```
App::uses('HeadlineRoute', 'Routing/Route');

Router::connect('/:year/:month', array(
    'controller' => 'headlines',
    'action' => 'listing'
), array(
    'year' => '[0-9]{4}',
    'month' => '[0-1]{0,1}[0-9]{1}',
    'routeClass' => 'HeadlineRoute'
));
```

2. Edit the `HeadlineRoute.php` file in `app/Routing/Route/` and add the following `parse()` method to it:

```
public function parse($url) {
    $params = parent::parse($url);
    if (empty($params)) {
        return false;
    }
    $cacheKey = $params['year'] . '-' . $params['month'];
    $headlines = Cache::remember($cacheKey, function () use
($params) {
        return ClassRegistry::init('Headline')->find('all', array(
            'conditions' => array(
                'Headline.year' => (int)$params['year'],
                'Headline.month' => (int)$params['month']
            )
        ));
    });
    if (!empty($headlines)) {
        return $params;
    }
    return false;
}
```

3. Define the following `listing()` method in the `HeadlinesController.php` file:

```
public function listing() {
    $year = $this->request->params['year'];
```

```
$month = $this->request->params['month'];
$headlines = Cache::read($year . '-' . $month);
$this->set(compact('year', 'month', 'headlines'));
}
```

4. Add the following content to the `listing.ctp` file:

```
<h2><?php echo __('Headlines for %s/%s', $year, $month); ?></h2>
<?php
$list = Hash::extract($headlines, '{n}.Headline.title');
echo $this->Html->nestedList($list);
```

5. Finally, navigate to `/2014/08` in your browser to see the headlines for that month. This is shown in the following screenshot:

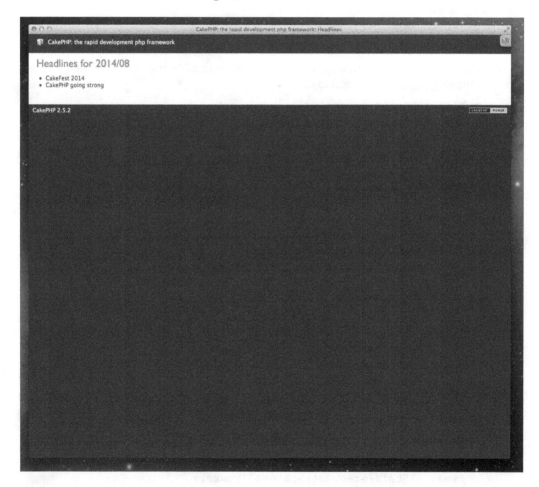

How it works...

For this recipe, we first created a custom route class to handle our routing logic. This class was created in a file named `HeadlineRoute.php`, which is located in `app/Routing/Route/`. There is no strict convention for the naming of route classes and they don't need to align with any controller or model, but it's best to name them wisely so that it's evident what their function entails. In these calls, we defined a `parse()` method, which processes the route. Note that the `HeadlineRoute` is only actioned when the `/:year/:month` template we defined matches. In this case, we also added some validation to our route, making sure that the year and month are valid for our request. The `routeClass` then defines that we want to use our custom route class for these routes. This is where our `parse()` method comes into play.

For our routing logic, we first resolve the `parent::parse()` call to obtain the underlying routing, and then check that we're in a valid route. We then build a cache key from the `year` and `month` values passed from our template in the request. Then, we use this key to call `Cache::remember()`, passing it an anonymous function that initializes the `Headline` model by calling the `ClassRegistry::init()` method and returns the headlines based on the values provided from our route. This greatly improves our application performance, as we will have the results cached for subsequent requests for the same year and month. If there are headlines, we return the `$params` array to signal that our route class has matched successfully. To the contrary, we return `false`, which means the route class did not resolve a possible resource.

When the route is successfully matched, we had defined in our configuration array for the request to be routed to the `listing()` action of the `HeadlinesController`. In this method, we only used the `year` and `month` values provided in the `CakeRequest::$params` array to construct our cache key and read the headlines our custom route class previously stored for us. Then, we just set those values as view variables using the `set()` method of our controller and used the `compact()` function to generate the `key => value` array from our variables.

Our view is just as simple. We created a header by using the `$year` and `$month` values passed via the URL, and we also processed the headlines to generate a list. For this, we first used the `Hash::extract()` method to parse our array of records to return an array of headline titles, and then we used the `nestedList()` method of the `Html` helper to build our HTML list.

There's more...

So far, we've successfully set up the logic to resolve the URL to a collection of headlines. However, it would now be ideal to also define the logic for reverse routing. This is where we generate a link based on the values of a headline.

For this, we want to be able to simply create a URL from the unique ID of a headline to generate the required path for the month's headlines. For this, we'll add a `match()` method to our `HeadlineRoute` class with the following logic:

```
public function match($url) {
   if ($url['controller'] === 'headlines' && $url['action'] ===
'listing' && !empty($url[0])) {
      $headline = ClassRegistry::init('Headline')->find('first', array(
         'conditions' => array(
            'id' => $url[0]
         )
      ));
      if (!empty($headline)) {
         $url['year'] = $headline['Headline']['year'];
         $url['month'] = $headline['Headline']['month'];
         unset($url[0]);
         return parent::match($url);
      }
   }
   return false;
}
```

In the preceding code, we've first checked that the URL configuration specified the `controller` as `Headline` and the `action` as `listing`, with the ID of the headline. We then instantiate the `Headline` model via `ClassRegistry::init()` method, using the ID provided. If a record is found, we set the `year` and `month` keys in the URL configuration and remove the ID. Finally, we call the `parent::match()` method to complete the translation of the route. To see how it works, add the following line to the `app/View/Headlines/listing.ctp` file:

```
debug(Router::url(array('controller' => 'headlines', 'action' =>
'listing', 1)));
```

It will output matching the `/2013/11` URL.

See also

▸ The *View caching* recipe from *Chapter 10, View Templates*.

Dispatch filter

The dispatch filters allow you to intercept the dispatch cycle, run code before or after the controller is built and dispatched, and even return early without completing the full cycle.

In this recipe, we'll create a dispatch filter that exposes an API without requiring the full dispatch cycle.

Getting ready

First, we'll create a file named `ApiDispatcher.php` in app/Routing/Filter/ as shown in the following code:

```php
<?php
App::uses('DispatcherFilter', 'Routing');
App::uses('ClassRegistry', 'Utility');

class ApiDispatcher extends DispatcherFilter {
}
```

We'll then need some data to serve from our API. For that, create a `libraries` table with the following SQL statement:

```sql
CREATE TABLE libraries (
    id INT NOT NULL AUTO_INCREMENT,
    name VARCHAR(100),
    details TEXT,
    created DATETIME,
    modified DATETIME,
    PRIMARY KEY(id)
);
```

Finally, populate the `libraries` table with the following SQL statement:

```sql
INSERT INTO libraries (name, details, created, modified)
VALUES
('Cake', 'Yummy and sweet', NOW(), NOW()),
('Cookie', 'Browsers love cookies', NOW(), NOW()),
('Helper', 'Helping you all the way', NOW(), NOW());
```

How to do it...

Perform the following steps:

1. Add the `ApiDispatcher` class name in the `Dispatcher.filters` configuration of your `bootstrap.php file`:

    ```php
    Configure::write('Dispatcher.filters', array(
      'AssetDispatcher',
      'CacheDispatcher',
      'ApiDispatcher'
    ));
    ```

2. Add the following `$priority` property to the `ApiDispatcher` class in `app/Routing/Filter/`:

    ```php
    public $priority = 9;
    ```

3. In the same `ApiDispatcher` class, add the following `beforeDispatch()` method;

    ```php
    public function beforeDispatch(CakeEvent $event) {
      $request = $event->data['request'];
      $response = $event->data['response'];
      $url = $request->url;
      if (substr($url, 0, 4) === 'api/') {
        try {
          switch (substr($url, 4)) {
            case 'libraries':
              $object = array(
                'status' => 'success',
                'data' => ClassRegistry::init('Library')->find('all')
              );
              break;
            default:
              throw new Exception('Unknown end-point');
          }
        } catch (Exception $e) {
          $response->statusCode(500);
          $object = array(
            'status' => 'error',
            'message' => $e->getMessage(),
            'code' => $e->getCode()
          );
          if (Configure::read('debug') > 0) {
            $object['data'] = array(
              'file' => $e->getFile(),
              'trace' => $e->getTrace()
    ```

```
        );
      }
    }
    $response->type('json');
    $response->body(json_encode($object));
    $event->stopPropagation();

    return $response;
  }
}
```

4. Navigating to `/api/libraries` in your browser will return the libraries in a JSON formatted response, as shown in the following screenshot:

{"status":"success","data":[{"Library":{"id":"1","name":"Cake","details":"Yummy and sweet","created":"2014-06-25 17:02:21","modified":"2014-06-25 17:02:21"}},{"Library":{"id":"2","name":"Cookie","details":"Browsers love cookies","created":"2014-06-25 17:02:21","modified":"2014-06-25 17:02:21"}},{"Library":{"id":"3","name":"Helper","details":"Helping you all the way","created":"2014-06-25 17:02:21","modified":"2014-06-25 17:02:21"}}]}

How it works...

In the first step, we added the `ApiDispatcher` class to the `Dispatch.filter` configuration array. When adding a class name, by setting it as a key of the `Dispatch.filters` array, you can pass an array of constructor `$settings` as the value. The class name may also use dot notation to load dispatch filters from a plugin.

The order here is also important, as the filters are executed in order of definition. However, we also set the `$priority` property on the class to a value of 9. The default priority is 10, with lower priorities executing first.

We then defined a `beforeDispatch()` method. The `DispatchFilter` class has two callback methods, `beforeDisptach()` and `afterDisptach()`, which executes before and after the dispatch cycle. These methods receive a single argument, which is the `CakeEvent` object. This contains the request and response objects, and it can also contain an array that is passed when the dispatch is triggered by a call to `requestAction()`.

In our callback method, we first extracted the request and response objects from `$event['reqesut']` and `$event['response']` respectively. We then read the URL of the request from `CakeRequest::$url`, which gave us the end-point for our API. We checked that we're dealing with an API call by confirming that the URL starts with `api/`. The remaining part of the URL string then represents the name of our endpoint. We then used a `switch()` statement to allow future extensions to the API, where adding a new endpoint would be as simple as just adding another case to our `switch()`.

In our case for `libraries`, we defined an array in an `$object` variable, which will later serve as our JSON object, following the *Jsend* spec. In this case, we define a `status` key with the value of `success`, and then use the `ClassRegistry` utility class to load our `Library` model on the fly, calling the `find()` method to return `all` records. These are stored in the `data` key of our JSON object. You'll notice that we defined all of this inside a `try/catch` statement. This is useful, as it allows us to capture and format any exceptions as a JSON formatted response. The `default` case for our switch throws an `Exception`, which advises that an end-point does not exist.

We finally prepare our response by calling the `CakeResponse::type()` method to set the `Content-Type` parameter of the HTTP response to `application/json`. The `CakeResponse` class has a significant list of predefined content types, which can be easily applied on demand. You can also define new content types if your application needs to support them. Following this, we use the `json_encode()` function to format our `$object` variable as a JSON object, and then apply that to the body of the HTTP response by using `CakeResponse::body()`. We then call `stopPropagation()` to stop any further dispatch filters from being executed and return the `$response` object to be returned to the client.

There's more...

If you didn't want to create a class for your dispatch filter, you can also define it as a PHP callable, for example:

```
Configure::write('Dispatcher.filters', array(
  'AssetDispatcher',
  'CacheDispatcher',
  'example' => array(
    'callable' => function(CakeEvent $event) {
      // your code here
    },
    'on' => 'before',
    'priority' => 9
  )
));
```

In the preceding code, the key is the name of your filter, while the array contains the configuration. `callable` is the function that is executed. This could be an anonymous function or any valid callable type. The exception here is that a string is not interpreted as a function name, but instead it is interpreted as a class name. The `on` setting defines the point at which the function is executed. This can either be `before` or `after`, to run before or after the dispatch cycle. Finally, the `priority` setting is the same as the `$priority` property we set in our class, and defines the execution order in relation to other dispatch filters.

3

HTTP Negotiation

In this chapter, we will cover the following topics:

- ▸ Parsing extensions
- ▸ Processing Ajax requests
- ▸ Building a response
- ▸ Uploading a file
- ▸ Using a detector
- ▸ Working with cookies
- ▸ Cache control
- ▸ Error handling

Introduction

Interpreting and manipulating HTTP is a fundamental area for any web-based application framework. Luckily, the framework comes well prepared to handle and work with HTTP.

In this chapter, we'll look at various scenarios where working with HTTP is greatly simplified by CakePHP.

Parsing extensions

It's common for applications to use a file extension as part of the URL. This can sometimes help orientate the user to the type of content found in that location or for your application to easily deal with data types such as JSON or XML.

In this recipe, we'll look at how easy it is to parse extensions using the framework.

Getting ready

For this recipe, we'll use a `books` controller from previous chapter, which will return a listing of books from the `books` database table as a JSON response. So, find a file named `BooksController.php` in `app/Controller/`.

How to do it...

Perform the following steps:

1. First, add the following line to your `routes.php` file located in `app/Config/`:

    ```
    Router::parseExtensions('json');
    ```

2. Then, we'll load the `RequestHandler` component in our `BooksController` class using the following code:

    ```
    public $components = array('RequestHandler');
    ```

3. We'll also add a `listing()` method with the following code:

    ```php
    public function listing() {
      $books = $this->Book->find('all', array('fields' =>
    array('name', 'stock')));
      $this->set(array(
        'books' => Hash::extract($books, '{n}.Book'),
        '_serialize' => array('books')
      ));
    }
    ```

4. Now, navigating to `/books/listing.json` in your browser will return a JSON listing of books similar to the following code:

    ```json
    {'books':[{'title':'1984','author':'George Orwell'},{'title':'
    Neuromancer','author':'William Gibson'},{'title':'The Cuckoo\'s
    Egg','author':'Cliff Stoll'}]}
    {
      "books": [
        {
          "name": "CakePHP Application",
          "stock": "2"
        },
        {
          "name": "PHP for Beginners",
          "stock": "3"
        },
        {
    ```

```
        "name": "Server Administration",
        "stock": "0"
      }
    ]
  }
```

How it works...

We first added a call to the static `parseExtensions()` method of the `Router` class. This method allows you to easily define extensions, which will be detected and handled automatically by the framework. By default, CakePHP provides both XML and JSON out of the box, but you can define any extension you like. You can also define multiple extensions by simply specifying the different extensions in the method call. An example can be seen in the following code:

```
Router::parseExtensions('xml', 'json');
```

Next, we included the `RequestHandler` component in our `BooksController` class, as this handles the internal logic to process the extension routing. You must include this component in any controller where you want extensions to be parsed correctly.

We then created a `listing()` action in our controller, which serves a list of books from the database for our JSON format. Here you'll notice our use of a `_serialize` key in our call to `set()`. This is a special view variable that defines other view variables to be serialized for use in data views. The value of `_serialize` can be a string, as the name of another view variable, or an array of various view variables to use. All variables defined for `_serialize` must also be defined using the `set()` method in the controller.

Internally, with the `json` extension defined to be parsed with `Router::parseExtensions()`, on every request with a `.json` URL extension or with the `Accept` header set to `application/json`, the framework will switch the standard view class for `JsonView`. This then handles the correct encoding and display of the JSON format.

See also

▸ Example usage of the Hash class is described at `http://book.cakephp.org/2.0/en/core-utility-libraries/hash.html`.

▸ More details on request handling can be found at `http://book.cakephp.org/2.0/en/core-libraries/components/request-handling.html`

Processing Ajax requests

It's no secret that Ajax has revolutionized web development and helped developers build and deliver engaging applications which have a real-time feel to them.

In this recipe, we'll look at how easy it is to handle Ajax requests in CakePHP and give you an introduction to the possibilities at your fingertips.

Getting ready

For this recipe, we'll reuse the `books` database table from the previous chapter. We'll also need a view for our `inventory_index()`. action, so create a file named `inventory_index.ctp` in `app/View/Books/`.

How to do it...

Perform the following steps:

1. Add the following `beforeFilter()` method to the `BooksController` class:

```
public function beforeFilter() {
  parent::beforeFilter();
  if ($this->request->is('ajax')) {
    $this->response->disableCache();
  }
}
```

2. In the same class, add the following `inventory_index()` method (we will utilize the `inventory` prefix added in the previous chapter):

```
public function inventory_index() {
  $this->set('books', $this->Book->find('all'));
}
```

3. In the same class, add the following `inventory_update()` method:

```
public function inventory_update() {
  $this->request->allowMethod('ajax');
  if (!$this->request->is('post')
    || !isset($this->request->data['id'])
    || !$this->Book->hasAny(array('id' => $this->request->data['id']))
    || !isset($this->request->data['stock'])
    || !is_numeric($this->request->data['stock'])
```

```php
    ) {
      throw new BadRequestException();
    }
    $this->autoRender = false;
    $this->Book->id = $this->request->data['id'];
    $this->Book->saveField('stock', $this->request->data['stock']);
    return true;
  }
```

4. Introduce the following content into the `inventory_index.ctp` file in `app/View/Books/`:

```php
<?php
  $this->Html->script('https://code.jquery.com/jquery-2.1.1.min.
js', array('block' => 'script'));
?>
<h2><?php echo __('Books stock'); ?></h2>
<ul>
  <?php foreach ($books as $book): ?>
    <li>
      <?php echo h($book['Book']['name']); ?>:
      <input id="<?php echo $book['Book']['id']; ?>" name="stock"
type="text" value="<?php echo $book['Book']['stock']; ?>"/>
      <?php
      echo $this->Html->scriptBlock(
        '$("#' . $book['Book']['id'] . '").keyup(function(e) { if
(e.keyCode === 13) { update($(this)); } });'
      );
      ?>
    </li>
  <?php endforeach; ?>
</ul>
<?php
$url = $this->Html->url(array('action' => 'update'));
$success = __('Updated!');
$error = __('Could not update stock');
$script = <<<JS
function update(node) {
  var stock = node.val();
  if (stock === '' || stock.match(/[^\d]+/)) {
    node.val('0');
    stock = '0';
  }
  var data = {
    id: node.attr('id'),
```

```
        stock: stock
    };
    $.post("$url", data)
        .done(function() { alert("$success"); })
        .fail(function() { alert("$error"); });
}
JS;

    $this->Html->scriptBlock($script, array('block' => 'script'));
```

5. Finally, navigate to /inventory/books in your browser and update the stock number of any book—just change some stock number and press the *Enter* key. The result can be seen in the following screenshot:

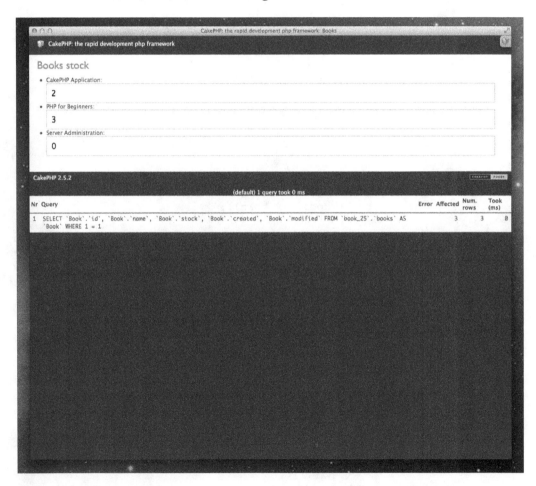

How it works...

In this recipe, we first defined a `beforeFilter()` callback method. This checks that the request was made via Ajax using the `is()` method of the `CakeRequest` object and passing the `ajax` value. If this is the case, we'll disable caching, as we always want to serve our Ajax calls fresh. Here, you could also consider turning debugging off by setting `Configure::write('debug', 0)` or any other feature you may have in your application which could output content.

We then defined our `inventory_index()` action, which simply reads all of the records in our `books` table and sets them to a `$books` variable in our view, which we'll see in a moment.

After that, we also added an `inventory_update()` action, which serves as our exclusive Ajax call. Here, we first restricted the request to only allow `ajax` calls. You could define HTTP methods here, but the framework provides a special `ajax` type that checks whether the call was made via Ajax, specifically by checking for an `X_REQUESTED_WITH` header in the HTTP request.

You'll notice that we subsequently checked whether the parsing body of the `POST` request was successful by checking whether the structure of that content, if it exists, is as we expect. In case it isn't, we throw `BadRequestException`, which is translated into a 400 HTTP status code, thus resulting in the Ajax call from the browser that understands the request as failed.

After parsing the content of the request, we updated the model with the ID and value of the stock to update with. Here, we not only validate that `id` and `stock` values exist in posted data, but also that a proper record exists and stock is numeric, to make sure that the data provided by the user is in line with what we would expect. The golden rule is to *never* trust data submitted by the users, *ever*!

We finally set the `$autoRender` property to `false` to avoid rendering a view and layout, after which we simply return `true`. Note that PHP would actually return 1 in the response body, as that's the way Boolean `true` is cast (the string `true` is not the same as a Boolean `true`, as the string `false` would also be `true`).

Once we had all of our logic in place, we created the view for our `inventory_index()` action. First, we called the `script()` method of the `Html` helper to include jQuery from the public CDN in our view. Notice that we set the `block` option to `script`, to make sure that the script wasn't included inline and, instead, was added to the view block named `script`. This isn't the best practice, as you should really include these assets in your layout or they should be delegated via a package/asset manager. We've included it in our view simply for this tutorial.

Following on, we then just output a list of the products available, with an input to update the stock value. Here, we included some JavaScript code using the `scriptBlock()` method, again from the `Html` helper, to output some jQuery code for each book.

After that, we again used the `scriptBlock()` method to output the `update()` JavaScript function used by our previous JavaScript code. Here, you probably noticed the use of heredoc syntax to specify the JavaScript code. This can help improve your code, especially if you find the need to inject PHP into your client-side scripts (try to avoid that as much as possible). It's always a much better practice to keep your JavaScript APIs and CSS styles in external files, as this greatly helps with development and maintenance down the road.

See also

▶ More details on heredoc syntax can be found at `http://www.php.net/manual/en/language.types.string.php#language.types.string.syntax.heredoc`

▶ The *Building a response* recipe

Building a response

CakePHP is designed to take most of the work out of building applications. However, sometimes you may want to handle things yourself, which the framework can also facilitate.

In this recipe we'll process a response ourselves, generating it exactly as we want.

Getting ready

As this recipe is straight to the point, we'll simply enhance an existing example controller to build our response. For this, open a file named `ExampleController.php` in `app/Controller/` and add the following `respond()` method to the `ExampleController` class:

```php
public function respond() {
  if (!$this->request->query('text')) {
    $this->response->statusCode(404);
  }
  $this->response->header('X-Timestamp', date('H:i:s'));
  $this->response->type('txt');
  $this->response->body($this->request->query('text'));
  $this->response->send();
  $this->_stop();
}
```

Navigate to `/example/respond?text=Hello` in your browser, which should output
Hello, as shown in the following screenshot:

How it works...

The framework usually handles the building of the response output as part of its dispatch
cycle; however, here we configured the response to our liking. First, in our `respond()` action,
we checked whether the request was sent with a query string parameter named `text` by
calling the `query()` method on the `CakeRequest` object. If the parameter is not found, we
update the status code of the response to 404 by calling the `statusCode()` method of the
`CakeResponse` object. Note that we update the status code, as its set to `200` by default.

Both the request and response objects are instantiated on the controller on the `$request` and `$response` properties, respectively. It's also possible to intercept these via a controller's `__construct()` method before they're set to the properties.

We then called the `type()` method to set the type of the content we're returning in the response. As we'll simply output the value of the `text` parameter, we'll set the type to `txt`. The HTTP header that's set by the `type()` method is named `Content-Type`. This header is responsible for defining the type of content the browser or client calling the URL should expect to be returned. In this case, we used `txt`, which CakePHP translates as `plain/text`. As many of the values used for the `Content-Type` header are long or have various alternatives, the framework helps by letting you simply reference the type by its associated file extension.

After handling the query string parameter and setting the `Content-Type` of the response, we also set a custom `X-Timestamp` header to the response via the `header()` method. You can also override standard headers or use the equivalent methods provided through the `CakeResponse` object's API, as we did with `type()`.

The `body()` method was then used to assign the actual content for the body of the response. In our example, this was the value of the `text` parameter, which we access via `$this->request->query('text')`. This can be any type of content, as long as it's a string or can be cast to a string in PHP. However, remember to set the `Content-Type` correctly if you're returning anything other than HTML (the default content type).

Now that our response object was configured as we wanted it, we just call `send()` to send it to the browser. It's important to note here that there are certain things that cannot be done after sending a response from PHP to the browser, and they become caveats for new developers, such as setting headers.

Finally, we also called the `_stop()` method. You might have seen others use `die()` or `exit()`, or you might even do so yourself. However, the correct way to stop the framework's execution is via the `_stop()` method. This is like correctly shutting down your computer, instead of just turning it off from the power button. This also allows you to hook in at a future point in time to perform certain operations before stopping the dispatch process.

Uploading a file

Creating forms and submitting data is usually easy until you have to deal with file uploads. Luckily, the framework doesn't tread on any toes here and lets you build the process as your application demands.

In this recipe, we'll look at a file upload scenario and build a process that is clean and helps maintain the separation of concerns in our application.

Getting ready

To begin with, we'll need to create a table to track our file uploads. For this, create a table named `uploads` with the following SQL statement:

```sql
CREATE TABLE uploads (
    id INT(11) NOT NULL AUTO_INCREMENT,
    name VARCHAR(100) NOT NULL,
    size INT(4) UNSIGNED NOT NULL,
    mime VARCHAR(50) NOT NULL,
    path TEXT NOT NULL,
    created DATETIME,
    modified DATETIME,
    PRIMARY KEY(id)
);
```

We'll also need a model for our `uploads` table, so create a file named `Upload.php` in `app/Model/` with the following content:

```php
<?php
App::uses('AppModel', 'Model');

class Upload extends AppModel {
}
```

We're still missing a controller to deal with our file uploads and view the files uploaded. So, create a file named `UploadsController.php` in `app/Controller/`, and introduce the following content:

```php
<?php
App::uses('AppController', 'Controller');

class UploadsController extends AppController {
}
```

We will use `SessionComponent` in this controller, but we have its usage already declared in the `AppController` parent class. Finally, we'll also need some views for our controller, so also create two files named `index.ctp` and `upload.ctp` in `app/View/Uploads/`.

How to do it...

Perform the following steps:

1. Define an `index()` method in our `UploadsController` class as shown in the following code:

```
public function index() {
  $this->set('uploads', $this->Upload->find('all'));
}
```

2. Define an `upload()` method in the same class:

```
public function upload() {
  if ($this->request->is('post')) {
    $this->Upload->create();
    if ($this->Upload->save($this->request->data)) {
      $this->Session->setFlash(__('New file uploaded'));
      return $this->redirect(array('action' => 'index'));
    }
    $this->Session->setFlash(__('Could not upload file'));
  }
}
```

3. Add a protected `_processFile()` method to our `Upload` model:

```
protected function _processFile() {
  $file = $this->data['Upload']['file'];
  if ($file['error'] === UPLOAD_ERR_OK) {
    $name = md5($file['name']);
    $path = WWW_ROOT . 'files' . DS . $name;
    if (is_uploaded_file($file['tmp_name'])
      && move_uploaded_file($file['tmp_name'], $path)
    ) {
      $this->data['Upload']['name'] = $file['name'];
      $this->data['Upload']['size'] = $file['size'];
      $this->data['Upload']['mime'] = $file['type'];
      $this->data['Upload']['path'] = '/files/' . $name;
      unset($this->data['Upload']['file']);
      return true;
    }
  }
  return false;
}
```

4. Add the `beforeSave()` callback method to the same model:

```php
public function beforeSave() {
  if (!parent::beforeSave($options)) {
    return false;
  }
  return $this->_processFile();
}
```

5. Add the following content to your `index.ctp` file in `app/View/Uploads/`:

```php
<h2><?php echo __('Uploads'); ?></h2>
<p>
  <?php echo $this->Html->link(__('Upload'), array('action' =>
'upload')); ?>
</p>
<table>
  <tr>
    <th><?php echo __('Name'); ?></th>
    <th><?php echo __('Uploaded'); ?></th>
  </tr>
  <?php foreach ($uploads as $upload): ?>
  <tr>
    <td>
      <?php
        echo $this->Html->link($upload['Upload']['name'],
$upload['Upload']['path'], array('target' => '_blank'));
      ?>
    </td>
    <td>
      <?php
        echo $this->Time->nice($upload['Upload']['created']);
      ?>
    </td>
  </tr>
  <?php endforeach; ?>
</table>
```

6. In your `upload.ctp` file, add the following content:

```php
<h2><?php echo __('Upload file'); ?></h2>
<?php
  echo $this->Form->create('Upload', array('type' => 'file'));
  echo $this->Form->file('file');
  echo $this->Form->end(__('Upload'));
```

7.   Finally, make the `app/webroot/files/` folder writable for web server's user account. The easiest way to do this is by executing `chmod 777 app/webroot/files` from the console, navigating to `/uploads` to view the files, and clicking on the **Upload** button to add a file.

How it works...

For this recipe, we built a small application to upload and store files of any type. Note that you cannot create a model class named `File`, so we named ours `Upload`.

We started by creating an `index()` action, which shows us a listing of all the uploaded files by calling the `find()` method on our `Upload` model requesting all records. We then set this data as a variable for our view using the `set()` method on our controller. We didn't preload any data into our `uploads` table, so this starts blank.

Next, we also created an `upload()` action, which handles our file uploads. Here, we first checked if the HTTP method used is "post", by calling the `is()` method on the `CakeRequest` object, located in the `$request` property of our controller. If this was the case, we then called the `create()` method on our `Upload` model, which tells it that we're about to define the data for a new record. We followed this by calling the `save()` method on our model, passing it the `$data` property of our `CakeRequest` object. If saving was successful, we call the `setFlash()` method of our `Session` component to send a notification to the user that the upload was completed and then redirect to our `index()` action. If the uploads fails, we simply notify the user of the issue.

After setting up our controller, we created a protected `_processFile()` method on our `Upload` model. This method handles all of the upload logic required for our file. We start by extracting information about our file from the data array sent by our form. The `error` key informs us of any problems encountered when handling the upload. Usually checking against the `UPLOAD_ERR_OK` constant is enough, but there are other PHP constants available for finer tuning, which are as follows:

▶   `UPLOAD_ERR_INI_SIZE`: This shows that the uploaded file exceeds the `upload_max_filesize` directive in your `php.ini` file

▶   `UPLOAD_ERR_FORM_SIZE`: This shows that the uploaded file exceeds the `MAX_FILE_SIZE` directive that was specified in the HTML form

▶   `UPLOAD_ERR_PARTIAL`: This shows that the uploaded file was only partially uploaded

▶   `UPLOAD_ERR_NO_FILE`: This shows that no file was uploaded

▶   `UPLOAD_ERR_NO_TMP_DIR`: This shows that a temporary folder is missing

▶   `UPLOAD_ERR_CANT_WRITE`: This shows that the writing operation to the disk has failed

▶   `UPLOAD_ERR_EXTENSION`: This shows that a PHP extension stopped the file upload

If no error was reported, we then proceeded to create a unique filename for our file (stored on the filesystem). For this, we simply used the md5() function, but you could use anything to name your files, even a composition of the file information. After that, we defined a $path for where we want to store the file as, by default, PHP uploads files to a temporary location, which by default is usually your system's temp directory. Here, we're moving our files to the files/ directory in webroot/. We then used the is_uploaded_file() and move_uploaded_file() functions to validate and move the uploaded file to our new path. The remaining logic simply populates the new record, unsets the file data originally uploaded, and returns true. You may have also noticed that we didn't use the $path variable as the value of our path field. This is because the $path variable is a filesystem path, while we want the URL to view or download the file. It's also worth noting here that you should remember to handle postprocessing on file upload, not on every request for a file. This reduces the load on your server to only when the file is initially uploaded and not continuously afterwards.

Now, we had our file processing defined; it needed to be called when saving a new file. To do this, we used the beforeSave() callback method to execute the logic before the record is saved. This helps avoid saving records where the file upload fails, as the callback would halt the process in case of a failure. We could even improve this user experience by adding some validation to our model and providing explicit details on failure. This is obviously down to each application to specify, as not all apps are built the same.

For the view for our index() action, we simply list the uploaded files in a table using the link() method of the Html helper to open the file. We set the target option to _blank here so that it opens in a new browser tab. Our upload() view was also quite simple, where we just output the form used to upload the file using the Form helper. You would have seen that we set the Upload model as the target but also specified the form type as file. This is important as it tells CakePHP to create a form capable of handling file uploads. We also used the file() method of the Form helper to create a file input for us.

There's more...

In this recipe, we saw what was required to deal with a basic file upload. However, you can save yourself a lot of time simply using an existing plugin to do most of the work for you. Additionally, there are some plugins available that offer extensive configuration options and features to build powerful and robust upload systems. Some of them are listed as follows:

- **CakePHP Upload**: The Upload plugin is a feature-rich option to help take the pain out of handling single and multifile uploads, while also providing some extensive behaviors, image, and even PDF thumbnail processing, and a wide range of validation rules for models.

  You can find more info on the Upload plugin at https://github.com/josegonzalez/cakephp-upload.

- **CakePHP File Storage**: The FileStorage plugin is not just another upload plugin, but a complete solution for file handling in your CakePHP applications. Instead of putting file metadata directly into tables, it organizes them into a separate table. All other entities can then use associations to access their associated files. For example, a User might have an Avatar, a Product may have many Images, or a Gallery could have and belong to many Pictures.

  At its core, the plugin wraps the Gaufrette library, which is an abstraction layer for virtually any kind of storage backend. It doesn't matter where you want to store a file; you can store it in a local drive, over FTP, on Amazon S3 or Dropbox, or even in a zip file. Another bonus is that you can very easily migrate files between different storage backends, which are configured via an array. You can find more on the FileStorage plugin at https://github.com/burzum/cakephp-file-storage.

- **CakePHP Imagine**: Image processing is not directly included in the plugin but can be with the Imagine plugin, which wraps the Imagine library. Image processing follows the best practice and is built with enterprise-level scalability in mind. Each version of the image is represented as a unique file and directly created after upload. Information on the Imagine plugin can be found at https://github.com/burzum/cakephp-imagine-plugin.

Using a detector

Detectors are used by the framework to analyze a request and make quick assertions about the incoming data or petition. CakePHP provides a set of default request detectors, such as post, ajax, or ssl. However, you can easily extend the available detectors using CakeRequest::addDetector(). There are four different types of detectors that you can create:

- **Environment Value Comparison**: This compares a value from env() for equality with the given value

- **Pattern Value Comparison**: This compares a value from env() with a regular expression

- **Options-based Comparison**: This uses a list of options to create a regular expression (options will be merged for subsequent calls to add an already defined options-based detector)

- **Callback**: This uses a *callable* type to handle the comparison (the callback function receives the request object as the first and only argument)

We'll focus on the callback detector here, as it's by far the most powerful.

Getting ready

For this recipe, we'll define a controller that uses a detector to verify access to a private API, requiring a shared key to be provided on all requests.

We'll create an `ApiController` class in a file named `app/Controller/ApiController.php` with the following code.

```php
<?php
App::uses('AppController', 'Controller');

class ApiController extends AppController {
}
```

This controller won't be using a view file, as we'll be using it exclusively to handle API requests.

How to do it...

Perform the following steps:

1. Define a detector that checks for a certain header in the HTTP request:

```php
public function __construct($request = null, $response = null) {
    parent::__construct($request, $response);

    $this->request->addDetector('verified', array(
        'callback' => function ($request) {
            $header = $request->header('X-Api-Key');
            return ($header === Configure::read('Api.key'));
        }
    ));
}
```

2. Create a `beforeFilter()` callback method in our `ApiController`:

```php
public function beforeFilter() {
    parent::beforeFilter();

    $this->Components->disable(array('Auth', 'Session'));

    if (!$this->request->is('verified')) {
        throw new ForbiddenException('Request not verified');
    }
}
```

Now, you can implement any number of actions in this controller, and all of them will require a valid API key passed in the `X-Api-Key` request header.

How it works...

In this recipe, we first defined a callback detector, which checks whether a certain HTTP header (`X-Api-Key`) was provided with the request and whether the value of that header was identical to the key that is stored locally on the server which exposes the API.

We then created the `beforeFilter()` callback method, which uses the `CakeRequest::is()` method to call the verified detector. If it fails, returning `false`, we throw a `ForbiddenException`, signaling that the request had not been authenticated earlier. We're also disabling the `Session` and `Auth` components for this particular controller—it inherits them from the `AppController` parent class, but we have no use for them in a private API authenticated against a key from the configuration.

See also

- ▶ The *Authentication API* recipe from *Chapter 4, API Strategies*
- ▶ The *The HTTP authorization* recipe from *Chapter 5, Using Authentication*

Working with cookies

Cookies allow you to persist data across requests, thus allowing you to keep track of certain aspects of the navigation, user, or anything that needs to be referenced from one action to another.

In this recipe, we'll create a basic example scenario that shows how to use cookies in the framework.

Getting ready

For this recipe, we'll use a controller to work with, so let's use our existing `ExampleController.php` file in `app/Controller/`. We'll also need a view for one of our actions, so also create a file named `cookie.ctp` in `app/View/Example/`.

How to do it...

Perform the following steps:

1. Add the `$components` property to the `ExampleController` class with the `Cookie` component, as shown in the following code:

   ```
   public $components = array(
     'Cookie' => array(
   ```

```
        'time' => '+1 day'
    )
);
```

2. Define the following `cookie()` method:

```php
public function cookie() {
  $value = __('No value defined');
  if ($this->Cookie->check('value')) {
    $value = $this->Cookie->read('value');
  }
  $this->set('value', $value);
}
```

3. Define the following `cookie_update()` method:

```php
public function cookie_update($value) {
  $this->Cookie->write('value', $value);
  $this->redirect(array('action' => 'cookie'));
}
```

4. You also need to define the following `cookie_remove()` method:

```php
public function cookie_remove() {
  $this->Cookie->delete('value');
  $this->redirect(array('action' => 'cookie'));
}
```
```
Finally, view app/View/Example/cookie.ctp
<h2>Cookie example</h2>
<p>
  Value: <?php echo h($value); ?>
</p>
```

How it works...

For this recipe, we've created a simple example that demonstrates how cookie handling works in CakePHP.

To test it out, visit /example/cookie in your browser. You should see a view similar to the following screenshot:

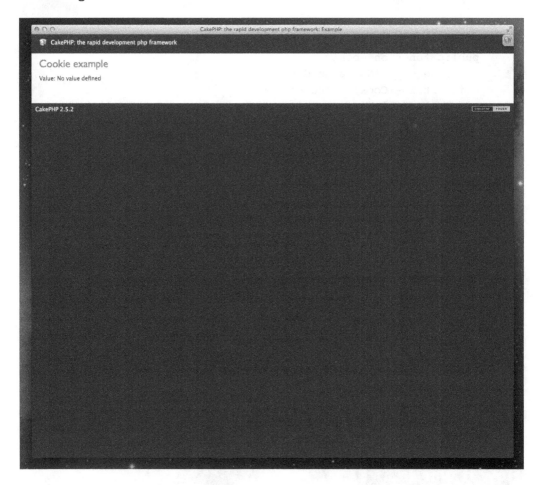

The view will state **No value defined**. This is because we haven't yet populated our cookie. So, now visit /example/cookie_update/test. The same view that you saw earlier will load, but this time, it will show **Value: test,** as shown in the following screenshot:

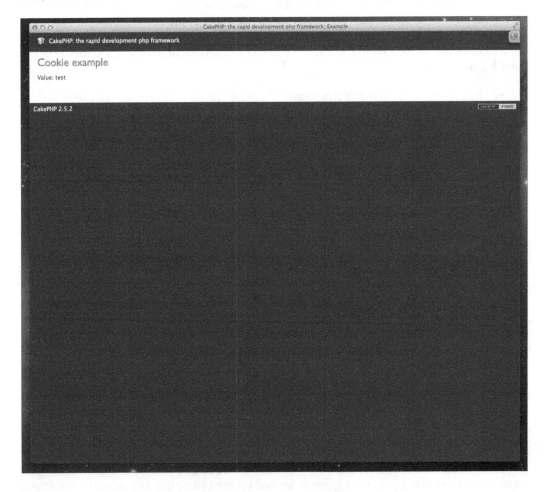

Likewise, if you now navigate to `/example/cookie_remove`, the view will reload again and again display **No value defined**.

Here, we first loaded the `Cookie` component in our controller. We also defined a `time` setting with the value of `+1 day`. This determines the expiry of the cookie. There are various configuration options, which can be set upon including the component or as properties of the `Cookie` component, typically in the `beforeFilter()` callback of the controller. Some of them are as follows:

- `name`: This is the name of the cookie.
- `time`: This is the duration the cookie will remain valid for.
- `path`: This is the server path that the cookie is available from. Default to the whole domain.
- `domain`: This is the domain the cookie applies to. To include subdomains, use `.example.com`.
- `secure`: This defines if the cookie is only available via HTTPS.
- `key`: This is the encryption key to use.
- `httpOnly`: This determines if the cookie is only available via HTTP (no access via JavaScript).

Then, in our `cookie()` method, we first defined a default text in our `$value` variable. We then called the `check()` method of the `Cookie` component to determine if a value key has been set earlier on the cookie. If so, we update the `$value` variable with the content of the value key in our cookie. We then finally used the `set()` method to register the `$value` variable to the view.

It's worth mentioning that there is no convention as to the naming of the keys in cookies; however, you can use the dot notation to define depths and namespace values. This way, if you were to define a `Product.status` key, you could only modify or delete the value of `status` by calling `Product.status`, or all values stored under `Product` by providing only that.

Now, in the `cookie_update()` method, we called the `write()` method of the `Cookie` component, to write the `$value` argument passed via the URL to the `value` key of the cookie after which, we redirect back to the `cookie()` action to display the result. The write method takes `key` as the first argument, and the value to write as the second. There are additionally two optional arguments, the first being a Boolean to determine if the value should be encrypted, and the other a specific timeout for this value. This can be an integer representing the number of seconds, or a string compatible with `strtotime()`.

Finally, we also created a `cookie_remove()` action, which calls the `delete()` method of the `Cookie` component to completely remove the `value` key from our cookie. This then also redirects to the `cookie()` method to again display that no value is defined.

Cache control

Manipulating the HTTP cache is a great way to control the impact of visitors and users on your application's resources. CakePHP provides a range of options to control both expiration and validation, and manage how clients and proxies engage with your content.

In this recipe, we'll look at the various ways you can handle the HTTP cache to your advantage.

Getting ready

In this recipe, we'll use a simple controller to show each of the caching options available. So, create a file named `CacheController.php` in `app/Controller/`, with the following content:

```php
<?php
App::uses('AppController', 'Controller');

class CacheController extends AppController {

    public $autoRender = false;
}
```

How to do it...

Perform the following steps:

1. Add a `cached()` method to the `CacheController` class, as shown in the following code:

   ```php
   public function cached() {
       $this->response->cache('-1 hour', '+1 day');
       return __('I am cached!');
   }
   ```

2. In the same class, also add an `expire()` method:

   ```php
   public function expire() {
       $this->response->expires('+2 days');
       return __('We all expire');
   }
   ```

3. In the same class, add a `modified()` method:

   ```php
   public function modified() {
       $record = array(
           'content' => __('Some old content'),
   ```

```
      'modified' => '2013-08-29 17:31:49'
    );
    $this->response->modified($record['modified']);
    if ($this->response->checkNotModified($this->request)) {
      return $this->response;
    }
    return $record['content'];
  }
```

4. Again, add an `etagged()` method:

```
public function etagged() {
  $record = array(
    'content' => __('Some old content'),
    'modified' => '2013-08-29 17:31:49'
  );
  $this->response->etag(md5($record['content']));
  if ($this->response->checkNotModified($this->request)) {
    return $this->response;
  }
  return $record['content'];
}
```

5. Finally, add a `cache_control()` method:

```
public function cache_control() {
  $this->response->sharable(true, 86400);
  return __('Caching under control');
}
```

How it works...

In this recipe, we've created a couple of actions, each of which show off how you can control the HTTP cache through the framework. In our first example, the `cached()` action, we used the `cache()` method of the `CakeResponse` object. This is the most general form of cache control in CakePHP, which sets a couple of HTTP together. The value of the first argument is used as the `Last-Modified` header value, which tells the browser when the content was last updated. In our example, we set this to a negative value (in the past), so it's not interpreted as new content. It also sets the `Cache-Control` header with the `public` directive and also sets the `max-age` directive with the value of the second argument. Even though the `Cache-Control` header overrides the `Expires` header, this is also set as a precaution.

In our next example, the `expire()` action, we used the `expires()` method of the `CakeResponse` object to directly set the value of the `Expires` header in the HTTP response. Here, the returned content would be cached by the client for two days.

Following on, we then created a `modified()` action, which used the `last_modified()` method to set the `Last-Modified` header in the HTTP response. Here, we created a record to use in our example. This would typically be a record from a model or some content you generate for the response. We first set the timestamp of the last time this content was modified (you would generally know this some way, such as the date a post was published in a blog, for example) by calling the `modified()` method of the `CakeResponse` object. We then checked if that date is stale (is old content, not fresh) by calling the `checkNotModified()` method and passing it the instance of the `CakeRequest` object found in the `$request` property of the controller. If the content has not been modified since the current date and time, we return `$response` as the content. If not, we return the content to be cached, in this case, the value in `$record['content']`.

For the next example, in the `etagged()` action, we used an Etag (entity tag). This works in a way that is similar to the `last_modified()` method, except here, we call the `etag()` method, passing it our value (in this case, a hash of the content). In HTTP, an Etag is used to reference a resource, so the client can determine if it has changed by a change in the Etag. You can also share Etags across common content with the `W/` prefix that specifies the Etag as weak. We then called the `checkNotModified()` method, again passing it the instance of the `CakeRequest` object. If the content has not been modified, as the Etags match, we return `$response` as the content. If not, as we did earlier, we return the content to be cached, which is the value in `$record['content']`.

For our final example, the `cache_control()` action, we used the `sharable()` method of the `CakeResponse` object to set the `Cache-Control` header in the HTTP response. This header provides a couple of directives to define how the cache is controlled. The first argument defines that we want this cache to be `public`. This means that it will be shared between users. For user-specific content, you would set this to `false`, making it `private`. The second argument then sets the timeout in seconds for the cache, before it must be revalidated. This value is set as the `max-age` directive of this header. The `CakeResponse` object also provides the `maxAge()`, `sharedMaxAge()`, and `mustRevalidate()` methods to control the values of the `Cache-Control` header independently.

It's also worth noting that you can also disable the cache just as easily, by simply calling the `disableCache()` method of the `CakeResponse` object, as we did in another recipe earlier. Additionally, in cases where we called the `checkNotModified()` method, you can also achieve the same by simply including the `RequestHandler` component in your controller. You can disable the automatic cache check in the component by setting the `checkHttpCache` configuration option to `false`, for example:

```
public $components = array(
  'RequestHandler' => array(
    'checkHttpCache' => false
  )
);
```

For most of the methods where a date and time is required, you can also use an instance of the `DateTime` object in PHP or a string that is `strtotime()` compatible and can be parsed by the class.

See also

► The *View caching* recipe from *Chapter 10, View Templates*

Error handling

By default, the framework handles most situations where errors occur, displaying an error page to the user when 4xx and 5xx HTTP exceptions are thrown, with a backtrace and code preview when the debug mode is enabled.

In this recipe, we'll see how you can customize this experience for your users and also some more advanced techniques to gain full control over error handling.

Getting ready

As we'll simply use this recipe to demonstrate a custom exception, let's create a controller that will serve as an example. So, create a file named `BrokenController.php` in `app/Controller/`, and introduce the following code in it:

```
<?php
App::uses('AppController', 'Controller');

class BrokenController extends AppController {
}
```

How to do it...

Perform the following steps:

1. Create a file named `CustomException.php` in `app/Error/` with the following content:

```php
<?php
class CustomException extends HttpException {
  public function __construct($message = null, $code = 417,
Exception $previous = null) {
    if (empty($message)) {
      $message = 'This is a custom error message';
    }
    parent::__construct($message, $code, $previous);
  }
}
```

2. Open the `error400.ctp` file in `app/View/Errros/error400.ctp`, and modify it with the following content:

```php
<h2><?php echo $message; ?></h2>
<p class="error">
  <strong><?php echo __d('cake', 'Error'); ?>: </strong>
  <?php echo __('Uh oh, it looks like something went wrong!'); ?>
</p>
<?php
if (Configure::read('debug') > 0) {
  echo $this->element('exception_stack_trace');
}
```

3. Include the following code at the beginning of the `BrokenController.php` file:

```php
<?php
App::uses('CustomException', 'Error');
```

4. Also, in the `BrokenController` class, add the following `index()` method:

```php
public function index() {
  throw new CustomException(__('Break all the things'));
}
```

5. Finally, calling /broken in your browser will return our modified error page with a custom exception, as shown in the following screenshot:

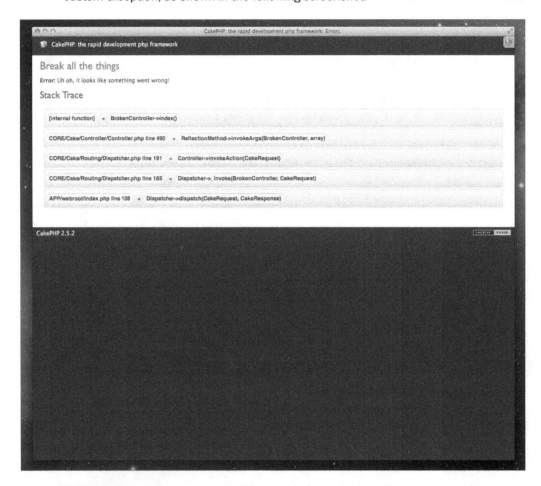

How it works...

The first thing we did in this recipe was to create our own custom exception. CakePHP comes with a selection of default out-of-the-box exceptions, which extend the CakeException class and include:

- MissingConnectionException
- MissingDatabaseException
- MissingTableException

- MissingBehaviorException
- MissingControllerException
- MissingComponentException
- MissingActionException
- PrivateActionException
- MissingLayoutException
- MissingViewException
- MissingHelperException
- MissingTaskException
- MissingShellException
- MissingShellMethodException

Here, we created a class named CustomException, which extends the HttpException base. These are special exceptions that are HTTP aware, allowing you to not only show an error page but also have your responses keep inline with the HTTP status codes. This makes your responses all the more RESTful. The exceptions available include:

- BadRequestException
- ForbiddenException
- NotFoundException
- MethodNotAllowedException
- InternalErrorException
- NotImplementedException

It's worth noting that all exception classes should aim to either extend the CakeException or HttpException class, which in turn extends the CakeBaseException class. This, of course, extends the core Exception class in PHP. Doing so allows the framework to make assumptions about your errors; otherwise, it will treat anything as an Internal Server Error.

Once we created our custom exception class, we then proceeded to modify the error400. ctp view file in app/View/Errors/ (we're rendering the exception_stack_trace. ctp CakePHP core element in it). This file, as well as the error500.ctp file, is the template used to display errors to the user. You can customize these directly to adapt them to your application. Additionally, if you wanted to display them with a different layout, simply add the following to the view files themselves:

```php
<?php $this->layout = 'custom_layout'; ?>
```

It's probably clear from the naming of these files that the 400 file is used for HTTP 4xx status codes while the other is used for 5xx. As mentioned earlier, anything that isn't clear about the status code it refers to or doesn't extend the `HttpException` class will use the `error500. ctp` template.

We then included our custom exception class in our controller using `App::uses()`, and created an `index()` action to test our new toys. Note that if you wanted to avoid calling `App::uses()` to load your custom exceptions, you could preload these via your `bootstrap.php` file in `app/Config/`.

See also

- More details on error handling and advanced options can be found at `http://book.cakephp.org/2.0/en/development/errors.html`
- More details on exceptions in `CakePHP` can be found at `http://book.cakephp. org/2.0/en/development/exceptions.html`

4
API Strategies

In this chapter, we will cover the following recipes:

- RESTful resources
- Exposing a web service
- Consuming a service
- Authentication API
- API versioning

Introduction

When building web applications, you will almost always find yourself building an API at some point. This is a data interface to your application; it is exposed via endpoints, which are consumed by another application or script, instead of a normal user.

Here, we'll look at a couple of ways to expose an API using CakePHP, so you can then decide which fits best with your application.

RESTful resources

You may have heard of REST at some point during your time in development. Representational State Transfer is an API architecture design which exposes resources over a stateless communication, using the HTTP methods of the protocol to facilitate polymorphism through a simplified and uniform API interface.

In this recipe we'll look at how easily REST can be implemented in CakePHP by leveraging the functionality provided by the framework.

Getting ready

For this recipe, we'll set up some standard and custom REST endpoints, which will act against a model. For this, create a table named `posts` using the following SQL statement:

```
CREATE TABLE posts (
    id INT NOT NULL AUTO_INCREMENT,
    title VARCHAR(255) NOT NULL,
    content TEXT,
    created DATETIME,
    modified DATETIME,
    PRIMARY KEY(id)
);
```

Then, we'll add some sample data using the following SQL statement:

```
INSERT INTO posts (title, content, created, modified)
VALUES
('Baking cakes', 'Baking is easy with CakePHP', NOW(), NOW()),
('How to create cookies', 'Browsers love cookies', NOW(), NOW()),
('Consuming a cake', 'Extra tasty with JSON', NOW(), NOW());
```

We'll also need a `posts` controller, so create a file named `PostsController.php` in `app/Controller/` with the following content:

```php
<?php

App::uses('AppController', 'Controller');

class PostsController extends AppController {
}
```

How to do it...

Perform the following steps:

1. Add the following lines to the beginning of your `routes.php` file in `app/Config/`:
    ```
    Router::mapResources('posts');
    Router::parseExtensions();
    ```

2. Edit your `PostController.php` file, and add the following `$components` property:
    ```
    public $components = array('RequestHandler');
    ```

3. In the same class, add the following methods:
    ```
    public function index() {
        $this->set(array(
    ```

```
      'posts' => $this->Post->find('all'),
      '_serialize' => array('posts')
    ));
  }

  public function view($id) {
    $this->set(array(
      'post' => $this->Post->findById($id),
      '_serialize' => array('post')
    ));
  }

  public function edit($id) {
    $this->Post->id = $id;
    $status = $this->Post->save($this->request->data);
    $this->set(array(
      'status' => ($status)? 'Post updated' : 'Error updating post',
      '_serialize' => array('status')
    ));
  }

  public function delete($id) {
    $status = $this->Post->delete($id);
    $this->set(array(
      'status' => ($status)? 'Post deleted' : 'Error deleting post',
      '_serialize' => array('status')
    ));
  }
```

4. Navigate to /posts.xml to see the XML of the posts data or to /posts/1.xml to view the first post, as shown in the following screenshot:

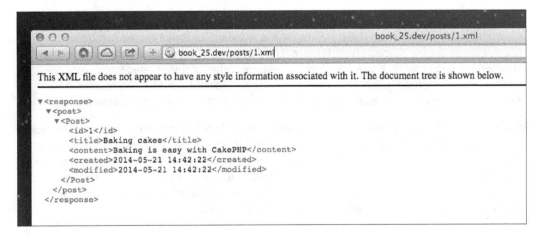

How it works...

In this recipe, we've created a basic REST interface to our `posts` table. To do this, we first mapped `posts` as a resource exposed by the framework. For this, we called the static `mapResources()` method of the `Router` class, passing the name of our resource to it, in this case, our `PostsController`.

When a resource is mapped, a collection of routes are automatically set up for it; they respond to a certain URL and HTTP method and route through to a specific action of the mapped controller.

The `/posts.xml` URL requested with `GET` maps to the `index()` action. The `/posts/{$id}.xml` requested with `GET` maps to the `view($id)` action, expecting an ID. The `/posts.xml` URL requested with `POST` maps to the `add()` action. The `/posts/{$id}.xml` URL requested with `POST` or `PUT` maps to the `edit($id)` action, expecting an ID. The `/posts/{$id}.xml` URL requested with `DELETE` maps to the `delete($id)` action, expecting an ID.

If you didn't want to use these settings, you could also configure the resource map to use different default actions. For this, you can call the static `resourceMap()` method of the `Router` class, passing an array of arrays to it; which contain the action name, the HTTP method, and whether an ID is expected. For example:

```
Router::resourceMap(array(
    array('action' => 'index', 'method' => 'GET', 'id' => false),
    array('action' => 'view', 'method' => 'GET', 'id' => true),
    array('action' => 'add', 'method' => 'POST', 'id' => false),
    array('action' => 'edit', 'method' => 'PUT', 'id' => true),
    array('action' => 'delete', 'method' => 'DELETE', 'id' => true)
));
```

Additionally, the way in which the HTTP method is resolved for these routes can depend on a couple of factors. Based on preference, the framework first checks for a `_method` parameter in the request. If this parameter is set, the value of this is used to emulate the defined request method. Otherwise, first, the `X_HTTP_METHOD_OVERRIDE` header is considered, or finally, in it's absence, the value of `REQUEST_METHOD` is considered.

In this recipe we're using XML, but you can also use JSON out of the box or even create your own formats. When a format is requested, it's linked to a custom `View` class. For example, `.json` is linked to the `JsonView` class, which is included by default in the framework. In our examples, we're using the `_serialize` view variable to automatically process the variables we include for the view, but you can also handle the formatting of the output manually by simply creating a view for your action, as you typically would.

We also enabled extensions in the URL to be parsed by CakePHP, using the static `parseExtensions()` method of the `Router` class. There is a recipe included for this, which will provide you with details on how to process file extensions in your URL.

After setting up our resource, we proceeded to create the logic for our REST actions in the `PostsController`. We first made sure that the `RequestHandler` component is included. This is important, as it handles much of the processing logic internally for your actions. You can also take advantage of this component to accept content in different formats. For example, request formats such as XML and JSON are automatically processed by CakePHP with this component; they simply provide the resulting content in the `$data` property of the `CakeRequest` object located in the `$request` property of the controller. You can even define your own input content types using the `addInputType()` method of the `RequestHandler` component, as shown in the following code:

```
$this->RequestHandler->addInputType('foo', array(function() {
  // parsing logic for "foo" input types
}));
```

Once our component was in place, we simply created the methods for each REST action, as defined by our default resource map. Here, you'll notice that our logic is minimal; however, this could be particular to each resource, where some may even affect other resources in your business layer.

As you can see, setting up REST endpoints is not only simple but flexible; it allows you to easily build and maintain your RESTful interfaces without hassle.

See also

*   ▶ The definition of REST can be found at `http://www.ics.uci.edu/~fielding/pubs/dissertation/rest_arch_style.htm`
*   ▶ The *Parsing extensions* recipe from *Chapter 3, HTTP Negotiation*
*   ▶ The *Building an XML view* recipe from *Chapter 10, View Templates*

Exposing a web service

When you first build an application, you'll most likely imagine how the user will interact with it and how it will be designed and structured for your content and features. However, there also comes a time when you'll want to expose certain functionality of your website as web services.

CakePHP comes well-prepared for this, so in this recipe, we'll look at how you can easily create a data-focused controller to serve certain functionality of your application via a service.

Getting ready

For this recipe, we'll start with a basic controller to serve as our endpoint. So, create a file named `ApiController.php` in `app/Controller/` with the following content:

```php
<?php
App::uses('AppController', 'Controller');

class ApiController extends AppController {
}
```

How to do it...

Perform the following steps:

1. Add the following line to your `routes.php` file in `app/Config/`:

```php
Router::connect('/api/:object/:command', array(
  'controller' => 'api',
  'action' => 'delegate'
), array(
  'pass' => array(
    'object',
    'command'
  )
));
```

2. Add the following `delegate()` method to the `ApiController` class:

```php
public function delegate($object, $command) {
  $result = null;
  try {
    if ($this->request->is('post') || $this->request->is('put')) {
      $args = $this->request->data;
    } else {
      $args = $this->request->query;
    }
    $component = Inflector::camelize($object);
    $this->{$component} = $this->Components->load($component);
    $this->{$component}->initialize($this);
    $action = Inflector::camelize($command);
    $return = $this->{$component}->{$action}($args);
    if ($this->{$component}->status === 'success') {
```

```
      $result = $this->_success($return);
    } else {
      $result = $this->_fail($return);
    }
  } catch(Exception $e) {
    $result = $this->_error($e->getMessage(), $e->getCode(),
$result);
  }
  $this->response->type('json');
  $this->response->statusCode(200);
  $this->response->body($result);
  $this->response->send();
  $this->_stop();
}
```

3. Also, add the following protected utility methods to the same class:

```
protected function _format($status, $response = array()) {
  $object = new stdClass();
  $object->status = $status;
  foreach ($response as $param => $value) {
    $object->{$param} = $value;
  }
  return json_encode($object);
}


protected function _success($data = null) {
  return $this->_format('success', array('data' => $data));
}


protected function _fail($data = null) {
  return $this->_format('fail', array('data' => $data));
}


protected function _error($message = 'Unknown', $code = 0, $data =
array()) {
  return $this->_format('error', array(
    'message' => $message,
    'code' => $code,
    'data' => $data
  ));
}
```

4. Now, create a file named `ExampleComponent.php` in `app/Controller/Component/` with the following content:

```php
<?php
App::uses('Component', 'Controller');

class ExampleComponent extends Component {

  public $status = 'success';

  public function hello($args) {
    return 'Hello World';
  }

  public function say($args) {
    if (empty($args['text'])) {
      throw new Exception('Missing argument: text');
    }
    return 'You said: ' . $args['text'];
  }
}
```

5. Navigate to `/api/example/hello` in your browser to see the following output:

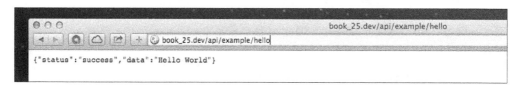

6. Alternatively, go to `/api/example/say?text=Bingo` to see the following output:

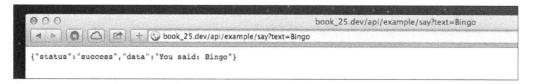

If you were to call the same URL, but *without* passing the `?text=Bingo` query string, you would get the following error response:

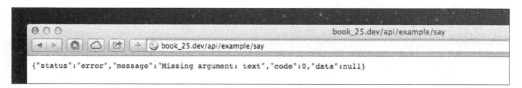

How it works...

When building an API, there are many ways you can approach the design. CakePHP is flexible, in that it doesn't lock you into any specific architecture or pattern; instead, it allows you to tackle the design as you see fit. In this recipe, we've used a component-based approach; it serves well for extensive APIs, which work well in object/command design.

For this example, we created a base `ApiController` class, which serves as the foundation to delegate calls to our components to the API. We also defined a route template in our `app/Config/routes.php` file for calls to the API, namespacing it with `/api/` to avoid clashing with the other URLs in our web application.

The `delegate()` method in the `ApiController` class is the receiving action that processes the actual calls to the API. The `$object` and `$command` arguments here are passed through from our route template, which captures them via the `:object` and `:command` tokens. You may have noticed that a significant part of our method's logic is encapsulated in a try/catch statement. This is important, as it allows our API to catch unforeseen exceptions that could potentially come from a component and process them accordingly.

We then captured the arguments passed to our API from the `$data` property of the `CakeRequest` object in `$this->request` if the HTTP request method was `post` or `put`, or from the `$query` property if any other HTTP method was used. The name of the component that is passed as the `$object` argument to the `delegate()` method is then formatted using the static `camelize()` method of the `Inflector` utility class. This changes the format of the component name from a URL value to a class name. You'll notice that we do the same with the action from the `$command` argument further below that.

We then use the `load()` method of the `ComponentCollection` class to correctly load our component, followed by a call to `initialize()` to process any setup logic that the component may have. The return value of the action is stored in a variable after the execution of the method, passing the arguments provided to the API call to it. As we're using the *Jsend* spec in this example, we also check the result of the call. In this case, the spec allows for `success` or `fail`, and we're reserving `error` for any exceptions we capture in our try/catch. Each of these is treated and built using our formatting helper methods to process the content for the HTTP response body.

Finally, the response object is configured. First, set the response content type to `json`, and the status code to `200`. We do this even for exceptions, as the response from the server is valid, with the result of the API call detailed in the response body. We then just send our response to the client and stop the framework's dispatch cycle when we're done.

The great thing about this design is it easily allows for extensibility. You can include auth validation, arguments processing, HTTP method checks, and much more in your `delegate()` method, with very little effort. It also allows growth and modularity, as areas of your API are broken into components, thus helping you maintain your code with ease. However, this is just one approach. You might prefer to have your API calls in each of their relevant controllers or, maybe, hack it and build out your endpoints in a dispatch filter or even a custom route class. You could also take the REST approach from a previous recipe. As always, CakePHP provides the tools to build your code as you see fit, thus offering flexibility and power at your fingertips.

See also

▸ The hyper-text transfer protocol at `http://www.w3.org/Protocols/rfc2616/rfc2616.html`

▸ The Jsend spec at `http://labs.omniti.com/labs/jsend`

▸ The *RESTful resources* recipe

Consuming a service

While it's great that you can expose certain functionality of your application via web services, you'll also want to consume services of your own or by other third parties. CakePHP comes equipped with a very useful HTTP socket class, which allows you to easily interact with other resources.

In this recipe, we'll consume the service from our previous example, which exposes its interface as JSON, and see how easy it is to quickly get the results you need.

Getting ready

For this recipe, we'll use a simple test controller to interact with our API. Create a file named `ServiceController.php` in `app/Controller/` with the following content:

```php
<?php
App::uses('AppController', 'Controller');
App::uses('HttpSocket', 'Network/Http');

class ServiceController extends AppController {
}
```

We'll also need a view file for the action we'll define, so create a file named `call.ctp` in `app/View/Service`.

How to do it...

Perform the following steps:

1. Create a file named `JsonResponse.php` in `app/Lib/Network/Http/` with the following content:

    ```php
    <?php
    App::uses('HttpSocketResponse', 'Network/Http');

    class JsonResponse extends HttpSocketResponse {

      public function __toString() {
        return json_encode($this->body);
      }

      public function body() {
        return $this->body;
      }

      public function isOk() {
        if (parent::isOk()) {
          return ($this->body['status'] === 'success');
        }
        return false;
      }

      public function parseResponse($message) {
        parent::parseResponse($message);
        $this->body = json_decode($this->body, true);
      }
    }
    ```

2. Add the following `call()` method to your `ServiceController` class:

    ```php
    public function call($value) {
      $config = array(
        'request' => array(
          'uri' => array(
            'host' => env('HTTP_HOST')
          )
        )
      );
    ```

```
$http = new HttpSocket($config);
$http = new HttpSocket();
$http->responseClass = 'JsonResponse';
$response = $http->get('/api/example/say', array('text' =>
$value));
  if ($response->isOk()) {
    $this->set('result', $response->body['data']);
  } else {
    throw new CakeException('Web service error');
  }
}
```

3. Introduce the following content into the `call.ctp` file in app/View/Service/:

    ```
    <h2><?php echo __('Service Response'); ?></h2>
    <p><?php echo $result; ?></p>
    ```

4. Navigate to `/service/call/Hello` in your browser to see the
    following output:

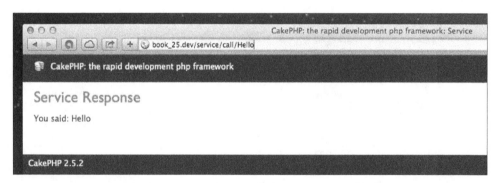

How it works...

In this recipe, we interfaced with the web service we set up in our previous example. For this, we first created a custom response class, so we can transparently handle the JSON returned by the API endpoint. To do this, we created a file named `JsonResponse.php` in app/Lib/ Network/Http/, which overrides a couple of methods.

The most relevant method here is the `parseResponse()` method, which handles the processing of the HTTP response message. Here, we called the parent method to execute the underlying logic and then made sure that the $body property of the response is correctly a JSON-decoded value. In this case, it is an associative array through our use of `true` as the second argument of the `json_decode()` function to force an array over an object representation of the JSON string.

We then also changed `body()` to return an array, instead of forcing it to be cast as a string as it does by default, and also `json_encode()` the array again in any case where the response object is cast to string with the `__toString()` method.

The final method that we override is `isOk()`. By default, this method simply checks whether the HTTP status code is within the expected range for a successful response. However, as the *Jsend* spec includes the actual result in the body of the response, we want our `isOk()` method to be more intelligent and check this too. For this, we first call the `parent::isOk()` method to make sure that the HTTP status code is within an acceptable range, and if it is, then check whether the `status` key of the JSON response also has the `success` value.

Once we had our custom response class ready, we proceeded to create our `call()` action, which serves to test our API call. Here, we first created a new instance of the `HttpSocket` class and set up our new `JsonResponse` class through the `$responseClass` property. When then made our call to the API using the `get()` method of the `HttpSocket` class, passing the URL of the endpoint, followed by an array with the query string parameter to pass in the call. Here, we could also pass the query string as an actual string. This then returns an instance of our `JsonResponse` class, with the specifics of the HTTP response.

We continue by calling our `isOk()` method on the `$response` object to determine if the request was successful. If it was, we assign a view variable named `result` with the value returned in the JSON response. Otherwise, we throw a nice `CakeException`. Here, you could become more explicit with the error message giving the HTTP status code from the `$code` property of the `$response` object or attempting to detail the actual issue if it is provided in the response from the service provider. Obviously, the more detailed your error messages, the quicker you're going to get to the bottom of the problems with your requests. Our view then simply outputs the value from our API call.

This is just an introduction to interfacing with services over HTTP, but the `HttpSocket` class provides an extensive interface to customize and control interactions with any HTTP endpoint. The ability to build your own response objects and manipulate the content returned is just the beginning to what you can build.

See also

- Details on the HTTP socket class are available at `http://book.cakephp.org/2.0/en/core-utility-libraries/httpsocket.html`
- More information on JavaScript Object Notation can be found at `http://json.org`
- The *Exposing a web service* recipe

Authentication API

When exposing features of your application via web services, you may want to control who has access. For this, you'll need to keep track of who is making the requests and allow these parties to authenticate themselves.

In this recipe, we'll look at how you can easily set up an authentication API, which persists the session through the use of an `auth` token.

Getting ready

We'll continue to build on our API from the previous recipes, adding a `users` table to control access to our services:

```
CREATE TABLE users (
    id INT NOT NULL AUTO_INCREMENT,
    username VARCHAR(20) NOT NULL,
    password VARCHAR(100) NOT NULL,
    token VARCHAR(32) DEFAULT NULL,
    ip VARCHAR(45) DEFAULT NULL,
    created DATETIME DEFAULT NULL,
    modified DATETIME DEFAULT NULL,
    PRIMARY KEY(id)
);
```

How to do it...

Perform the following steps:

1. Create a file named `AccessComponent.php` in `app/Controller/Component/` with the following content:

```php
<?php
App::uses('Component', 'Controller');
App::uses('Security', 'Utility');
App::uses('ClassRegistry', 'Utility');

class AccessComponent extends Component {

    public $components = array('Cookie');

    public $status = 'success';
```

```
public function register($args) {
  if (empty($args['username'])) {
    throw new Exception('Missing argument: username');
  }
  if (empty($args['password'])) {
    throw new Exception('Missing argument: password');
  }
  $User = ClassRegistry::init('User');
  $User->create();

  return $User->save(array(
    'username' => $args['username'],
    'password' => Security::hash($args['password'], null, true)
  ));
}

public function login($args) {
  if (empty($args['username'])) {
    throw new Exception('Missing argument: username');
  }
  if (empty($args['password'])) {
    throw new Exception('Missing argument: password');
  }
  $User = ClassRegistry::init('User');
  $data = $User->find('first', array(
    'conditions' => array(
      'User.username' => $args['username'],
      'User.password' => Security::hash($args['password'], null,
true)
    )
  ));
  if (!empty($data)) {
    if (empty($data['User']['token'])) {
      $request = $this->_Collection->getController()->request;
      $data['User']['token'] = md5(uniqid());
      $data['User']['ip'] = $request->clientIp(false);
      $User->save($data);
    }
    $this->Cookie->write('auth_token', $data['User']['token']);

    return true;
  }
```

```
        return false;
    }

    public function logout($args) {
      if ($this->Cookie->check('auth_token')) {
        $request = $this->_Collection->getController()->request;
        $User = ClassRegistry::init('User');
        $data = $User->find('first', array(
          'conditions' => array(
            'User.token' => $this->Cookie->read('auth_token'),
            'User.ip' => $request->clientIp(false)
          )
        ));
        if (!empty($data)) {
          $data['User']['token'] = null;
          $data['User']['ip'] = null;
          $User->save($data);
          $this->Cookie->delete('auth_token');

          return true;
        }
      }

      return false;
    }

    public function validate($args) {
      if ($this->Cookie->check('auth_token')) {
        $request = $this->_Collection->getController()->request;
        $User = ClassRegistry::init('User');
        $data = $User->find('first', array(
          'conditions' => array(
            'User.token' => $this->Cookie->read('auth_token'),
            'User.ip' => $request->clientIp(false)
          )
        ));
        if (!empty($data)) {
          return true;
        }
      }

      return false;
    }
}
```

2. Update the `delegate()` method in your `ApiController` with the following change (highlighted):

```php
public function delegate($object, $command) {
  $result = null;
  try {
    if ($this->request->is('post') || $this->request->is('put')) {
      $args = $this->request->data;
    } else {
      $args = $this->request->query;
    }
    $component = Inflector::camelize($object);
    if ($component !== 'Access') {
      $this->_validateAccess($args);
    }
    $this->{$component} = $this->Components->load($component);
    $this->{$component}->initialize($this);
    $action = Inflector::camelize($command);
    $return = $this->{$component}->{$action}($args);
    if ($this->{$component}->status === 'success') {
      $result = $this->_success($return);
    } else {
      $result = $this->_fail($return);
    }
  } catch (Exception $e) {
    $result = $this->_error($e->getMessage(), $e->getCode(),
$result);
  }
  $this->response->type('json');
  $this->response->statusCode(200);
  $this->response->body($result);
  $this->response->send();
  $this->_stop();
}
```

3. Add the following protected `_validateAccess()` method to the same class:

```php
protected function _validateAccess($args) {
  $this->Access = $this->Components->load('Access');
  if (!$this->Access->validate($args)) {
    throw new ForbiddenException();
  }
}
```

4. Make sure that you have no model named `User` in your application (or check out its callbacks) and then navigate to `/api/example/hello`—it will return an error, as access is forbidden, as shown in the following screenshot:

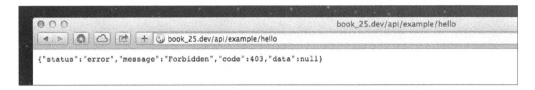

5. Register a user by navigating to `/api/access/register?username=test&pass word=12345`.

6. Login by navigating to `/api/access/login?username=test&password=12345`. This will register the `auth_token` cookie by the web service.

7. Navigate again to `/api/example/hello` to see the following output:

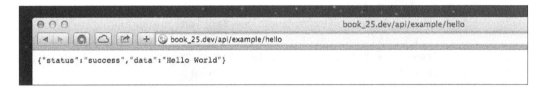

How it works...

In this recipe, we've extended the scope of our web service from the previous recipes to include an authentication layer that requires a consumer of the API to identify themselves. For this, we've kept with the modular architecture of our API and created an authentication service called `Access`. This provisions the actions necessary for users to register, log in, and log out, as well as provide us with a means to test whether a user has a valid session.

To track the user, we're using an `auth_token`, which we're persisting via a cookie. You'll notice that we're loading the `Cookie` component in our `Access` component. This is a great feature of CakePHP; it allows maximum reuse of your code through the likes of components.

In our first method, `register()`, we first checked whether the required `username` and `password` arguments have been provided with the API call, and if not, we throw an exception. We then used the static `init()` method of the `ClassRegistry` class to create an instance of the `User` model. In a real application, validate data in the model layer. After this, we called the `create()` method of our model to notify the framework of our intent to create a new row in the `users` table. Finally, we simply returned the result of saving the new data, hashing the password in the process with the `hash()` method of the `Security` utility class. Note that this method automatically handles the salt in our hash, using the value set in the `core.php` file in `app/Config/` under the `Security.salt` configuration setting.

In the `login()` method, we also checked for the required `username` and `password` arguments. Then, again, we used the static `init()` method of the `ClassRegistry` class to create the instance of our `User` model. We then called `find()` to locate the "first" row that matches the provided `username` and `password`, the latter hashed with the `hash()` method of the `Security` utility class. After this, we checked if a result was returned by making sure that the `$data` variable is not empty, and we also checked whether `$data` does not already have a token defined. For a case where there is no token, we use the `uniqid()` function to create a unique ID, and then hash this as an MD5 string and set it to `$data['User']['token']`. We also set the user's IP address to `$data['User']['ip']`, so we can *marry* the user to their token; otherwise, the user's `auth_token` could be easily hijacked. Note that we're setting the first argument of the `clientIp()` method of the `CakeRequest` class to `false`, as this is preferable when the request cannot be entirely trusted. We complete the login process by saving the data and setting the `auth_token` cookie to persist the user's session.

Our `logout()` method then checks for the existence of the `auth_token` cookie using the `check()` method of the `Cookie` component. If it is found, we then check whether the token is valid by looking up a user that has both the token and a matching IP address stored for that token. If they are found, we simply save the user by setting both the `token` and `ip` fields to `null`, and then proceed to delete the `auth_token` cookie using the `Cookie` component's `delete()` method.

Finally, the `validate()` method of the `Access` component is our utility method to determine if a user who makes a request to our API has a valid token and if it matches a known user with the same IP address.

To take advantage of our new authentication layer, we then modified the `delegate()` method of the `ApiController` to contemplate an `auth` check upon every request. For this, we also checked whether the request isn't for the `Access` service itself, and if it is not, we call our protected `_validateAccess()` method. The great thing about this method is that it also reuses our authentication service by simply throwing a `ForbiddenException` if the user's token doesn't validate. This aligns well with the mantra of "eat your own dog food", in which you should always aim to consume your own services as any other consumer and avoid hacking around your API internally or creating back doors for yourself at all costs.

The authentication system outlined in this recipe isn't the greatest and, for sure, isn't the most secure, but it gives you a heads-up into understanding the options available when securing your API. If you wanted to build a more robust authentication system, you could also look at using *OAuth* or even integrate directly with a third party-service. Either way, you'll find the token system very common among APIs out there in the wild.

See also

- ▶ The OAuth 2.0 specification at `http://tools.ietf.org/html/rfc6749`
- ▶ The *Exposing a web service* recipe

API versioning

As time goes by, you'll find that an API changes and evolves. However, when others are interacting with your API, it's important to be coherent about where certain functionality exists and maintain a clear versioning of the actions available and their characteristics.

In this recipe, we'll look at how you can implement different API-versioning techniques to help maintain consistency in your API and promote a stable longevity.

Getting ready

We'll be using the code we created in a previous recipe to create a web service and extend it to allow for versioning of the API we defined.

How to do it...

Perform the following steps:

1. Update the route for the API action that we added in a previous recipe; it will be used just for authentication purposes:

```
Router::connect('/api/access/*', array(
  'controller' => 'api',
  'action' => 'delegate',
  '',
  'access'
));
```

2. Add a new route for the versioned API:

```
Router::connect('/api/:version/:object/:command', array(
  'controller' => 'api',
  'action' => 'delegate'
), array(
  'pass' => array(
    'version',
    'object',
    'command'
  )
));
```

3. Change the `delegate()` action in the `ApiController` to the following:

```
public function delegate($version, $object, $command) {
  $result = null;
  try {
```

```php
    if ($this->request->is('post') || $this->request->is('put')) {
      $args = $this->request->data;
    } else {
      $args = $this->request->query;
    }
    $component = Inflector::camelize($object);
    if ($component !== 'Access') {
      $this->_validateAccess($args);
      $component .= strtoupper($version);
    }
    $this->{$component} = $this->Components->load($component);
    $this->{$component}->initialize($this);
    $action = Inflector::camelize($command);
    $return = $this->{$component}->{$action}($args);
    if ($this->{$component}->status === 'success') {
      $result = $this->_success($return);
    } else {
      $result = $this->_fail($return);
    }
  } catch(Exception $e) {
    $result = $this->_error($e->getMessage(), $e->getCode(),
$result);
  }
  $this->response->type('json');
  $this->response->statusCode(200);
  $this->response->body($result);
  $this->response->send();
  $this->_stop();
}
```

4. Update the file name of the `ExampleComponent` class to
   `ExampleV1Component.php` and also the class declaration in the file to the following:

```php
<?php
App::uses('Component', 'Controller');

class ExampleV1Component extends Component {

  public $status = 'success';

  public function hello($args) {
    return 'Hello World';
  }

  public function say($args) {
```

```php
    if (empty($args['text'])) {
      throw new Exception('Missing argument: text');
    }
    return 'You said: ' . $args['text'];
  }
}
```

5. We'll also duplicate this file by changing the file name to `ExampleV2Component.php` and also the class declaration to the following:

```php
<?php
App::uses('ExampleV1Component', 'Controller/Component');

class ExampleV2Component extends ExampleV1Component {

  public function hello($args) {
    return 'Hey there!';
  }

  public function foo($args) {
    return 'bar';
  }
}
```

6. Navigating to `/api/v1/example/hello` will return the following output, as it did in the previous recipe:

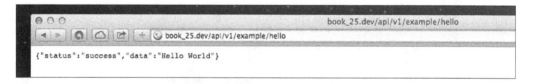

However, when you o to `/api/v2/example/hello`, you will see the new output we defined, as shown in the following screenshot:

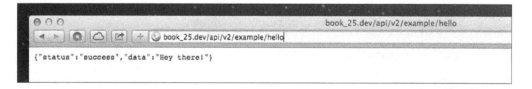

7. Navigating to `/api/v2/example/foo` will return the output (seen in the first screenshot that follows) we defined, while navigating to `/api/v1/example/foo` (notice the change in the API version) will return an error (as seen in the second screenshot that follows):

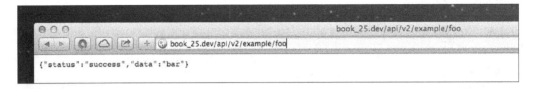

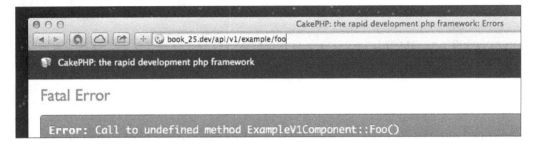

How it works...

In this recipe, we built on the web service we created earlier. The first thing you probably noticed is how easy it was to add versioning to our API. We are not interested in a versioned `AccessComponent` now, so we changed our API route to be used just for registration and authentication purposes. The second step we took was to create our route for the API to include a new `:version` token, which captures the version of the API requested. Here, we simply changed the `delegate()` method of the `ApiController` class to contemplate the new `$version` argument, as defined in our `pass` array from the route.

The magic then comes from the component name, which now changes to have the version added in the file and class names. You may have also noted that we extended the `ExampleV2Component` component from the `ExampleV1Component` class, which allows us to easily inherit the functionality from the previous version of our API. It's worth pointing out that if you wanted to deprecate an action in a newer version or remove it all together, you could have related component method return the `410 Gone` HTTP status code. Alternatively, if you have an upcoming feature, you could also use the `501 Not Implemented` status to communicate it's current unavailability.

You'll now see that by simply changing the version in the URL of the request, the call gets routed to the relevant component internally by our `delegate()` method. However, what happens if we're not a fan of including the version in the URL?

There's more...

So, we want to maintain a cleaner URL interface for our API, and not mess it up with versioning. Not to worry; let's change our implementation to accept the version via the HTTP request headers.

First, remove the two routes that we added for access control and versioned API, and add the route for the API endpoint back with its original definition, as shown in the following code:

```
Router::connect('/api/:object/:command', array(
  'controller' => 'api',
  'action' => 'delegate'
), array(
  'pass' => array(
    'object',
    'command'
  )
));
```

Then, open your `ApiController.php` file and modify the `delegate()` method to the following:

```
public function delegate($object, $command) {
  $result = null;
  try {
    if ($this->request->is('post') || $this->request->is('put')) {
      $args = $this->request->data;
    } else {
      $args = $this->request->query;
    }
    $component = Inflector::camelize($object);
    if ($component !== 'Access') {
      $this->_validateAccess($args);
      $version = $this->request->header('X-API-Version');
      $component .= strtoupper($version);
    }
    $this->{$component} = $this->Components->load($component);
    $this->{$component}->initialize($this);
    $action = Inflector::camelize($command);
    $return = $this->{$component}->{$action}($args);
    if ($this->{$component}->status === 'success') {
      $result = $this->_success($return);
    } else {
```

```
      $result = $this->_fail($return);
    }
  } catch (Exception $e) {
    $result = $this->_error($e->getMessage(), $e->getCode(), $result);
  }
  $this->response->type('json');
  $this->response->statusCode(200);
  $this->response->body($result);
  $this->response->send();
  $this->_stop();
}
```

Now, we could make a call to the API with a HTTP request as follows (using the domain you have defined):

```
GET http://example.com/api/example/hello HTTP/1.1
Host: example.com
X-API-Version: v1
```

Keep in mind that this method of reading the API version does have drawbacks. For example, creating an API call now requires that we set a request header, which could be a limiting factor in some scenarios. Also, earlier, the client that made the call only needed to know the URL to make the request; now, it needs to also know the specifics of the HTTP request itself. You may also want to use a more standard format to specifying the version, such as via the Content-Type header, using something similar to the following line of code:

```
application/vnd.example.v1+json
```

See also

▶ The *Exposing a web service* recipe

5
Using Authentication

In this chapter, we will cover the following recipes:

- ▸ The HTTP authentication
- ▸ Custom authorize class
- ▸ Facebook authentication
- ▸ Custom RBAC
- ▸ Working with ACL

Introduction

Not all applications are created equal, and in many scenarios, you'll want to control how your application is accessed and by whom. It just so happens that CakePHP includes a flexible authentication system, which aims to take the pain out of users and session handling.

In this chapter, we'll look at various ways of handling authentication and access control when using the framework.

The HTTP authentication

Authentication logic covers the matching between user credentials (usually, a username and password combination) and an existing user defined in your system.

CakePHP is packed with several authentication classes, which provide you with the most widely used types for use in your application:

- ▸ `FormAuthenticate`: This is used to provide a login page and submit user credentials via a `POST` request to your login action.

- ▶ `BasicAuthenticate`: This lets the browser ask you for the credentials, using a standard HTTP basic authentication. The credentials are sent in plain text to the web server. This could be a security risk in your application, so using SSL is *strongly* advised.

- ▶ `DigestAuthenticate`: This uses the HTTP digest authentication method. It is slightly more secure than the basic HTTP authentication, as the credentials are hashed before sending them to the server. However, security risk still exists, so using SSL is suggested.

In this recipe, we'll explore the basic HTTP authentication, which is usually ignored but is useful when you combine this method with an SSL-protected web server.

Getting ready

For this recipe, we'll create a `users` table, using the following SQL statement:

```
CREATE TABLE users (
  id VARCHAR(36) NOT NULL,
  username VARCHAR(255) NOT NULL,
  password VARCHAR(128) NOT NULL,
  active TINYINT(1) DEFAULT '0',
  created DATETIME DEFAULT NULL,
  modified DATETIME DEFAULT NULL,
  PRIMARY KEY(id)
);
```

Then, optionally, set up SSL for your domain or local virtual host. Check your web server documentation about setting up SSL certificates. This is strongly recommended but not required if you're testing this recipe in a development environment.

How to do it...

Perform the following steps:

1. Create a new `AuthsController` in a file named `app/Controller/AuthsController.php` using the following code:

```php
<?php
App::uses('AppController', 'Controller');

class AuthsController extends AppController {

    public $components = array(
        'Auth' => array(
            'authenticate' => array('Basic' => array(
```

```
        'fields' => array(
          'username' => 'username',
          'password' => 'password'
        ),
        'userModel' => 'User',
        'scope' => array(
          array('User.active' => 1)
        ),
        'recursive' => -1,
        'realm' => 'Speak, friend, and enter.'
      )),
      'authorize' => array('Controller')
    )
);

public function beforeFilter() {
  parent::beforeFilter();
  AuthComponent::$sessionKey = false;
  $this->Auth->allow('saveTestUser');
}

public function isAuthorized($user = null) {
  return true;
}

public function saveTestUser() {
  $data = array(
    'id' => 1,
    'username' => 'friend',
    'password' => Security::hash('mellon', null, true),
    'active' => 1
  );
  debug(ClassRegistry::init('User')->save($data));
  $this->autoRender = false;
}

public function index() {
}
}
```

If you have the `User` model from the previous recipes, it handles password hashing for you—in this case, send the password in plaintext, `mellon`, to the `User` model (remove the use of `Security::hash()` from the `saveTestUser()` method). Otherwise, your passwords will be hashed twice, and you'll be unable to log in.

2. Add a view for the `index()` action, by convention, in a file named `app/View/Auths/index.ctp`, as shown in the following code:

```php
<?php
echo $this->Html->tag('h2', __('You are allowed to pass, %s', Auth
Component::user('username')));
```

3. Now, use the `saveTestUser()` utility action that we created to generate a new test user for your application by opening a browser and navigating to `/auths/saveTestUser`:

```
book_25.dev/auths/saveTestUser

/app/Controller/AuthsController.php (line 40)

array(
        'User' => array(
                'password' => '*****',
                'id' => (int) 1,
                'username' => 'friend',
                'active' => (int) 1,
                'created' => '2014-06-02 16:00:25',
                'modified' => '2014-06-02 16:00:25'
        )
)
```

4. Open the `/auths/index` protected page.

   You'll get an HTTP basic browser popup that requests the username and password to access this website. Type the following for each field:

   ```
   Username: friend
   Password: mellon
   ```

   You'll get access to the index page, and a **You are allowed to pass, friend** welcome message will be displayed, as shown in the following screenshot:

5. Once you're able to log in, remove the `saveTestUser()` method from the `AuthsController` class.

How it works...

In this recipe, we're using CakePHP basic authentication and controller authorization to protect the `AuthsController::index()` action.

We started with an empty `users` table, so we added a utility action to generate the first user in our system with the username, `friend`, and password, `mellon`.

First, we created a new `AuthsController` controller and used the `$components` public attribute to indicate that we're going to use the core `AuthComponent` along with a custom configuration. This configuration will be passed to the component when CakePHP creates the instance of the component that will be attached to the `AuthsController`, as shown in the following code:

```
public $components = array(
  'Auth' => array(
    'authenticate' => array('Basic' => array(
      'fields' => array(
        'username' => 'username',
        'password' => 'password'
      ),
      'userModel' => 'User',
      'scope' => array(
        array('User.active' => 1)
      ),
      'realm' => 'Speak, friend, and enter.',
    )),
    'authorize' => array('Controller')
  )
);
```

Here, we're setting how the CakePHP core `AuthComponent` will manage the authentication and authorization in this controller. If we want to protect all of our controllers, we could use the base `AppController` class instead, so all of the controllers in our application (extending `AppController`) will share the same auth settings.

In this case, we're setting the authenticate class as `Basic` and passing an array of settings to it:

```
array(
  'fields' => array(
    'username' => 'username',
    'password' => 'password'
  ),
```

```
    'userModel' => 'User',
    'scope' => array(
      array('User.active' => 1)
    ),
    'realm' => 'Speak, friend, and enter.'
)
```

The `fields` key allows us to change the matching between the `username` and `password` credential fields and the columns present in our `users` table. In this case, we have columns with the same name, so we could simply remove the `fields` key and use CakePHP defaults by convention. However, we've left this key specifically to show you this setting, in case your `users` table has different names for the fields and you need to configure them properly.

The `userModel` key is used to configure the name of the model that we'll use. In our case, we haven't even created a class file for it in this recipe (although it was mentioned in the previous ones), as we don't have any additional business logic to be added to the `User` model. CakePHP will use an instance of the `AppModel` when no model file is present. The `scope` key is used to filter our query to the `users` table; in this case, we'll allow only active users to log in. The `realm` parameter is then used to configure the HTTP Basic realm string, displayed to the user when the credentials are requested (in the username/password popup).

```
    'authorize' => array('Controller')
```

We also set the authorize option to implement our authorization logic per `Controller`, using a callback function named `isAuthorized($user)`. Once logged in, the authorization logic will determine if the user has the rights to access a given resource or not. Depending on the `$user` and the resource requested, we can return `true` to allow access or `false` to deny it. In this case, we are setting the following:

```
public function isAuthorized($user = null) {
    return true;
}
```

So here, all authenticated users will have access to all of the actions in this controller.

We've then used the `beforeFilter()` controller callback that will be executed before any action in this controller to configure a couple of items related to `AuthComponent`, as shown in the following code:

```
public function beforeFilter() {
    parent::beforeFilter();
    AuthComponent::$sessionKey = false;
    $this->Auth->allow('saveTestUser');
}
```

By setting the `AuthComponent::$sessionKey` property to `false`, we'll ensure that the session will not be checked and the user credentials will be rechecked again on every request.

Using `$this->Auth->allow('saveTestUser')`, we ensure that the action named `saveTestUser` will be available for all users, even for those not logged in. This is important if we want to run this utility action while the `AuthComponent` is protecting the controller.

```php
public function saveTestUser() {
  $data = array(
    'id' => 1,
    'username' => 'friend',
    'password' => Security::hash('mellon', null, true),
    'active' => 1
  );
  debug(ClassRegistry::init('User')->save($data));
  $this->autoRender = false;
}
```

Once we've created an initial user, we can safely delete this method from our controller. Then, the only action present in the `AuthsController` class is an empty `index()` action, which will render the associated view file in `app/View/Auths/index.ctp`. The content of this file is as follows:

```php
<?php
echo $this->Html->tag('h2', __('You are allowed to pass, %s', AuthComp
onent::user('username')));
```

Here, we use the `tag()` method of the `Html` helper to render a `<h2>` tag with a content message. We're using the static `AuthComponent::user()` method to retrieve the username of the currently logged-in user. You can use this static method from any place in your CakePHP application to inspect and retrieve any user data.

Using this recipe, you can easily protect any controller action to log in users, or even your complete application if you apply the same recipe directly to your base `AppController` class.

See also

▸   `http://en.wikipedia.org/wiki/Basic_access_authentication`

Custom authorize class

As we saw in our previous recipe, CakePHP provides several core authorization classes out of the box, but it also provides the ability to customize the process using your own authorization and authentication classes.

In this recipe, we'll introduce a custom authorization process based on an `is_admin` flag in our `users` table, where we'll restrict access to all our admin-prefixed routes.

Getting ready

For this recipe, we'll be using the basic authenticate protected controller from our previous tutorial. So, first create a `users` table using the following SQL statement, or update it with the highlighted field:

```
CREATE TABLE users (
    id VARCHAR(36) NOT NULL,
    username VARCHAR(255) NOT NULL,
    password VARCHAR(128) NOT NULL,
    active TINYINT(1) DEFAULT '0',
    is_admin TINYINT(1) DEFAULT '0',
    created DATETIME DEFAULT NULL,
    modified DATETIME DEFAULT NULL,
    PRIMARY KEY(id)
);
```

As suggested in our previous recipe, it's strongly recommended that you set up SSL for your domain. Check your web server documentation about setting up SSL certificates

Now, create a file named `AuthsController.php` in `app/Controller/` if you don't have it already:

```php
<?php
App::uses('AppController', 'Controller');

class AuthsController extends AppController {

    public $components = array(
        'Auth' => array(
            'authenticate' => array('Basic' => array(
                'fields' => array(
                    'username' => 'username',
                    'password' => 'password'
                ),
                'userModel' => 'User',
                'scope' => array(
                    array('User.active' => 1)
                ),
                'recursive' => -1,
                'realm' => 'Speak, friend, and enter.'
            )),
            'authorize' => array('Controller')
        )
    );

    public function beforeFilter() {
```

```
      parent::beforeFilter();
      AuthComponent::$sessionKey = false;
   }

   public function isAuthorized($user = null) {
     return true;
   }

   public function index() {
   }
}
```

Then, add the view file for the `index()` action, by convention, in a file named `app/View/Auths/index.ctp`:

```php
<?php
echo $this->Html->tag('h2', __('You are allowed to pass, %s', AuthComponent::user('username')));
```

How to do it...

Perform the following steps:

1. First, ensure that your `admin` prefixes are enabled in the `core.php` file in `app/Config/` by uncommenting this line:

   ```
   Configure::write('Routing.prefixes', array('admin'));
   ```

2. Create a new custom authorization class file named `AdminAuthorize.php` in `app/Controller/Component/Auth/` with the following content:

   ```php
   <?php
   App::uses('BaseAuthorize', 'Controller/Component/Auth');

   class AdminAuthorize extends BaseAuthorize {

     public function authorize($user, CakeRequest $request) {
       $isAdminPrefix = (Hash::get($request->params, 'prefix') ===
   'admin');
       if (!$isAdminPrefix) {
         return true;
       }

       $isAdminUser = (bool)Hash::get($user, 'is_admin');
       return $isAdminUser;
     }
   }
   ```

3. Update your `AuthsController` controller in `app/Controller/`
    `AuthsController.php` as follows:

```php
<?php
App::uses('AppController', 'Controller');

class AuthsController extends AppController {

  public $components = array(
    'Auth' => array(
      'authenticate' => array('Basic' => array(
        'fields' => array(
          'username' => 'username',
          'password' => 'password'
        ),
        'userModel' => 'User',
        'scope' => array(
          array('User.active' => 1)
        ),
        'recursive' => -1,
        'contain' => null,
        'realm' => 'Speak, friend, and enter'
        )),
        'authorize' => array('Admin')
    )
  );

  public function beforeFilter() {
    AuthComponent::$sessionKey = false;
    $this->Auth->allow('saveTestUser');
  }

  public function saveTestUser() {
    $User = ClassRegistry::init('User');
    $data = array(
        'id' => 1,
        'username' => 'admin',
        'password' => Security::hash('admin', null, true),
        'active' => 1,
        'is_admin' => 1
    );
```

```
        $User->create();
        $User->save($data);
        $data = array(
          'id' => 2,
          'username' => 'user',
          'password' => Security::hash('user', null, true),
          'active' => 1,
          'is_admin' => 0
        );
        $User->create();
        $User->save($data);
        $this->autoRender = false;
    }

    public function index() {
        // all logged in users should have access
    }

    public function admin_index() {
        // all admin users should have access
        $this->render('index');
    }
}
```

4. Use the `saveTestUser()` utility action to generate two new test users for your application by opening a browser, and navigate to `/auths/saveTestUser`.

5. Open the protected page, `/admin/auths/index`.

   You'll get an HTTP basic browser popup that requests the username/password to access this website. Type the following for each field:

   ```
   Username: admin
   Password: admin
   ```

   You'll then get access to the admin index page, and a **You are allowed to pass, friend** welcome message will be displayed:

6. Once you're able to log in, remove the `saveTestUser()` method from the `AuthsController.php` file in app/Controller/.

7. Finally, open a new browser window and log in again, but instead of using the `admin` user, try `user`. You'll get a **You are not authorized to access that location** message.

How it works...

In this recipe, we first enabled the `admin` prefix routing option for our application, using the following code:

```
Configure::write('Routing.prefixes', array('admin'));
```

Prefixes are useful here to add a layer of actions that are only accessible by the `admin` user. The `admin` prefixes are managed by the framework transparently, using `admin/` in this case prior to the controller name in your URL. CakePHP will then match this string with the `admin` prefix (we could have several prefixes configured) and then resolve the specific action with this prefix by convention, for example, `admin_index()`. This action would be called in your controller, instead of the regular `index()` action. So, in our recipe, we are using the following:

```
/admin/auths/index
```

The magic then happens in our newly customized authorize class. Let's focus on the following method:

```
public function authorize($user, CakeRequest $request) {
  $isAdminPrefix = (Hash::get($request->params, 'prefix') ===
'admin');
  if (!$isAdminPrefix) {
    return true;
  }

  $isAdminUser = (bool)Hash::get($user, 'is_admin');
  return $isAdminUser;
}
```

The `authorize()` method takes two parameters: the currently logged-in `$user` (after our authentication logic was executed) and the current `$request` object. We'll be able to inspect the `$request` object to determine the current action and parameters, and based on this information as well as the user, return `true` for authorized or `false` for denied.

In our scenario, we're first inspecting the `$request` object to determine if the current prefix is an admin or not:

```
$isAdminPrefix = (Hash::get($request->params, 'prefix') === 'admin');
```

Remember to always use the `Hash::get()` function to safely retrieve an array value. In using it this way, we'll avoid getting warnings if the key is not set in the `$request->params` array and cut down on the typical logic for this. Here, we expect this value to be `string`, so we compare it to our `admin` prefix to cast it to a `(bool)` value.

Here, we'll return `true` for all nonadmin-prefixed actions, so users logged in will have access to all of the actions except for the admin-prefixed ones. We then perform a similar check to inspect the `$user` data and determine if the user is an admin or not:

```
$isAdminUser = (bool)Hash::get($user, 'is_admin');
```

After that, we'll return `true` only in case the user is an admin.

We then updated the `AuthsController` to use our newly created `AdminAuthorize` class:

```
'authorize' => array('Admin')
```

As we're following the CakePHP conventions for the naming and placing of our custom `Auth` classes, we only need to specify the name, and the full path will be assumed as the following:

```
app/Controller/Component/Auth/AdminAuthorize.php
```

Now, we could also remove the unused `isAuthorized()` method of `AuthsController`. Once everything was in place, we updated the `saveTestUser()` method to save two test users instead of one. Note that the admin user is saved with the is_admin flag set to 1. We also added the following new `admin` prefixed `admin_index()` action to our controller:

```
public function admin_index() {
    // all admin users should have access
    $this->render('index');
}
```

This new action is reusing the index view but will allow us to test the `admin` prefix authentication we just created.

Testing our auth-protected URLs would be the next step:

- ▸ `/admin/auths/index` is allowed for `admin` but not allowed for `user`, as this is prefixed with `admin/`
- ▸ `/auths/index` is allowed for any logged-in user, either `admin` or `user`

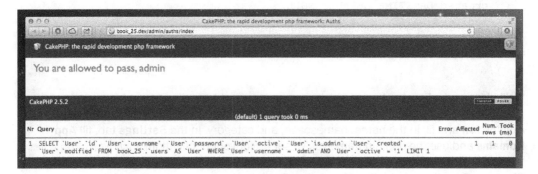

See also

▶ For more details on routing prefixes, visit `http://book.cakephp.org/2.0/en/development/routing.html#prefix-routing`

▶ The *The HTTP authentication* recipe

Facebook authentication

These days, you don't always need to worry about creating user accounts; you can simply use an external service instead, and let the user connect their third-party or social account with your application.

Popular services such as Facebook, Google, and Twitter all provide an API to define and connect a new application. Focusing on Facebook, their services rely on OAuth for a token-based authorization system. OAuth is an open protocol for authentication and authorization; it allows you to use a third-party service to identify a user without directly accessing their credentials (password).

In this recipe, we'll be using Opauth to connect our CakePHP application with Facebook.

Getting ready

For this recipe, we'll need a table for our users, so create one with the following SQL statement:

```
CREATE TABLE users (
    id VARCHAR(36) NOT NULL,
    username VARCHAR(255) NOT NULL,
    password VARCHAR(128) DEFAULT NULL,
    email VARCHAR(255) DEFAULT NULL,
    active TINYINT(1) DEFAULT '1',
    created DATETIME DEFAULT NULL,
    modified DATETIME DEFAULT NULL,
    remote_id VARCHAR(255) NOT NULL,
    PRIMARY KEY(id)
);
```

We'll also need a Facebook app, which you can create at `https://developers.facebook.com/apps/`. Log in using your Facebook credentials. Click on **Create New Application** and fill in the name, namespace, and category. In the **Settings** tab, fill **App Domains** and use the domain name you've set up for your application, such as `myapp.com`. Click on **+ Add platform** and select **Website**; fill **Site URL** with `myapp.com`. Click on **Save Changes**. Copy the **Application ID** and **App Secret** values; we'll need them later.

How to do it...

Perform the following steps:

1. First, download and install the Opauth plugin for CakePHP by running the following commands (we'll use git for this):

   ```
   $ git submodule add git://github.com/uzyn/cakephp-opauth.git app/
   Plugin/Opauth
   ```

   ```
   $ git submodule update --init --recursive
   ```

   ```
   Submodule 'Vendor/Opauth' (git://github.com/uzyn/opauth.git)
   registered for path 'Vendor/Opauth'
   ```

   ```
   Cloning into 'Vendor/Opauth'...
   ```

   ```
   remote: Counting objects: 2611, done.
   ```

   ```
   remote: Compressing objects: 100% (1155/1155), done.
   ```

   ```
   remote: Total 2611 (delta 1111), reused 2609 (delta 1110)
   ```

   ```
   Receiving objects: 100% (2611/2611), 507.36 KiB | 275.00 KiB/s,
   done.
   ```

   ```
   Resolving deltas: 100% (1111/1111), done.
   ```

   ```
   Checking connectivity... done.
   ```

   ```
   Submodule path 'app/Plugin/Opauth/Vendor/Opauth': checked out
   'bea7c46f7568c2f37301f284c1e907cffa03bb6b
   ```

2. Install the Facebook strategy for Opauth:

   ```
   $ cd app/Plugin/Opauth/Strategy
   ```

   ```
   $ git clone https://github.com/opauth/facebook.git Facebook
   ```

3. Add this line at the end of your `bootstrap.php` file in `app/Config/`:

   ```
   CakePlugin::load('Opauth', array(
     'routes' => true,
     'bootstrap' => true
   ));
   Configure::write('Opauth.Strategy.Facebook', array(
     'app_id' => 'YOUR APP ID',
     'app_secret' => 'YOUR APP SECRET',
     'scope' => 'email'
   ));
   ```

4. Also, add this line to your `routes.php` file, again in `app/Config/`:

   ```
   Router::connect('/opauth-complete/*', array(
     'controller' => 'users',
     'action' => 'opauth_complete'
   ));
   ```

5. Now, create a file named `UsersController.php` in `app/Controller/` with the following content:

```php
<?php
App::uses('AppController', 'Controller');

class UsersController extends AppController {

  public function beforeFilter() {
    parent::beforeFilter();
    $this->Auth->allow('opauth_complete');
  }

  public function opauth_complete() {
    $uid = $this->request->data('auth.uid');
    $username = $this->request->data('auth.info.email');
    $user = $this->User->getRemote($uid, $username);
    $this->Auth->login($user['User']);
    $this->redirect(array('action' => 'dashboard'));
  }

  public function dashboard() {
  }
}
```

6. Also, create a file named `User.php` in `app/Model/` with the following content:

```php
<?php
App::uses('AppModel', 'Model');

class User extends AppModel {

  public function getRemote($remoteId, $username) {
    $user = $this->find('first', array(
      'conditions' => array(
        'remote_id' => $remoteId,
        'username' => $username
      )
    ));
    if (empty($user)) {
      // register a new user
      $user = $this->save(array(
        'remote_id' => $remoteId,
        'username' => $username,
        'password' => md5(String::uuid())
      ));
```

```
    }
        return $user;
    }
}
```

7. Create a file named `dashboard.ctp` in `app/View/Users/` with the following content:

```php
<?php
echo $this->Html->tag('h2', __('Welcome back, %s', AuthComponent::
user('username')));
```

8. Now, configure the `Auth` component in your `AppController` in `app/Controller/AppController.php`:

```php
<?php
App::uses('Controller', 'Controller');

class AppController extends Controller {

  public $components = array(
    'Auth' => array(
      'authorize' => array('Controller'),
      'loginAction' => '/auth/facebook'
    )
  );

  public function isAuthorized($user = null) {
    return true;
  }
}
```

9. Finally, log in using Facebook by navigating to `/auth/facebook` from your application in your browser.

  You'll be redirected to Facebook to enter your user credentials and authorize the application you created earlier in this recipe to access your basic data and e-mail. Click on **Accept** on this page to be redirected back to your application by Facebook.

10. After redirection, you'll land on the `/users/dashboard` view where a **Welcome back, your@facebook.email.here.com** welcome message will be displayed:

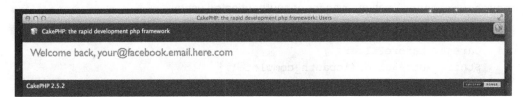

How it works...

Opauth uses strategies to provide vendor-specific logic, which you can use to implement multiple vendors in your applications such as Twitter or Linkedin. In this recipe, we're only covering Facebook.

We first created a new Facebook app and configured the application to allow our domain name as an authorization source. In this step, it's important to note that you'll need to set up a virtual host in your web server to allow your application to work using a real (or test) domain instead of `localhost`. Check out the details on this at `http://book.cakephp.org/2.0/en/installation/url-rewriting.html`. Also ensure that you can access your application using a domain such as `http://myapp.com`, as we'll need to use `myapp.com` to identify our application in the Facebook application's list of domain names.

```
CakePlugin::load('Opauth', array(
  'routes' => true,
  'bootstrap' => true
));

Configure::write('Opauth.Strategy.Facebook', array(
  'app_id' => 'YOUR APP ID',
  'app_secret' => 'YOUR APP SECRET',
  'scope' => 'email'
));
```

The `scope` is important to request Facebook to share the e-mail of the user, as we're going to use this e-mail address to fill in the `users` table when a new Facebook user is accessing our application but does not have an associated row in our `users` table.

We then configured the application routes with the following:

```
Router::connect('/opauth-complete/*', array(
  'controller' => 'users',
  'action' => 'opauth_complete'
));
```

This route is used by the Opauth plugin to redirect to any application-specific code once the user has been validated and we have the data provided by Facebook. In this case, we're redirecting to the `opauth_complete()` action of the `UsersController`.

In the same controller, we first set the `Auth` component to allow access to the `opauth_complete()` action, even for nonauthenticated users:

```
public function beforeFilter(){
  parent::beforeFilter();
  $this->Auth->allow('opauth_complete');
}
```

We then implement the `opauth_complete()` action itself in the following way:

```
public function opauth_complete() {
  $uid = $this->request->data('auth.uid');
  $username = $this->request->data('auth.info.email');
  $user = $this->User->getRemote($uid, $username);
  $this->Auth->login($user['User']);
  $this->redirect(array('action' => 'dashboard'));
}
```

Here, we're inspecting the returned user data (from the Facebook API) to get the unique ID and e-mail address; then, we retrieve or create a new user in our `users` table linked to the Facebook user, and redirect to the `dashboard()` action. We then log in the user, thus effectively managing the user data from the `Auth` component.

The `dashboard()` action then simply presents a welcome message to the user:

```
echo $this->Html->tag('h2', __('Welcome back, %s', AuthComponent::user
('username')));
```

The user has now been logged in, so we have their data available through the `Auth` component.

In the `User` model, we then created a method to retrieve a Facebook user or create a new one if the user data is not found in our users table:

```
public function getRemote($remoteId, $username) {
  $user = $this->find('first', array(
    'conditions' => array(
      'remote_id' => $remoteId,
      'username' => $username
    )
  ));
  if (empty($user)) {
    // register a new user
    $user = $this->save(array(
      'remote_id' => $remoteId,
      'username' => $username,
      'password' => md5(String::uuid())
    ));
  }
  return $user;
}
```

Note that we're storing a random password here, as we don't have access to the Facebook password. This new user will only be able to log in to our system using the Facebook callback.

We've also configured the `Auth` component in our `AppController` class to enable auth in all of the controllers application wide:

```
public $components = array(
  'Auth' => array(
    'authorize' => array('Controller'),
    'loginAction' => '/auth/facebook'
  )
);
```

Setting `loginAction` will redirect the browser to `/auth/facebook` when we visit any page of our website and we're not authenticated yet. This page is managed by the Opauth plugin to trigger the Facebook redirect by passing all of the required parameters to Facebook to identify our application and redirect back to the right URL once the user is authenticated:

```
public function isAuthorized($user = null) {
  return true;
}
```

We're also setting all pages as authorized, so any user currently logged in will be allowed to access it.

Of course, there are several things needed before we can finish a full Facebook integration, such as the ability to log a user out, set a local password, enable additional vendors, and improve security. However, in this recipe, we focused on the minimum steps you'll need to be able to link your application to Facebook and log in users via this service.

See also

- The steps for installation of Opauth for CakePHP can found at `https://github.com/uzyn/cakephp-opauth#how-to-use`
- Information on the Facebook API is found at `https://developers.facebook.com/docs/facebook-login/overview/v2.0`
- Read more about the OAuth protocol at `http://oauth.net`
- More details on Opauth can be found at `http://opauth.org`
- The list of Opauth strategies are available at `https://github.com/opauth/opauth/wiki/List-of-strategies`
- The *The HTTP authentication* recipe

Custom RBAC

Role Based Access Control (**RBAC**) is where a user belongs to one or several roles. There are then permissions assigned to a specific role; they allow or deny user access to subjects.

In this recipe, we're going to use a simplified approach, where users will belong to exactly one role, and permissions will be set to allow access to controller actions. By default, all actions will be denied, and we'll configure which roles can access which actions in our application. For this, we'll use a custom authenticate class and a configuration file to define the permissions. Easy to maintain and human readable.

Getting ready

For this recipe, we'll again create a `users` table, using the following SQL statement:

```sql
CREATE TABLE users (
    id VARCHAR(36) NOT NULL,
    username VARCHAR(255) NOT NULL,
    password VARCHAR(128) NOT NULL,
    active TINYINT(1) DEFAULT '0',
    created DATETIME DEFAULT NULL,
    modified DATETIME DEFAULT NULL,
    PRIMARY KEY(id)
);
```

How to do it...

Perform the following steps:

1. First, add the following content to your `AppController.php` file in `app/Controller/`:

```php
<?php
App::uses('Controller', 'Controller');

class AppController extends Controller {

    public $components = array(
        'Auth' => array(
            'authenticate' => array('Basic' => array(
                'fields' => array(
```

```
          'username' => 'username',
          'password' => 'password'
        ),
        'userModel' => 'User',
        'scope' => array(
          array('User.active' => 1)
        ),
        'recursive' => -1,
        'contain' => null,
        'realm' => 'Speak, friend, and enter'
      )),
      'authorize' => array('SimpleRbac')
    )
  );

  public function beforeFilter() {
    parent::beforeFilter();
    AuthComponent::$sessionKey = false;
  }
}
```

2. Create a new custom authorize class named `SimpleRbacAuthorize.php` in `app/Controller/Component/Auth/`:

```php
<?php
App::uses('BaseAuthorize', 'Controller/Component/Auth');

class SimpleRbacAuthorize extends BaseAuthorize {

  public function authorize($user, CakeRequest $request) {
    $role = Hash::get($user, 'role');
    if ($role === ROLE_ADMIN) {
      return true;
    }
    $permissions = Configure::read('app.permissions.' . $this->action($request));
    if (empty($permissions)) {
      return false;
    } elseif ($permissions === '*') {
      return true;
    }
    $roles = is_array($permissions) ? $permissions : explode(',', $permissions);
    return in_array($role, $roles);
  }
}
```

3. Add the following line to the end of your `bootstrap.php` file in `app/Config/`:

```
config('permissions');
```

4. Create a new configuration file named `permissions.php` in `app/Config/`, with the following content:

```php
<?php
define('ROLE_ADMIN', 'admin');
define('ROLE_MANAGER', 'manager');
define('ROLE_REGISTERED', 'registered');

Configure::write('app.permissions', array(
  'Auths/index' => '*',
  'Auths/admin_index' => array(ROLE_MANAGER)
));
```

5. Add a `role` column to the `users` table, using the following SQL statement:

```
ALTER TABLE users ADD role VARCHAR( 255 ) DEFAULT NULL;
```

6. Create a file named `AuthsController.php` in `app/Controller/` with the following content:

```php
<?php
App::uses('AppController', 'Controller');

class AuthsController extends AppController {

  public function beforeFilter() {
    parent::beforeFilter();
    $this->Auth->allow('saveTestUser');
  }

  public function saveTestUser() {
    $User = ClassRegistry::init('User');
    $data = array(
      'id' => 1,
      'username' => 'admin',
      'password' => Security::hash('admin', null, true),
      'active' => 1,
      'role' => ROLE_ADMIN
    );
    $User->create();
    $User->save($data);
    $data = array(
      'id' => 2,
```

```
                'username' => 'registered',
                'password' => Security::hash('registered', null, true),
                'active' => 1,
                'role' => ROLE_REGISTERED
            );
            $User->create();
            $User->save($data);
            $this->autoRender = false;
        }

        public function index() {
        }

        public function admin_index() {
            $this->render('index');
        }
    }
```

7. Create a view for the `index()` action, by convention, in a file named `app/View/Auths/index.ctp`:

    ```php
    <?php
    echo $this->Html->tag('h2', __('You are allowed to pass, %s', Auth
    Component::user('username')));
    ```

8. Create a couple of test users, using the `saveTestUser()` utility action by navigating to `/auths/saveTestUser` in your browser.

9. Check whether you're able to access all the configured pages as the user `admin` (password = `admin`):

    ```
    /auths/index
    /admin/auths/index
    ```

10. Also, check whether you're able to access only the nonprefixed index action as the `registered` user (password = `registered`):

    ```
    /auths/index
    ```

How it works...

In this recipe, we've implemented a custom, quick, and easy RBAC authorization class. We started by adding application-wide `Auth` component settings as follows:

```
'Auth' => array(
    'authenticate' => array('Basic' => array(
        'fields' => array(
```

```
      'username' => 'username',
      'password' => 'password'
    ),
    'userModel' => 'User',
    'scope' => array(
      array('User.active' => 1)
    ),
    'recursive' => -1,
    'contain' => null,
    'realm' => 'Speak, friend, and enter'
  )),
  'authorize' => array('SimpleRbac')
)
```

As all of our application controllers extend the `AppController` class, we effectively protected our entire application using basic HTTP authentication, using a new authorization custom class named `SimpleRbac`.

By reviewing the `authorize()` method (shown in the following code) in this class, we can inspect how the roles and users are managed to determine whether we're allowed to access the current action or not:

```
public function authorize($user, CakeRequest $request) {
  $role = Hash::get($user, 'role');
  if ($role === ROLE_ADMIN) {
    return true;
  }
  $permissions = Configure::read('app.permissions.' . $this-
>action($request));
  if (empty($permissions)) {
    return false;
  } elseif ($permissions === '*') {
    return true;
  }
  $roles = is_array($permissions) ? $permissions : explode(',',
$permissions);
  return in_array($role, $roles);
}
```

The `role` field in our `users` table is used to extract a role name for every user. We then compare this role's name with the specific array of allowed roles in a configuration file named `permissions.php` in app/Config/, loaded at bootstrap time.

The `permissions.php` file contains a list of role names and an array of permissions that match the current controller name (capitalized) and the action requested. If the name of the role is not listed in the `controller+action` key in the permissions array, the current user will not be allowed. There is a special `*` key defined in roles that allows any role to access specific actions. We're also detecting `ROLE_ADMIN` and allowing them to access any action in the application, as shown in the following code:

```
Configure::write('app.permissions', array(
  'Auths/index' => '*',
  'Auths/admin_index' => array(ROLE_MANAGER)
));
```

Note that we're also using the `beforeFilter()` callback method in the `AuthsController` class to ensure that we can access the `saveTestUser()` action even if we aren't logged in.

With the permission configuration that we set up, the registered users will be allowed to access the `/auths/index` page but not allowed to access `/admin/auths/index` (note the `admin` prefix used). You can read more about routing prefixes at `http://book.cakephp.org/2.0/en/development/routing.html#prefix-routing`.

The good thing about this implementation is its simplicity. You got a centralized place to set up your permissions application wide, and it's very easy to understand when a user is allowed to access a specific action. The main flaw in this is the lack of flexibility, as adding a new role to an existing (complex) application would be tedious. However, from here, you can extend and build out this base implementation to suit your needs.

See also

- ▸ RBAC definition at `http://en.wikipedia.org/wiki/Role-based_access_control`
- ▸ The *The HTTP Basic authentication* recipe

Working with ACL

When your application needs a powerful and flexible authentication mechanism, it's probably time to use the **Access Control Lists** (**ACL**) component, included with CakePHP.

Although you can use a file to manage your ACL configuration, storing all of the data in the database is the most common option, as we'll see in this recipe.

Getting ready

For this recipe, we'll use a `users` table as well as a `roles` table to allow us to define roles and inherit their permissions. For this, we'll use the following SQL statements:

```sql
CREATE TABLE users (
    id VARCHAR(36) NOT NULL,
    username VARCHAR(255) NOT NULL,
    password VARCHAR(128) NOT NULL,
    active TINYINT(1) DEFAULT '0',
    role_id VARCHAR(36) DEFAULT NULL,
    created DATETIME DEFAULT NULL,
    modified DATETIME DEFAULT NULL,
    PRIMARY KEY(id)
);

CREATE TABLE roles (
    id VARCHAR(36) NOT NULL,
    name VARCHAR(255) NOT NULL,
    role_id VARCHAR(36) DEFAULT NULL,
    created DATETIME DEFAULT NULL,
    modified DATETIME DEFAULT NULL,
    PRIMARY KEY(id)
);
```

We'll also create a file named `AuthsController.php` (shown in the following code) in `app/Controller/` to test our ACL application later:

```php
<?php
App::uses('AppController', 'Controller');

class AuthsController extends AppController {

    public function index() {
    }

    public function admin_index() {
        $this->render('index');
    }
}
```

We'll also need a view file for the `index()` action, which is created by convention in a file named `app/View/Auths/index.ctp`, with the following content:

```php
<?php
echo $this->Html->tag('h2', __('You are allowed to pass, %s', AuthComp
onent::user('username')));
```

Next, install the `AclExtras` plugin, which you can download from `https://github.com/ markstory/acl_extras/archive/master.zip`.

Then, uncompress the file contents into a directory named `AclExtras` in `app/Plugin/` and load the plugin in your `bootstrap.php` file by adding this line:

```php
CakePlugin::load('AclExtras');
```

How to do it...

Perform the following steps:

1. First, initialize the ACL related tables, using the ACL shell provided by CakePHP:

   ```
   $ Console/cake acl initdb
   ```

   ```
   Welcome to CakePHP v2.5.2 Console
   ---------------------------------------------------------------
   App : app
   Path: /home/user/app/
   ---------------------------------------------------------------


   Welcome to CakePHP v2.5.2 Console
   ---------------------------------------------------------------
   App : app
   Path: /home/user/app/
   ---------------------------------------------------------------
   Cake Schema Shell
   ---------------------------------------------------------------


   The following table(s) will be dropped.
   acos
   aros
   aros_acos
   ```

```
Are you sure you want to drop the table(s)? (y/n)
[n] > y
Dropping table(s).
acos updated.
aros updated.
aros_acos updated.

The following table(s) will be created.
acos
aros
aros_acos
Are you sure you want to create the table(s)? (y/n)
[y] > y
Creating table(s).
acos updated.
aros updated.
aros_acos updated.
End create.
```

2. Create a file named `User.php` in `app/Model/`, with the following content:

```php
<?php
App::uses('AppModel', 'Model');
App::uses('SimplePasswordHasher', 'Controller/Component/Auth');

class User extends AppModel {

  public $belongsTo = array('Role');

  public $actsAs = array('Acl' => array('type' => 'requester'));

  public function parentNode() {
    if (empty($this->id)) {
      return null;
    }
    $roleId = Hash::get($this->data, 'User.role_id');
    if (empty($roleId)) {
      $roleId = $this->field('role_id');
    }
    if (empty($roleId)) {
      return null;
```

```php
      } else {
        return array('Role' => array('id' => $roleId));
      }
    }


    public function beforeSave($options = array()) {
      if (!parent::beforeSave($options)) {
        return false;
      }

      if (isset($this->data[$this->alias]['password'])) {
        $hasher = new SimplePasswordHasher();
        $this->data[$this->alias]['password'] = $hasher->hash($this->data[$this->alias]['password']);
      }

      return true;
    }
}
```

3. Also, create a file named `Role.php`, again, in `app/Model/`, with the following content:

```php
<?php
App::uses('AppModel', 'Model');

class Role extends AppModel {

  public $hasMany = array('User');

  public $actsAs = array('Acl' => array('type' => 'requester'));

  public function parentNode() {
    if (empty($this->id)) {
      return null;
    }
    $roleId = Hash::get($this->data, 'Role.role_id');
    if (empty($roleId)) {
      $roleId = $this->field('role_id');
    }
    if (empty($roleId)) {
      return null;
    } else {
      return array('Role' => array('id' => $roleId));
    }
  }
}
```

4. Now, configure the `Auth` component in `app/Controller/AppController.php` with the following setup:

```php
<?php
App::uses('Controller', 'Controller');

class AppController extends Controller {

    public $components = array(
        'Acl',
        'Auth' => array(
            'authenticate' => array('Basic' => array(
                'fields' => array(
                    'username' => 'username',
                    'password' => 'password'
                ),
                'userModel' => 'User',
                'scope' => array(
                    array('User.active' => 1)
                ),
                'recursive' => -1,
                'contain' => null,
                'realm' => 'Speak, friend, and enter'
            )),
            'authorize' => array('Actions' => array('actionPath' =>
'controllers'))
        )
    );

    public function beforeFilter() {
        parent::beforeFilter();
        AuthComponent::$sessionKey = false;
    }
}
```

5. Update the content in the `AuthsController` with the following code:

```php
<?php
App::uses('AppController', 'Controller');

class AuthsController extends AppController {

    public function beforeFilter() {
        parent::beforeFilter();
```

```
      $this->Auth->allow('saveTestUser');
}

public function saveTestUser() {
  $Role = ClassRegistry::init('Role');
  $Role->create();
  $Role->save(array(
    'id' => 1,
    'name' => 'registered',
    'role_id' => null
  ));
  $Role->create();
  $Role->save(array(
    'id' => 2,
    'name' => 'manager',
    'role_id' => 1
  ));
  $Role->create();
  $Role->save(array(
    'id' => 3,
    'name' => 'admin',
    'role_id' => 2
  ));
  $User = ClassRegistry::init('User');
  $User->create();
  $User->save(array(
    'id' => 1,
    'username' => 'admin',
    'password' => 'admin',
    'active' => 1,
    'role_id' => 3
  ));
  $User->create();
  $User->save(array(
    'id' => 2,
    'username' => 'manager',
    'password' => 'manager',
    'active' => 1,
    'role_id' => 2
  ));
  $User->create();
  $User->save(array(
```

```
          'id' => 3,
          'username' => 'registered',
          'password' => 'registered',
          'active' => 1,
          'role_id' => 1
      ));
      $this->autoRender = false;
  }

  public function index() {
      // all logged in users should have access
  }

  public function admin_index() {
      // all admin users should have access
      $this->render('index');
  }
}
```

Ensure that your `users` and `roles` tables are empty, using the following SQL statement:

```
TRUNCATE users;
TRUNCATE roles;
```

 Be warned that the table contents will be removed.

6. Create a couple of test users and roles using the `saveTestUser()` utility action by navigating to `/auths/saveTestUser` in your browser.

7. Verify that the users and roles were created correctly using the ACL console shell as follows:

```
$ Console/cake acl view aro


Welcome to CakePHP v2.5.2 Console
---------------------------------------------------------------
App : app
Path: /home/user/app/
---------------------------------------------------------------
```

```
Aro tree:
---------------------------------------------------------------

   [1] Role.1
     [2] Role.2
       [3] Role.3
         [4] User.1
       [5] User.2
     [6] User.3

---------------------------------------------------------------
```

8. Use the AclExtras plugin to generate the ACOs for all of your controller actions, using the plugin's shell:

    ```
    $ Console/cake AclExtras.acl_extras aco_sync
    ```

    ```
    Welcome to CakePHP v2.5.2 Console
    ---------------------------------------------------------------
    App : app
    Path: /home/user/app/
    ---------------------------------------------------------------
    Created Aco node: controllers/Auths
    Created Aco node: controllers/Auths/saveTestUser
    Created Aco node: controllers/Auths/index
    Created Aco node: controllers/Auths/admin_index
    Aco Update Complete
    ```

9. Check whether the ACOs were created successfully with the following command:

    ```
    $ Console/cake acl view aco
    ```

    ```
    Welcome to CakePHP v2.5.2 Console
    ---------------------------------------------------------------
    App : app
    Path: /home/user/app/
    ---------------------------------------------------------------
    Aco tree:
    ---------------------------------------------------------------

       [1] controllers
         [2] Auths
    ```

```
[3]  saveTestUser
[4]  index
[5]  admin_index
```
----

10. Grant some permissions using the ACL shell as follows:

    `$ Console/cake acl grant Role.3 controllers/Auths/admin_index`

    `$ Console/cake acl grant Role.2 controllers/Auths/index`

11. Check the permissions for your `AuthsController` actions by either logging in as the test user or using the ACL console shell.

    For example, logging in as the manager user:

    ```
    http://yoursite.com/auths/index
    username: manager
    password: manager
    User is allowed to access this page
    ```

    ```
    http://yoursite.com/admin/auths/index
    username: manager
    password: manager
    User is NOT allowed to access this page
    ```

    ```
    http://yoursite.com/auths/index
    username: admin
    password: admin
    User is allowed to access this page
    ```

    ```
    http://yoursite.com/admin/auths/index
    username: admin
    password: admin
    User is allowed to access this page
    ```

    ```
    http://yoursite.com/auths/index
    username: registered
    password: registered
    User is NOT allowed to access this page
    ```

    ```
    http://yoursite.com/admin/auths/index
    username: registered
    password: registered
    User is NOT allowed to access this page
    ```

Alternatively, you can use the ACL shell:

```
Admin user (User.id = 1)
$ Console/cake acl check User.1 controllers/Auths/index
User.1 is allowed.
$ Console/cake acl check User.1 controllers/Auths/admin_index
User.1 is allowed.


Manager user (User.id = 2)
$ Console/cake acl check User.2 controllers/Auths/index
User.2 is allowed.
$ Console/cake acl check User.2 controllers/Auths/admin_index
User.2 is not allowed.


Registered user (User.id = 3)
$ Console/cake acl check User.3 controllers/Auths/index
User.3 is not allowed.
$ Console/cake acl check User.3 controllers/Auths/admin_index
User.3 is not allowed.
```

How it works...

In this recipe, we implemented a flexible access-control system using the CakePHP core ACL component and behaviors.

In the ACL world, there are the following:

- ► Subjects to be managed, called **Access Control Objects** (**ACO**). A subject could be a controller action, a model method, or a high-level abstract definition such as *PDF Reports or Export to external FTP server* that does not directly match any of your actions, objects, or methods in your code but represents a feature that needs to be managed in your application.

- ► Requesters to be allowed or denied when accessing a specific subject, called **Access Request Objects** (**ARO**). A requester is usually a user logged in to your application after your authentication logic validates their credentials.

- ► Permissions, matching AROs with ACOs. Note that all of the permission checks return denied access unless an allowed permission is set.

▶ Both ACOs and AROs are saved using a tree structure, thus allowing us to inherit permissions. When the `closer` permission set to any ARO is used, we can override permissions for specific nodes. For example, we could define a `denied` permission for all users in a given group and allow one specific user to access the ACO. The ACL-related logic will determine if a given ARO is allowed to access a specific ACO.

Here, we're managing all of our controllers and actions as ACOs, using one main node for all of the controllers and then a child node for each controller and specific actions:

```
/controllers
  /AuthsController
    /index
    /admin_index
```

All of our roles and users are AROs to let the roles inherit permissions from parent roles. In this example, all of the allowed permissions set to `registered` users will be inherited by the `manager` users:

```
/Registered
  /Manager
    /Admin
       /User1 (is an admin)
    /User2 (is a manager)
  /User3 (is a registered user)
```

We've started initializing the ACOs and AROs tables using the ACL shell. Both tables will store the respective ACO and ARO entities in a tree-like structure.

$ Console/cake acl initdb

Once the tables are created, we configured ACL to link both our `User` and `Role` models into the AROs table. Setting our models with a requester behavior as shown in the following code in ACL will ensure that every time a new user or role is created, a related ARO entry will also be created:

```php
<?php
App::uses('AppModel', 'Model');
App::uses('SimplePasswordHasher', 'Controller/Component/Auth');

class User extends AppModel {

  public $belongsTo = array('Role');

  public $actsAs = array('Acl' => array('type' => 'requester'));

  public function parentNode() {
```

```
        if (empty($this->id)) {
          return null;
        }
        $roleId = Hash::get($this->data, 'User.role_id');
        if (empty($roleId)) {
          $roleId = $this->field('role_id');
        }
        if (empty($roleId)) {
          return null;
        }else {
          return array('Role' => array('id' => $roleId));
        }
      }
    }

    public function beforeSave($options = array()) {
      if (!parent::beforeSave($options)) {
        return false;
      }

      if (isset($this->data[$this->alias]['password'])) {
        $hasher = new SimplePasswordHasher();
        $this->data[$this->alias]['password'] = $hasher->hash($this-
>data[$this->alias]['password']);
      }

      return true;
    }
  }
```

We also defined the `parentNode()` method to let the ACL system know who is the parent of this specific node. In this case, the parent node of any user will be the associated role.

We've also defined a `beforeSave()` callback to automatically hash the password for newly created users.

The same approach is taken in the `Role` model, but in this case, the parent node is configured to return the role associated as the parent role to the current one. We're doing it this way because we want to be able to create roles "below" other roles in our ACO tree structure.

```
    public $components = array(
      'Acl',
      'Auth' => array(
        'authenticate' => array('Basic' => array(
        'fields' => array(
          'username' => 'username',
```

```
      'password' => 'password'
    ),
    'userModel' => 'User',
    'scope' => array(
      array('User.active' => 1)
    ),
    'recursive' => -1,
    'contain' => null,
    'realm' => 'Speak, friend, and enter'
    )),
    'authorize' => array('Actions' => array('actionPath' =>
  'controllers'))
  )
);
```

We also set up our base `AppController` class to use both the `Acl` and `Auth` components and configured the `Auth` component to use the `Actions` authorization, using a root path called `controller`. The `actionPath` configuration will allow us to check all of the actions under the `/controllers` root path in our ACO tree structure. This way, we don't populate the root path of our ACO tree structure but keep all of the controller-related ACOs well organized below a unique root path.

We then prepared the following utility method in our `AuthsController` class to create the roles and users we'll have available in our application:

```
public function saveTestUser() {
  $Role = ClassRegistry::init('Role');
  $Role->create();
  $Role->save(array(
    'id' => 1,
    'name' => 'registered',
    'role_id' => null
  ));
  $Role->create();
  $Role->save(array(
    'id' => 2,
    'name' => 'manager',
    'role_id' => 1
  ));
  $Role->create();
  $Role->save(array(
    'id' => 3,
    'name' => 'admin',
    'role_id' => 2
  ));
```

```
$User = ClassRegistry::init('User');
$User->create();
$User->save(array(
    'id' => 1,
    'username' => 'admin',
    'password' => 'admin',
    'active' => 1,
    'role_id' => 3
));
$User->create();
$User->save(array(
    'id' => 2,
    'username' => 'manager',
    'password' => 'manager',
    'active' => 1,
    'role_id' => 2
));
$User->create();
$User->save(array(
    'id' => 3,
    'username' => 'registered',
    'password' => 'registered',
    'active' => 1,
    'role_id' => 1
));
$this->autoRender = false;
}
```

Saving new roles now will create and link a new ARO row too. The AROs will be saved using the model alias and the foreign key of the model saved. For example, the ARO row for the first role created will be saved as `Role.1` and will be the parent node of the `Role.2` node. Note that the `roles` and `users` tables have a `role_id` column filled with the ID of the parent role to be assigned.

As we did in our previous recipes, the `beforeFilter()` callback allows us to execute the `saveTestUser()` method even for users who are not logged in. Once we've run this action, we can safely delete the `saveTestUser()` method from the `AuthsController` class.

Note that we need to ensure that no users or roles are created earlier in their respective tables. If not, an ACL-related exception will be raised, as the related row is not present in the `aros` table.

We then used the ACL console shell to inspect our ARO entries, with the following command:

```
$ Console/cake acl view aro
```

The ACL shell can be used to inspect both AROs and ACOs and also to create new nodes as well as grant or check the current permissions. We could use the ACL console to generate our ACO nodes, but instead, we're using a smarter approach to sync all of the controllers and actions we have in our application to the `acos` table. For this, we used the AclExtras plugin as follows:

```
$ Console/cake AclExtras.acl_extras aco_sync
```

The `aco_sync` task inspects all our controllers and actions, and checks if they're already created in our `acos` table, under the root key, "controllers." Once executed, you could inspect your ACOs using the following command:

```
$ Console/cake acl view aco
```

With this, you'll get the tree of all of your controllers and actions (below their respective controller). These ACOs will then be used to check if the current user is allowed to access it.

The `Actions` authenticate class will extract the currently requested controller and action name, and match it against the related ACO row. Based on the permissions assigned to the current user and parent role(s), we'll return `true` or `false` to allow or deny access.

The last thing that we did is to actually create the permissions:

```
$ Console/cake acl grant Role.3 controllers/Auths/admin_index
```

```
$ Console/cake acl grant Role.2 controllers/Auths/index
```

This allows `Role.3` (admin) to access the `admin_index()` action in `AuthsController` and also allows `Role.2` (manager) to access the `index()` action.

Once done, we've granted access to all of the child nodes too, for example:

```
User.1 (admin) is allowed to access controllers/Auths/admin_index
because his parent role Role.3 (admin) is allowed.
User.1 (admin) is allowed to access controllers/Auths/index because
one of his parent roles Role.2 (manager) is allowed.
```

Remember that our ARO tree is as follows:

```
/Role.1 (=Registered)
  /Role.2 (=Manager)
    /Role.3 (=Admin)
      /User.1
```

We've used this ARO structure because we want the roles in our application to inherit all parent role permissions, but this may not be the case for you. Nothing stops us now from creating new top-level roles and starting clean with a new permission list.

See also

- ▸ The RBAC definition at `http://en.wikipedia.org/wiki/Role-based_access_control`
- ▸ The *The HTTP Basic authentication* recipe

6
Model Layer

In this chapter, we will cover the following topics:

- ► Has and belongs to many (HABTM)
- ► Joining through
- ► Containing models
- ► Custom finders
- ► On-the-fly associations
- ► Using transactions

Introduction

The model layer is the driving factor behind applications in CakePHP. It offers a powerful abstraction of your database by exposing your tables as model objects, allowing the framework to make assumptions about your data structure through conventions and for you to work on a business-domain level instead of raw SQL.

In this chapter, we will take a look at the various aspects of the models and how to wield their power.

Has and belongs to many (HABTM)

Has and belongs to many (HABTM) is the most complex model association available in CakePHP. This association type allows you to define many-to-many relationships in your data model, for example, in an inventory management application, where packages might be stored in different warehouses, and each warehouse might have several packages. This is a typical many-to-many relationship between packages and warehouses.

To model this association, you'll need to use three tables in your database: the `packages` table to store the data related to your packages, the `warehouses` table, and the `packages_warehouses` table, where the association itself is defined. The `packages_warehouses` table will have three columns by convention: `id`, `package_id`, and `warehouse_id`. We'll use this table to store the IDs of the associated models.

Of course, you *could* manage this table manually, keeping track of the association data and performing the changes that are required. However, CakePHP provides a way to easily manage this association using the framework's model layer to translate your models and associations into the SQL statement, which is required to retrieve and update the model and associated data.

There are simpler association types you could use, where the association data is stored in a column added to one of the models belonging to the association. You can learn more about simple CakePHP associations at `http://book.cakephp.org/2.0/en/models/associations-linking-models-together.html`.

In this recipe, we'll be focusing on the HABTM association.

Getting ready

First, we'll create the two new database tables, `packages` and `warehouses`, using the following SQL statement:

```
CREATE TABLE packages (
    id INT NOT NULL AUTO_INCREMENT,
    recipient VARCHAR(255) NOT NULL,
    address VARCHAR(255) NOT NULL,
    created DATETIME,
    modified DATETIME,
    PRIMARY KEY(id)
);

CREATE TABLE warehouses (
    id INT NOT NULL AUTO_INCREMENT,
    name VARCHAR(255) NOT NULL,
    created DATETIME,
    modified DATETIME,
    PRIMARY KEY(id)
);
```

We'll also insert some sample data into our tables with the following SQL statement:

```
INSERT INTO packages (recipient, address, created, modified)
VALUES
('John Doe', 'Sunset Boulevard 1, Los Angeles, CA', NOW(), NOW());
```

```
INSERT INTO warehouses (name, created, modified)
VALUES
('Main Warehouse', NOW(), NOW()),
('Auxiliar Warehouse 1', NOW(), NOW());
```

Then, create the models for both tables in `app/Model/` (the first in a file named `Package.php`), as shown in the following code:

```php
<?php
App::uses('AppModel', 'Model');

class Package extends AppModel {
}
```

Create another file named `Warehouse.php`:

```php
<?php
App::uses('AppModel', 'Model');

class Warehouse extends AppModel {
}
```

How to do it...

Perform the following steps:

1. First, create a new table to hold the HABTM association data. Following the name conventions, you'll use the existing table names, separated by an underscore character:

```sql
CREATE TABLE packages_warehouses (
  id INT NOT NULL AUTO_INCREMENT,
  package_id INT NOT NULL,
  warehouse_id INT NOT NULL,
  PRIMARY KEY(id)
);
```

2. Then, add a new association in the `Package` model by adding a new `$hasAndBelongsToMany` property to the `Package` model class in `app/Model/Package.php`:

```php
public $hasAndBelongsToMany = array(
  'Warehouse' => array(
    'className' => 'Warehouse',
    'joinTable' => 'packages_warehouses',
    'foreignKey' => 'package_id',
    'associationForeignKey' => 'warehouse_id',
```

```
        'unique' => 'keepExisting',
        'conditions' => '',
        'fields' => '',
        'order' => '',
        'limit' => '',
        'offset' => '',
        'finderQuery' => ''
      )
    );
```

3. Now, add a new association in the `Warehouse` model by adding the following code to the `Warehouse` class declared in `app/Model/Warehouse.php`:

```
public $hasAndBelongsToMany = array(
  'Package' => array(
    'className' => 'Package',
    'joinTable' => 'packages_warehouses',
    'foreignKey' => 'warehouse_id',
    'associationForeignKey' => 'package_id',
    'unique' => 'keepExisting',
    'conditions' => '',
    'fields' => '',
    'order' => '',
    'limit' => '',
    'offset' => '',
    'finderQuery' => ''
  )
);
```

How it works...

In this recipe, we first created a new table to store the association data (many-to-many relationship) between our packages and warehouses. Following the CakePHP conventions for the HABTM associations, this new table consists of three columns: an id for the row and the id of each member of the association, in this case, `package_id` and `warehouse_id`.

We then added a new `$hasAndBelongsToMany` association property to each model, as this is the way associations are configured in CakePHP models.

The new HABTM association is configured using an array. Let's take a look at the configuration used for the `Package` model:

```
public $hasAndBelongsToMany = array(
  'Warehouse' => array(
    'className' => 'Warehouse',
```

```
        'joinTable' => 'packages_warehouses',
        'foreignKey' => 'package_id',
        'associationForeignKey' => 'warehouse_id',
        'unique' => 'keepExisting',
        'conditions' => '',
        'fields' => '',
        'order' => '',
        'limit' => '',
        'offset' => '',
        'finderQuery' => ''
    )
);
```

Here, we're defining a HABTM association with the name `Warehouse` and configuring the association to use the `Warehouse` class. Note that we may call the association using a different name (this is called an *alias* in CakePHP), although in this case, we're using the same association name (key of the `Warehouse` array) and the class name of the model being associated (`'className' => 'Warehouse'`).

We're also configuring `packages_warehouses` as the table to use to store the association data and the column names in this table holding the IDs of the models being associated. The name of the column that stores the `id` of the model is `foreignKey`, where the association is defined (in this case, `Package`), and `associationForeignKey` is the name of the column where the `id` of each associated model is stored.

You might need to tweak other association parameters, such as using `unique`, `conditions`, `fields`, `order`, and so on. For example, you could limit this association to retrieve only active warehouses by adding the following code:

```
'conditions' => array('Warehouse.active' => true)
```

You can find more information on how to use these association keys at `http://book.cakephp.org/2.0/en/models/associations-linking-models-together.html#hasandbelongstomany-habtm`.

In this recipe, we defined the HABTM association on both models, slightly changing the HABTM association array to cover both sides of the relationship. Also, note that our association tables are following the CakePHP naming conventions, but you can customize this using the association properties, for example, by providing custom `joinTable` and `foreignKey` if you're using a legacy database.

Once set up, let's create an example of the data array for a `find` operation with an example controller. So, create a new file named `PackagesController.php` in app/Controllers/ with the following content:

```php
<?php
App::uses('AppController', 'Controller');
```

```
class PackagesController extends AppController {

  public function debug() {
    debug($this->Package->find('first', array('contain' =>
array('Warehouse'))));
    $this->autoRender = false;
  }
}
```

If you now call `/packages/debug` from your browser, the debug output would be the following:

```
array(
  'Package' => array(
    'id' => '1',
    'recipient' => 'John Doe',
    'address' => 'Sunset Boulevard 1, Los Angeles, CA',
    'created' => '2014-06-21 13:21:14',
    'modified' => '2014-06-21 13:21:14'
  ),
  'Warehouse' => array(
    (int) 0 => array(
      'id' => '1',
      'name' => 'Main Warehouse',
      'created' => '2014-06-21 13:18:11',
      'modified' => '2014-06-21 13:18:11',
      'PackagesWarehouse' => array(
        'id' => '1',
        'package_id' => '1',
        'warehouse_id' => '1'
      )
    ),
    (int) 1 => array(
      'id' => '2',
      'name' => 'Auxiliar Warehouse 1',
      'created' => '2014-06-21 13:18:11',
      'modified' => '2014-06-21 13:18:11',
      'PackagesWarehouse' => array(
        'id' => '2',
        'package_id' => '1',
        'warehouse_id' => '2'
      )
    )
  )
)
```

Note that this is the standard CakePHP array notation for data retrieved from a `find` operation on a model. The array that could be read as `package id = 1` is associated with two warehouses, with IDs 1 and 2.

See also

▸ The *Containing models* recipe

Joining through

Sometimes, you'll need to store additional data related to a HABTM association between your models. In this case, you can use a *join-through* association type, using a new model to hold the association details.

Join-through associations are similar to HABTM, but instead of having one table that stores the IDs of the associated models, we also store additional data related to the specific association. For example, if we follow our package's HABTM warehouses example from the previous recipe, we might want to store the number of packages we have stored in each warehouse, thus adding a new field to our association table to specify the required stock number for each association,.

Getting ready

Let's define a stock per package in each warehouse and redefine our HABTM association from our previous recipe to use a join-through association instead.

Note that we are using the tables and models created in our previous recipe.

How to do it...

Perform the following steps:

1. First, add a new `amount` column to the `packages_warehouses` table with the following SQL statement:

   ```
   ALTER TABLE packages_warehouses ADD amount INT NOT NULL DEFAULT
   '0';
   ```

2. Then, create a new model for the association in a file named `app/Model/Stock.php`:

   ```php
   <?php
   App::uses('AppModel', 'Model');

   class Stock extends AppModel {
   ```

```
public $useTable = 'packages_warehouses';

public $belongsTo = array(
  'Package',
  'Warehouse'
);
}
```

3. Now, change the model associations for `Package` and `Warehouse`, removing the current $hasAndBelongsToMany property and adding a new $hasMany property to define this association type:

```
public $hasMany = array(
  'Stock'
);
```

How it works...

In this recipe, we upgraded our HABTM association to a hasMany through association. We first added a new `amount` column to the `packages_warehouses` table to store the amount of packages stored in a given warehouse.

We then created a new `Stock` model to hold the association. This new model uses the `$useTable` model property to let the CakePHP model's **object relational mapper (ORM)** know how to link this model to one of our database tables, as it's not matching the model name. If we don't use this model property, CakePHP will link this model to the table named `stocks`, by convention. However, as this table doesn't exist in our database, an exception would be thrown.

Note that we've used two $belongsTo associations in the new `Stock` model, effectively breaking one HABTM into two belongs-to associations. We're now able to store the stock of our packages in each associated warehouse.

This way we'd be able to access the `Stock` itself (as it's a model now) and save or retrieve the current stock along with the associated packages or warehouses.

See also

► The *Containing models* recipe

Containing models

`Containable` is one of the must-have core behaviors in CakePHP. A behavior is added to a model to reuse logic, allowing you to configure your models by adding or removing specific behaviors to dynamically include or modify features or capabilities.

Using `Containable` allows you to determine which associations are retrieved for a specific `find` operation. So, instead of retrieving all the associated models on each `find` operation, you have the ability to select which specific associations you need for your next query. This is especially useful to optimize model queries when a large number of associations are defined. You also have the power to filter based on specific conditions and define which fields should be retrieved. When you combine the `Containable` behavior with associations, you'll resolve most of your data-retrieval needs.

Getting ready

For this recipe, we'll first define a new table and change our existing one using the following SQL statements:

```
CREATE TABLE categories (
    id INT NOT NULL AUTO_INCREMENT,
    name VARCHAR(255) NOT NULL,
    created DATETIME,
    modified DATETIME,
    PRIMARY KEY(id)
);

INSERT INTO categories (name, created, modified)
VALUES
('Paper Box', NOW(), NOW()),
('Wooden Box', NOW(), NOW());

ALTER TABLE packages ADD fragile TINYINT(1) NOT NULL DEFAULT '0';
ALTER TABLE packages ADD category_id INT NOT NULL DEFAULT '0';
UPDATE packages SET category_id = '1' WHERE id = 1;
```

Then, we'll also need our `Package.php` and `Warehouse.php` models with HABTM relations defined previously. To be able to use our stock model along with the HABTM association, add the following line of code to the HABTM definitions in the `Package` and `Warehouse` models:

```
'with' => 'Stock',
```

Also, add the following line to the `Package` model class:

```
public $belongsTo = array('Category');
```

Finally, create a file named `Category.php` in `app/Models` with the following content:

```php
<?php
App::uses('AppModel', 'Model');

class Category extends AppModel {

  public $hasMany = array(
    'Package'
  );
}
```

Just a quick reminder: these are the associations between these models:

- `Category` hasMany `Package`
- `Package` belongsTo `Category`
- `Package` hasAndBelongsToMany `Warehouse`
- `Warehouse` hasAndBelongsToMany `Package`
- `Package` and `Warehouse` hasMany `Stock`
- `Stock` belongsTo `Package` and `Warehouse`

How to do it...

Perform the following steps:

1. First, edit the `app/Model/AppModel.php` file, modify its contents to configure the models to use the `Containable` core behavior, and set recursive as `-1` by default for all models, as shown in the following code:

```php
<?php
App::uses('Model', 'Model');

class AppModel extends Model {

  public $recursive = -1;

  public $actsAs = array('Containable');
}
```

2. Now, create a new public function in the `Category` model:

```php
<?php
App::uses('AppModel', 'Model');

class Category extends AppModel {

    //…

    /** Retrieve the Products and Warehouse array for a given
$categoryId */
    public function getCategoryWarehouses($categoryId) {
        return $this->find('first', array(
            'conditions' => array(
                "{$this->alias}.{$this->primaryKey}" => $categoryId,
            ),
            'contain' => array(
                'Package' => array(
                    'Warehouse' => array(
                        'fields' => array(
                            'Warehouse.id',
                            'Warehouse.name'
                        )
                    ),
                    'conditions' => array(
                        'Package.fragile' => false
                    ),
                    'fields' => array(
                        'Package.id',
                        'Package.address'
                    )
                )
            )
        ));
    }

    //…

}
```

How it works...

In this recipe, we first used our AppModel class to set up all of our models to use the $recursive property as -1 by default and to use the Containable core behavior. Remember, all our models extend the AppModel class, so they can override these settings if needed. Setting the $recursive property to -1 will configure the CakePHP model object relational mapper to retrieve only the requested model on any find operation. Keep in mind that the default behavior has recursive set to 0 and retrieves all the associated models when a find operation is executed. For example, performing a $this->Category->find('all') would not only retrieve all of the categories, but also the packages associated with each category. Using recursive could lead to inefficient queries, so the best practice is to set it to -1 and use Containable to specify exactly what should be retrieved.

Note that behaviors in the framework are lazy loaded, so it's safe to declare them in AppModel, as they won't be used if not referenced directly in our model logic.

Then, using the Containable behavior, we retrieved an array with the Category model matching the $categoryId. Here, all of the fields in the categories row will be retrieved, along with the associated nonfragile packages and all of their associated warehouses.

The following code shows how these conditions are passed, using the containable array in the find operation:

```
'contain' => array(
  'Package' => array(
    'Warehouse' => array(
      'fields' => array(
        'Warehouse.id',
        'Warehouse.name'
      )
    ),
    'conditions' => array(
      'Package.fragile' => false
    ),
    'fields' => array(
      'Package.id',
      'Package.address'
    )
  )
)
```

As the Category model is associated to Package, and Package is also associated to Warehouse, we can cascade the *contain to retrieve models associations* inside other model associations, like we're doing in this recipe, deeply retrieving packages and warehouses.

We also set a condition at the `Package` level to retrieve only nonfragile packages and a field filter to retrieve only those two fields (`id` and `address`) at this level of the contain chain.

Let's quickly add a new controller to debug this new method. Create a file named `CategoriesController.php` in `app/Controller/`, with the following content:

```php
<?php

App::uses('AppController', 'Controller');

class CategoriesController extends AppController {

  public function debug() {
    debug($this->Category->getCategoryWarehouses(1));
    $this->_stop();
  }
}
```

By calling `/categories/debug` in your browser, you'll see that the resulting array would be similar to the following:

```
array(
  'Category' => array(
    'id' => '1',
    'name' => 'Paper Box',
    'created' => '2014-06-21 14:00:23',
    'modified' => '2014-06-21 14:00:23'
  ),
  'Package' => array(
    (int) 0 => array(
      'id' => '1',
      'address' => 'Sunset Boulevard 1, Los Angeles, CA',
      'category_id' => '1',
      'Warehouse' => array(
        (int) 0 => array(
          'id' => '1',
          'name' => 'Main Warehouse',
          'Stock' => array(
            'id' => '1',
            'package_id' => '1',
            'warehouse_id' => '1',
            'amount' => '0'
          )
        ),
```

```
            (int) 1 => array(
              'id' => '2',
              'name' => 'Auxiliar Warehouse 1',
              'Stock' => array(
                'id' => '2',
                'package_id' => '1',
                'warehouse_id' => '2',
                'amount' => '0'
              )
            )
          )
        )
      )
    )
```

See also

▸ The *Has and belongs to many (HABTM)* recipe

Custom finders

Instead of creating custom getter methods in your models, like we did in our previous recipe by running `find()` internally and returning an array of results, you can also use the built-in feature to define custom finder methods. These can modify the find options before the query is executed or even fix the returned results before they are used.

Custom finders provide a better interface to reuse common `find` operation parameters. Instead of working only with the result arrays (containing the database rows in array format), we'll be able to work with the find options first.

In this recipe, we'll create a custom finder to retrieve the latest products in our database, injecting a *stored in several warehouses* field on the fly, once the results are available.

Getting ready

We'll assume that you have the `Package` and `Warehouse` models and tables in place from our previous recipe, with the `Package hasAndBelongsToMany Warehouse` association.

How to do it...

Perform the following steps:

1. First, modify the `Package.php` file in `app/Model/`, add the following `$findMethods` property and `_findLatest()` protected function to the `Package` model class:

```
public $findMethods = array('latest' => true);


protected function _findLatest($state, $query, $results = array())
{
  if ($state === 'before') {
    $query['conditions']['Package.fragile'] = false;
    $query['order'] = array('Package.created' => 'desc');
    $query['contain'] = array('Warehouse');
    return $query;
  }
  foreach ($results as &$result) {
    $warehouseCount = count($result['Warehouse']);
    $result = Hash::insert($result, 'Package.multiple_warehouses',
$warehouseCount > 1);
  }
  return $results;
}
```

2. Now, use your new custom finder in your `PackagesController` class in the new `latest()` public function in `app/Controller/PackagesController.php`, as shown in the following code:

```
public function latest() {
  debug($this->Package->find('latest'));
  $this->_stop();
}
```

3. Finally, when you navigate to `/packages/latest`, you should expect an array output in the following format:

```
array(
    (int) 0 => array(
      'Package' => array(
        'id' => '1',
        'recipient' => 'John Doe',
```

```
                    'address' => 'Sunset Boulevard 1, Los Angeles, CA',
                    'created' => '2014-06-21 13:21:14',
                    'modified' => '2014-06-21 13:21:14',
                    'fragile' => false,
                    'category_id' => '1',
                    'multiple_warehouses' => true
                ),
                'Warehouse' => array(
                    (int) 0 => array(
                        'id' => '1',
                        'name' => 'Main Warehouse',
                        'created' => '2014-06-21 13:18:11',
                        'modified' => '2014-06-21 13:18:11',
                        'Stock' => array(
                            'id' => '1',
                            'package_id' => '1',
                            'warehouse_id' => '1',
                            'amount' => '0'
                        )
                    ),
                    (int) 1 => array(
                        'id' => '2',
                        'name' => 'Auxiliar Warehouse 1',
                        'created' => '2014-06-21 13:18:11',
                        'modified' => '2014-06-21 13:18:11',
                        'Stock' => array(
                            'id' => '2',
                            'package_id' => '1',
                            'warehouse_id' => '2',
                            'amount' => '0'
                        )
                    )
                )
            )
        )
    )
```

How it works...

Custom finders let you modify the normal `find` operation workflow, which consists of two main steps:

1. Before the query, where we're able to modify the query params, we need to add conditions; fix containable parameters, order, and fields; and so on.

2. After the query, where we have the results array available, we can tweak the results to add new fields and calculate values and inject them into the results array to have them available along with the database retrieved data.

Keep in mind that custom finders run *twice* per `find` operation: once before the query is executed and once after the results are read from the database.

We've defined a custom finder, which we'll now need to make the model aware of, so we can execute this logic when the custom `find` operation is called for this model. This is done by defining it in the `$findMethods` property of the model class, as shown in the following code:

```
public $findMethods = array('latest' => true);
```

You can define several custom finders per model, and are protected methods, named after the finder method name, using the `_find` prefix and camelCase by convention. In our recipe, the finder method we used is called `latest`, so the function name we used is `_findLatest()`.

Looking closer at our custom finder code, we started with a check for the "before" step:

```
if ($state === 'before') {
    $query['conditions']['Package.fragile'] = false;
    $query['order'] = array('Package.created' => 'desc');
    $query['contain'] = array('Warehouse');
    return $query;
}
```

We then specified a custom condition to retrieve only the nonfragile packages and ordering by the date on which the descending package was created. We then returned early so that only the `$query` is modified.

Then, for the "after" step, we did the following:

```
foreach ($results as &$result) {
    $warehouseCount = count($result['Warehouse']);
    $result = Hash::insert($result, 'Package.multiple_warehouses',
$warehouseCount > 1);
}
return $results;
```

Here, we iterated over the results and counted all the warehouses present per package, injecting this number into the `Package.multiple_warehouses` key to have it available later on in the controller or model, or whatever calls this custom finder.

See also

▶ The *Containing models* recipe

On-the-fly associations

Sometimes, you'll find it useful to create a new association on the fly before a `find` operation to retrieve specific data or filter unwanted result rows from your query.

In this recipe, we'll look at how associations can be defined at runtime on your models.

Getting ready

We'll assume you have the `Package`, `Stock`, and `Warehouse` models in place from our previous recipes, where `Stock` belongsTo `Warehouse` and `Stock` belongsTo `Package`.

We'll also add an `active` field to our `packages` and `warehouses` tables with the following SQL statement:

```
ALTER TABLE packages ADD active TINYINT(1) NOT NULL DEFAULT '1';
ALTER TABLE warehouses ADD active TINYINT(1) NOT NULL DEFAULT '1';
```

We want to retrieve only the stocks with a positive amount for both warehouses and packages that are active, so let's set `amount` for one join record, as shown in the following code:

```
UPDATE packages_warehouses SET amount = '1' WHERE id = 1;
```

Note that the ORM in CakePHP will translate the *belongsTo* associations to `left join` SQL queries by default, so we're going to restrict that to retrieve only the desired rows.

Finally, we'll also want a `StocksController` to view the output, so create a file named `StocksController.php` in `app/Controller/` with the following content:

```php
<?php
App::uses('AppController', 'Controller');

class StocksController extends AppController {
}
```

How to do it...

Perform the following steps:

1. First, we'll add a new custom finder to our `Stock` model in `app/Mode/Stock.php`:

   ```php
   <?php

   App::uses('AppModel', 'Model');
   ```

```
class Stock extends AppModel {

  public $useTable = 'packages_warehouses';

  public $belongsTo = array(
    'Package',
    'Warehouse'
  );

  public $findMethods = array('available' => true);

  protected function _findAvailable($state, $query, $results =
array()) {
    if ($state === 'before') {
      $this->bindModel(array(
        'belongsTo' => array(
          'Warehouse' => array(
            'conditions' => array('Warehouse.active' => true),
            'type' => 'inner'
          ),
          'Package' => array(
            'conditions' => array('Package.active' => true),
            'type' => 'inner'
          )
        )
      ));
      $query['conditions'] = array('Stock.amount >' => 0);
      $query['contain'] = array('Warehouse', 'Package');
      return $query;
    }
    return $results;
  }
}
```

2. Now, add a debug() method in the StocksController.php class:

```
public function debug() {
  debug($this->Stock->find('available'));
  $this->_stop();
}
```

How it works...

In this recipe, we first created a new custom finder for our stocks, using the following addition to our code:

```
$this->bindModel(array(
  'belongsTo' => array(
    'Warehouse' => array(
      'conditions' => array('Warehouse.active' => true),
      'type' => 'inner'
    ),
    'Package' => array(
      'conditions' => array('Package.active' => true),
      'type' => 'inner'
    )
  )
));
$query['conditions'] = array('Stock.amount >' => 0);
$query['contain'] = array('Warehouse', 'Package');
return $query;
```

Here, the `bindModel()` method of our model object is used to dynamically modify the model associations on the fly. In this recipe, we're binding two new *belongsTo* associations:

- Between `Stock` and `Warehouse`
- Between `Stock` and `Package`

These associations modify the previous ones with the same alias name. They will be used in the next `find` operation only, effectively allowing you to retrieve the required warehouses and packages using an inner join instead of the default left join with `'type' => 'inner'` and filtering by only active entities using `'conditions' => array('Package.active' => true)`.

Note that we're also filtering to return only stocks greater than `0` and using the `Containable` behavior to retrieve our warehouses and packages along with the stocks.

Notice that the array syntax to define on-the-fly associations is the same as defining associations in the model properties.

When you navigate to `/stocks/debug`, you should expect an array output in the following format:

```
array(
  (int) 0 => array(
    'Stock' => array(
```

```
      'id' => '1',
      'package_id' => '1',
      'warehouse_id' => '1',
      'amount' => '1'
    ),
    'Package' => array(
      'id' => '1',
      'recipient' => 'John Doe',
      'address' => 'Sunset Boulevard 1, Los Angeles, CA',
      'created' => '2014-06-21 13:21:14',
      'modified' => '2014-06-21 13:21:14',
      'fragile' => false,
      'category_id' => '1',
      'active' => true
    ),
    'Warehouse' => array(
      'id' => '1',
      'name' => 'Main Warehouse',
      'created' => '2014-06-21 13:18:11',
      'modified' => '2014-06-21 13:18:11',
      'active' => true
    )
  )
)
```

Also, the SQL generated by the framework for this is as follows:

```
SELECT
  'Stock'.'id',
  #... rest of the list of fields here
FROM
  myapp'.'packages_warehouses' AS 'Stock'
  inner JOIN
  myapp'.'packages' AS 'Package' ON ('Stock'.'package_id' =
'Package'.'id'
  AND 'Package'.'active' = '1')
  inner JOIN
  myapp'.'warehouses' AS 'Warehouse' ON ('Stock'.'warehouse_id' =
'Warehouse'.'id'
  AND 'Warehouse'.'active' = '1')
WHERE
  'Stock'.'amount' > 0
```

Once the `find` operation is executed, this on-the-fly association will be forgotten, and the association will be restored to the default values configured in the model class properties.

See also

▶ The *Containing models* recipe

▶ The *Custom finders* recipe

Using transactions

Saving data for several models at once could lead to orphaned data if some validation breaks along the way. It's always good practice to use atomic save operations when related data needs to make it to the database together.

CakePHP provides the `saveAssociated()`, `saveMany()`, and `saveAll()` model methods to store your data using an atomic operation, but sometimes, you'll want to use a database transaction to manage it. Find more details on these methods at `http://book.cakephp. org/2.0/en/models/saving-your-data.html#model-savemany-array-data- null-array-options-array`.

> Your database tables must allow transactions. For example, the InnoDB storage engine, which ships with MySQL, implements transactions. Please check your database documentation to confirm if your current storage engine allows transactions.

Getting ready

For this recipe, we'll use the `packages` and `warehouses` tables and related models from previous recipes, where `Package` hasMany `Stock` (or where `Stock` is defined as the `'with'` key in HABTM associations between the `Package` and `Warehouse` models).

How to do it...

Perform the following steps:

1. First, add a `saveComplexPackages()` method in your `Package` class in `app/Model/Package.php`, as shown in the following code:

```
public function saveComplexPackages($data) {
  $dataSource = $this->getDataSource();
  try {
    $dataSource->begin();
    $this->_complexSave1($data);
    $this->_complexSave2($data);
    $dataSource->commit();
```

```
  } catch (Exception $ex) {
    $dataSource->rollback();
  }
}
```

2. Then, create protected methods to perform every complex `save` operation, throwing an exception if validation fails:

```
protected function _complexSave1($data) {
  $saveResult = $this->saveAssociated($data);
  if (!$saveResult) {
    throw new OutOfBoundsException(__('Unable to save %s', __
METHOD__));
  }
}
```

```
protected function _complexSave2($data) {
  // do another complex save operation
  return true;
}
```

3. Now, create a new `save()` public function in the `PackagesController.php` file in `app/Controller/` containing the following code:

```
public function save() {
  $data = array(
    'Package' => array(
      'recipient' => 'John Doe',
      'address' => 'Sunset Boulevard 1, Los Angeles, CA'
    ),
    'Warehouse' => array(
      array(
        'name' => 'Main Warehouse'
      )
    )
  );
  $this->Package->saveComplexPackages($data);
  $this->_stop();
}
```

4. Finally, be sure to enable the SQL debug (if not already enabled) by setting the following in your `core.php` file in `app/Config/`:

```
Configure::write('debug', 2);
```

How it works...

Working with database transactions in CakePHP is easy. In this recipe, we've implemented a complex `save` method, which uses the following code:

```
$dataSource = $this->getDataSource();
```

This starts a transaction block, after which we've used several complex methods to simulate some complex logic in our application. Each of these methods may throw an exception, if their internal validation fails.

We detect these exceptions using the following code:

```
try {
    $dataSource->begin();
    $this->_complexSave1($data);
    $this->_complexSave2($data);
    $dataSource->commit();
} catch (Exception $e) {
    $dataSource->rollback();
}
```

The transaction is committed if all the complex `save` operations are executed without errors. In the case of an exception, the transaction is rolled back, and nothing is saved. You may also want to log errors at this point or take other measures to keep track of issues that occur.

Database transactions will allow you to break down a complex `save` operation; they cannot be processed directly by the CakePHP ORM `save` methods and save either all of the data or nothing.

See also

  ▸   More details on transactions in MySQL can be found at `http://dev.mysql.com/doc/refman/5.0/en/ansi-diff-transactions.html`

7
Search and Pagination

In this chapter, we will cover the following topics:

- ▶ Pagination
- ▶ Basic search and filter
- ▶ The Search plugin
- ▶ Advanced search

Introduction

Accessing and viewing data in your applications is fundamental to provide an engaging experience for your users. The model layer in CakePHP greatly simplifies access to data and relationships while also offering a powerful pagination system, which is painless to implement.

In this chapter, we'll introduce some recipes to help you get familiar with search and pagination in the framework.

Pagination

CakePHP provides a core Pagination component to process the request parameters in the controller and build the model queries to retrieve paginated data. Instead of getting all the rows from your table, based on the current request parameters, the Pagination component will retrieve only the current page, defined as a limited amount of rows. Of course, all of the pagination settings can be configured, such as to define a specific page limit or change the default ordering of the paginated data.

Just after creating your initial CRUD for any database table, you'll get a fully paginated index view. In this recipe, we'll tweak the pagination defaults to use some URL query string parameters instead of named parameters (named params are deprecated in CakePHP 3.0).

You'll identify named parameters when your website's URL looks something like the following:

```
http://localhost/myapp/packages/index/page:3
```

Query string parameters will generate a URL, which instead looks like this:

```
http://localhost/myapp/packages/index?page=3
```

We'll also set up some other defaults for a package's index page.

Getting ready

For this recipe, we'll first load some data into our `packages` table using the following SQL statement:

```sql
INSERT INTO packages (recipient, address, created, modified)
VALUES
('Recipient 1', 'Sunset Boulevard 1, Los Angeles, CA', NOW(), NOW()),
('Recipient 2', 'Sunset Boulevard 2, Los Angeles, CA', NOW(), NOW()),
('Recipient 3', 'Sunset Boulevard 3, Los Angeles, CA', NOW(), NOW()),
('Recipient 4', 'Sunset Boulevard 4, Los Angeles, CA', NOW(), NOW()),
('Recipient 5', 'Sunset Boulevard 5, Los Angeles, CA', NOW(), NOW()),
('Recipient 6', 'Sunset Boulevard 6, Los Angeles, CA', NOW(), NOW()),
('Recipient 7', 'Sunset Boulevard 7, Los Angeles, CA', NOW(), NOW()),
('Recipient 8', 'Sunset Boulevard 8, Los Angeles, CA', NOW(), NOW()),
('Recipient 9', 'Sunset Boulevard 9, Los Angeles, CA', NOW(), NOW()),
('Recipient 10', 'Sunset Boulevard 10, Los Angeles, CA', NOW(),
NOW()),
('Recipient 11', 'Sunset Boulevard 11, Los Angeles, CA', NOW(),
NOW());
```

How to do it...

Perform the following steps:

1. First, add the following properties and method to our existing `PackagesController.php` file in app/Controller/:

    ```php
    public $components = array('Paginator');

    public $helpers = array('Paginator');

    public function index() {
    ```

```
$this->Paginator->settings = array(
  'Package' => array(
    'paramType' => 'querystring',
    'imit' => 5,
    'order' => array(
      'Package.recipient' => 'asc'
    )
  )
);
$this->set('packages', $this->Paginator->paginate());
}
```

2. Then, create a new index view in a file named `app/View/Packages/index.ctp` with the following content:

```
<div class="packages index">
  <h2><?php echo __('Packages'); ?></h2>
  <table>
  <tr>
    <th><?php echo $this->Paginator->sort('recipient'); ?></th>
    <th><?php echo $this->Paginator->sort('address'); ?></th>
    <th><?php echo $this->Paginator->sort('modified'); ?></th>
    <th class="actions"><?php echo __('Actions'); ?></th>
  </tr>
    <?php foreach ($packages as $package): ?>
  <tr>
    <td><?php echo h($package['Package']['recipient']); ?> </td>
    <td><?php echo h($package['Package']['address']); ?> </td>
    <td><?php echo h($package['Package']['modified']); ?> </td>
    <td class="actions">
      <?php echo $this->Html->link(__('View'), array('action' => 'view', $package['Package']['id'])); ?>
    </td>
  </tr>
<?php endforeach; ?>
  </table>
  <p>
  <?php
  echo $this->Paginator->counter(array(
    'format' => 'range'
  ));
  ?>
```

```
    </p>
    <div class="paging">
    <?php
    echo $this->Paginator->prev('< ' . __('Previous Page'), array(),
null, array('class' => 'prev disabled'));
    echo $this->Paginator->next(__('Next Page') . ' >', array(),
null, array('class' => 'next disabled'));
    ?>
    </div>
    </div>
```

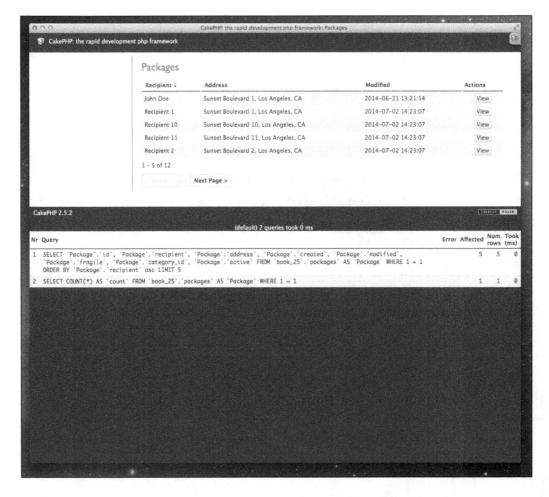

How it works...

Here, we changed the code of the controller for our `packages` table and started by including the `Paginator` component and helper as follows:

```
public $components = array('Paginator');

public $helpers = array('Paginator');
```

Note that when using helpers, we really don't need to add the `Paginator` helper in the controller, as helpers are automatically included by CakePHP when first used in a view.

We then added an `index()` action to our controller. Here, we're using the `$settings` property of the `Paginator` component to set up the pagination configuration for the `Package` model. We could also have different pagination settings applied to different models, using the model alias as the first key in the pagination settings and then using some configuration settings for each.

The `paramType` setting with `querystring` configures the `Paginator` component to detect and use paginator-specific query string parameters from the URL. It also configures the `Paginator` helper to generate query string parameters when we build the pagination links on our view.

We also set a limit of 5, so our "pages" of results will have five rows each, with a default ordering (by recipient, in ascending order). Note that the ordering could change if we click in the header column for any of our fields in the generated view. The `Paginator` component would take care of the newly specified order priority and merge this requested setting with the default settings before running the database query and retrieving the packages.
You don't need to code that logic yourself, which is great!

The last line in the controller is the actual call to the `Paginator` component to retrieve the packages. Only five packages will be retrieved, based on the paginator's default settings and the request's querystring values. For example, `/packages/index` will show records one to five, while `/packages/index?page=2` will show records six to ten. This is shown in the following screenshot:

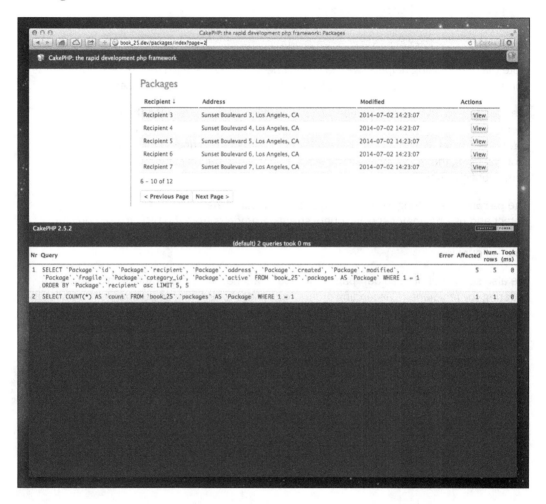

Next, we created a view file to display our `index()` action. The view uses the `Paginator` helper to do the following:

▶ It displays sortable header links using the `sort()` method. Clicking on these will change the query order; clicking on it again would use the inverse order.

▶ It displays a pagination counter below the results table using the `counter()` method and by setting `format` to `range`.

 ▶ It displays the `prev` and `next` buttons using the `prev()` and `next()` methods, respectively.

Note that we're tweaking the block formatting, the previous and next button classes, as well as the strings to be displayed in our view.

The `Paginator` component will take care of parsing the current pagination-related parameters in the URL and based on this, append the conditions in order to the find operation. We're using querystring parameters instead of named parameters in this recipe, mainly because named parameters will become deprecated in future versions of the framework.

See also

 ▶ `http://book.cakephp.org/2.0/en/core-libraries/components/pagination.html`

Basic search and filter

Displaying paginated records can be great to allow your users to easily navigate through large sets of data. However, it is even better when you can give them the option to search directly.

In this recipe, we're going to add a new search box for our packages. We'll use a `LIKE` condition in SQL to filter the resulting packages. This will do the trick for small datasets as a starting point.

Getting ready

For our recipe, we'll assume that you still have the `packages` table, `Package` model, and `PackagesController`, with the paginated `index()` action with the `index.ctp` view created from our previous recipe.

How to do it...

Perform the following steps:

1. First, add the following search box to `index.ctp` in `app/View/Packages/` right below the `<h2>` element:

```php
<?php
  echo $this->Form->create('Package', array('action' =>
'search'));
  if (!isset($searchQuery)) {
    $searchQuery = '';
  }
```

```
    echo $this->Form->input('searchQuery', array('value' =>
  h($searchQuery)));
    echo $this->Form->end(__('Search'));
  ?>
```

2. Then, add the following `search()` action to the `PackagesController` class:

```php
public function search() {
  if ($this->request->is('put') || $this->request->is('post')) {
    // poor man's Post Redirect Get behavior
    return $this->redirect(array(
      '?' => array(
        'q' => $this->request->data('Package.searchQuery')
      )
    ));
  }
  $this->Package->recursive = 0;
  $searchQuery = $this->request->query('q');
  $this->Paginator->settings = array(
    'Package' => array(
      'findType' => 'search',
      'searchQuery' => $searchQuery
    )
  );
  $this->set('packages', $this->Paginator->paginate());
  $this->set('searchQuery', $searchQuery);
  $this->render('index');
}
```

3. Next, in our `Package` model class, add the following code to the `$findMethods` property and the `_findSearch()` method to implement the search query:

```php
public $findMethods = array('search' => true);

protected function _findSearch($state, $query, $results = array())
{
  if ($state === 'before') {
    $searchQuery = Hash::get($query, 'searchQuery');
    $searchConditions = array(
      'or' => array(
        "{$this->alias}.recipient LIKE" => '%' . $searchQuery .
  '%',
        "{$this->alias}.address LIKE" => '%' . $searchQuery . '%'
      )
    );
```

```
    $query['conditions'] = array_merge($searchConditions,
(array)$query['conditions']);
    return $query;
  }
  return $results;
}
```

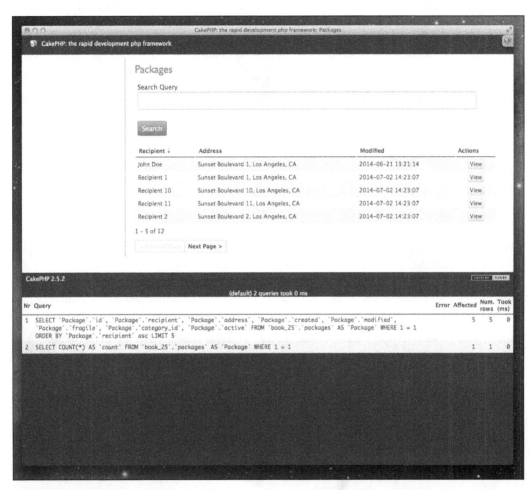

How it works...

In this recipe, we created a new search form in `app/View/Packages/index.ctp`. The form is configured to send the POST requests to the `search()` action (by default, CakePHP will use the current packages controller) upon submission.

We then created the new `search()` action in the `PackagesController`. This method first detects a `POST` request and then does a super-quick implementation of the *Post/Redirect/ Get* design pattern. We switched the posted `searchQuery` request data (sent using the input field in our search form) to a query string parameter and then issued a redirect to the same action, appending the new search query to the URL.

For example, if we fill the search box with the `example` text and then hit the **Submit** button, we'd post the form data to the `search()` action first and then issue a redirect to `/packages/index?q=example`. Using this pattern will provide a better search experience for users and also *remember* the query variable in all of the pagination and order columns of our page.

Following on, we then covered the rest of the implementation in our `PackagesController`, configuring the `Paginator` component using the following settings:

```
$this->Paginator->settings = array(
  'Package' => array(
    'findType' => 'search',
    'searchQuery' => $searchQuery
  )
);
```

This lets CakePHP use a custom finder to retrieve the packages from the database, instead of using the standard `find()` operation. We're passing a `searchQuery` parameter, with the query string value retrieved from the `POST` request. This `$searchQuery` parameter will be used in the new custom finder to filter the packages using a `LIKE` operation in the generated SQL condition.

Finally, we implemented the custom finder in our `Package` model. Here, we're using the custom finder to modify the find query before CakePHP builds the final SQL to be run against the database to retrieve the rows. Our logic is as follows:

```
$searchQuery = Hash::get($query, 'searchQuery');
$searchConditions = array(
  'or' => array(
    "{$this->alias}.recipient LIKE" => '%' . $searchQuery . '%',
    "{$this->alias}.address LIKE" => '%' . $searchQuery . '%'
  )
);
$query['conditions'] = array_merge($searchConditions,
(array)$query['conditions']);
return $query;
```

We first retrieve the `searchQuery` value attached to the `find` options. You'll remember that we just added this value in the `Paginator` settings setup, in the `search()` action of our `PackagesController`. We then built a new array of conditions, using the new `$searchQuery`, and merged it with any other possible conditions passed when using this custom finder.

The `Paginator` component will call our new custom finder and take care of the page management for us, filtering and displaying only those package rows that contain the word used in our search box. That's it; you can now search through your data!

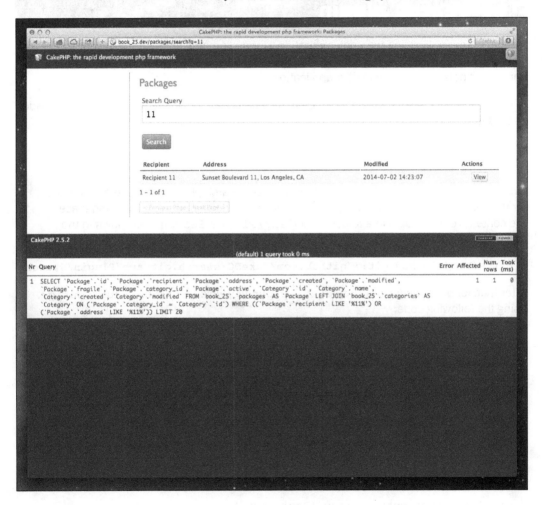

See also

▸ More on the Post/Redirect/Get design pattern at `http://en.wikipedia.org/wiki/Post/Redirect/Get`

▸ The *Custom finders* recipe from *Chapter 6, Model Layer*

▸ The *Pagination* recipe

The Search plugin

Instead of manually doing the implementation of the searching and filtering in your models, you may be interested in using the CakeDC Search plugin, a powerful and reusable way to implement database search in your application.

In this recipe, we'll see how easy it can be to include the plugin within an application and add some search power on the fly.

Getting ready

First, we'll need to download and install the CakeDC Search plugin. We'll use git modules for the setup, but if you're not using git, you can simply download the ZIP file and place the contents of the plugin in a folder named `app/Plugin/Search/`, as shown in the following command:

```
$ git submodule add git://github.com/CakeDC/search.git app/Plugin/Search
```

After that, load the plugin in your `bootstrap.php` file, which is located in `app/Config/`, using the following code:

```
CakePlugin::load('Search');
```

In this recipe, we're going to quickly build a search panel to filter our categories by their names (using `LIKE`) and by the amount of fragile packages. So, let's change our existing `categories` table and adjust its data using the following SQL statement:

```
ALTER TABLE categories ADD packages_fragile_count INT(20) UNSIGNED NOT
NULL DEFAULT '0';
```

We'll then update our controller file named `CategoriesController.php` in `app/Controller/` with the following content:

```
public $components = array('Paginator');

public function index() {
  $this->set('categories', $this->Paginator->paginate());
}
```

We will also update the index view file in `app/View/Categories/index.ctp` with the following content:

```
<div class="packages index">
  <h2><?php echo __('Categories'); ?></h2>
  <table>
    <tr>
      <th><?php echo $this->Paginator->sort('name'); ?></th>
      <th><?php echo $this->Paginator->sort('packages_fragile_count');
?></th>
      <th class="actions"><?php echo __('Actions'); ?></th>
    </tr>
    <?php foreach ($categories as $category): ?>
      <tr>
        <td><?php echo h($category['Category']['name']); ?> </td>
        <td><?php echo h($category['Category']['packages_fragile_
count']); ?> </td>
        <td class="actions">
          <?php echo $this->Html->link(__('View'), array('action' =>
'view', $category['Category']['id'])); ?>
        </td>
      </tr>
    <?php endforeach; ?>
  </table>
  <p>
    <?php
    echo $this->Paginator->counter(array(
      'format' => 'range'
    ));
    ?>
  </p>
  <div class="paging">
    <?php
    echo $this->Paginator->prev('< ' . __('Previous Page'), array(),
null, array('class' => 'prev disabled'));
    echo $this->Paginator->next(__('Next Page') . ' >', array(), null,
array('class' => 'next disabled'));
    ?>
  </div>
</div>
```

How to do it...

Perform the following steps:

1. First, add a new search form below h2 in the app/View/Categories/index.ctp file:

```php
<?php
  echo $this->Form->create();
  echo $this->Form->input('name');
  echo $this->Form->input('packages_fragile_count', array('label'
=> __('Minimum fragile packages')));
  echo $this->Form->end(__('Submit'));
?>
```

2. Then, add the Searchable behavior in the $actsAs property of your Category model class, and configure the search fields in the $filterArgs property:

```php
public $actsAs = array(
  'Search.Searchable'
);

public $filterArgs = array(
  'name' => array(
    'field' => 'Category.name',
    'type' => 'like'
  ),
  'packages_fragile_count' => array(
    'field' => 'Category.packages_fragile_count >=',
    'type' => 'value'
  )
);
```

3. Now, configure your CategoriesController to use the Search.Prg component as follows:

```php
public $components = array(
  'Paginator',
  'Search.Prg'
);
```

4. Also, in the same controller, change the index() action to process the search form data as follows:

```php
public function index() {
  $this->Category->recursive = 0;
```

```
$this->Prg->commonProcess(null, array(
    'paramType' => 'querystring'
));
$this->Paginator->settings = array(
    'Category' => array(
        'paramType' => 'querystring',
        'conditions' => $this->Category->parseCriteria($this->Prg-
>parsedParams())
    )
);
$this->set('categories', $this->Paginator->paginate());
}
```

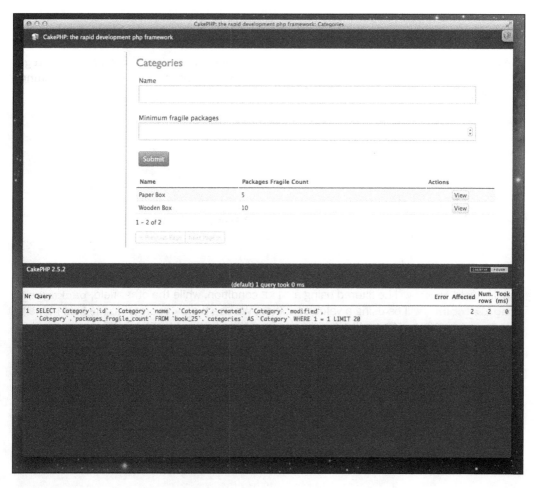

How it works...

In this recipe, we added a new form into the `app/View/Categories/index.ctp` file, to issue a `POST` request to the `index()` action of our `CaterogiesController` in our application. The form has two input fields: one for the category name (we'll be using a `LIKE` operation in the SQL condition to filter the categories) and another one for the minimum amount of fragile packages.

We then configured the `Category` model to use a behavior called `SearchableBehavior` that is distributed as part of the CakeDC Search plugin. We use this behavior in our model by configuring it in the `$actsAs` property, as shown in the following code:

```
public $actsAs = array(
  'Search.Searchable'
);
```

The `SearchableBehavior` uses a public property in the model class named `$filterArgs`, to configure how the search should be made against our database. In this case, we're setting up the configuration for two fields:

```
public $filterArgs = array(
  'name' => array(
    'field' => 'Category.name'
    'type' => 'like'
  ),
  'packages_fragile_count' => array(
    'field' => 'Category.packages_fragile_count >=',
    'type' => 'value'
  )
);
```

The first field, `name`, will be filtered using a `LIKE` condition, while the other field, `packages_fragile_count`, will be using a value condition. We use the `>=` operator in the field name to determine whether our filter will retrieve rows from the `categories` table greater or equal to the given value present.

After setting up our model, we then updated the controller code as follows to use the `Prg` component and refactored the `index()` action to use the component:

```
public function index() {
  $this->Category->recursive = 0;
  $this->Prg->commonProcess(null, array(
    'paramType' => 'querystring'
  ));
  $this->Paginator->settings = array(
    'Category' => array(
      'paramType' => 'querystring',
      'conditions' => $this->Category->parseCriteria($this->Prg-
>parsedParams())
    )
  );
  $this->set('categories', $this->Paginator->paginate());
}
```

Note that we're setting up both the `commonProcess()` method of the `Prg` and `Paginator` components to use the query string request parameters, as the default configuration is to use named parameters (named parameters will be deprecated in CakePHP 3.0).

As we did in our previous recipe, we first detect a `POST` request and then use the Post/Redirect/Get implementation provided by the CakeDC Search plugin. We also switch the posted request data (sent using the input field in the search form) to a query string parameter list and issue a redirect to the same action, appending the new search query to the URL. Now, we don't need to take care of implementing the PRG pattern manually, as it's done in a flexible way through the plugin.

Once we have set up the `$filterArgs` property in our model, calling the `parseCriteria()` method in the controller will detect and build the conditions based on the passed request data. Those parameters will be parsed by the `parsedParams()` method of the `Prg` component.

You may have noticed that we used the same field names in our search form and our `Category` model. However, we could have used any other name in our search form and then matched it with the `Category` model using the `field` configuration option in the `$filterArgs` property.

Finally, searching for categories with minimal fragile packages equal to 7 produces the following page and SQL query:

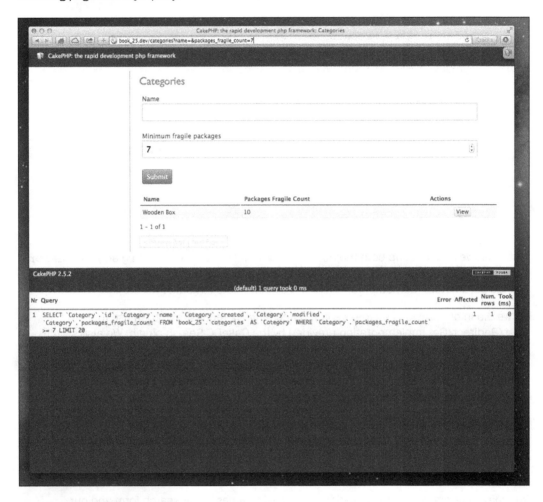

See also

▶ PRG design pattern at http://en.wikipedia.org/wiki/Post/Redirect/Get

▶ The CakeDC Search plugin can be found at https://github.com/CakeDC/search

▶ The *Pagination* recipe

Advanced search

Searching through your data isn't always as simple as filtering a value on a single model; sometimes, you need to take into account the relationship of a model with other models.

In this recipe, we're going to search and filter using a model association. We'll configure the CakeDC Search plugin from our previous recipe to create a recipients filter by gift name. This allows us to display our gift recipients, filtering by the recipient name, address, and the gift title.

Getting ready

In this recipe, we'll continue using the CakeDC Search plugin, for which you can find some installation instructions in our previous recipe. Then, we'll create both `gifts` and `recipients` tables in our database, using the following SQL statements:

```
CREATE TABLE gifts (
    id INT NOT NULL AUTO_INCREMENT,
    title VARCHAR(255) NOT NULL,
    created DATETIME NOT NULL,
    modified DATETIME NOT NULL,
    PRIMARY KEY(id)
);

CREATE TABLE recipients (
    id INT NOT NULL AUTO_INCREMENT,
    name VARCHAR(255) NOT NULL,
    address VARCHAR(255) NOT NULL,
    created DATETIME,
    modified DATETIME,
    gift_id INT NULL,
    PRIMARY KEY(id)
);
```

We'll also include some data in these tables to work with, using these SQL statements:

```
INSERT INTO gifts (title, created, modified)
VALUES
    ('T-Shirt Grey', NOW(), NOW()),
    ('T-Shirt Black', NOW(), NOW()),
    ('Mug Small', NOW(), NOW()),
    ('Mug Mega', NOW(), NOW());
```

```
INSERT INTO recipients (name, address, created, modified, gift_id)
VALUES
    ('John Doe', 'Sunset Boulevard 1, Los Angeles, CA', NOW(), NOW(),
1),
    ('Recipient 1', 'Hudson Street, New York', NOW(), NOW(), 2),
    ('Recipient 1', 'Hudson Street, New York', NOW(), NOW(), 3),
    ('Recipient 2', 'Collins Av., Vancouver', NOW(), NOW(), 4);
```

Now, we'll use the CakePHP `bake` shell to build all the CRUD files for your newly created tables, using the following commands from your `app/` directory in the shell:

```
$ Console/cake bake all Gift
$ Console/cake bake all Recipient
```

Note that the `bake` shell will generate controllers, models, and views for all the CRUD actions in your tables. Help on using `bake` can be found at `http://book.cakephp.org/2.0/en/console-and-shells/code-generation-with-bake.html`.

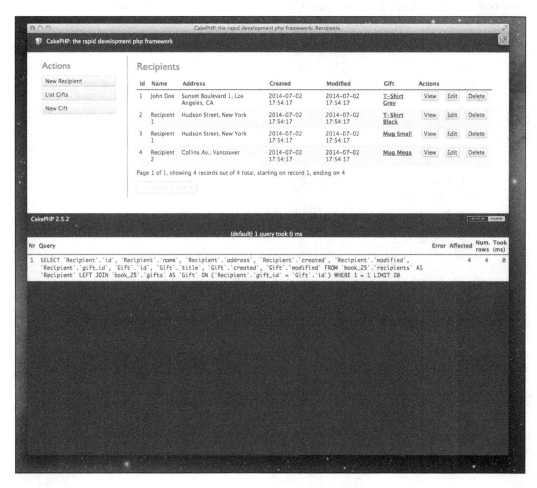

How to do it...

Perform the following steps:

1. First, create a new search form in the file named `index.ctp` in `app/View/Recipients/` by inserting the following code after the `<h2>` title tag:

```
<h2><?php echo __('Recipients'); ?></h2>
<!-- insert code below -->
<?php
  echo $this->Form->create();
  echo $this->Form->input('name', array('required' => false));
  echo $this->Form->input('address', array('required' => false));
  echo $this->Form->input('title', array('label' => __('Gift
Title')));
  echo $this->Form->end(__('Submit'));
?>
```

2. Then, include the `Paginator` and `Prg` components in the `$components` property of the `RecipientsController`:

```
public $components = array(
  'Paginator',
  'Search.Prg'
);
```

3. Also, replace the `index()` action in the same class with the following method:

```
public function index() {
  $this->Recipient->recursive = 0;
  $this->Prg->commonProcess(null, array(
    'paramType' => 'querystring'
  ));
  $this->Paginator->settings = array(
    'Recipient' => array(
      'paramType' => 'querystring',
      'conditions' => $this->Recipient->parseCriteria($this->Prg-
>parsedParams())
    )
  );
  $this->set('recipients', $this->Paginator->paginate());
}
```

4. Finally, configure your `Recipient` model to use the `Searchable` behavior with the following `$actsAs` and `$filterArgs` properties:

```
public $actsAs = array('Search.Searchable');

public $filterArgs = array(
  'name' => array(
    'field' => 'Recipient.name',
    'type' => 'like'
  ),
  'address' => array(
    'field' => 'Recipient.address',
    'type' => 'like'
  ),
  'title' => array(
    'field' => 'Gift.title',
    'type' => 'like'
  )
);
```

How it works...

In this recipe, we first added a new search form in the `app/View/Recipients/index.ctp` file, adding three fields. The `address` and `name` fields will be used to filter the parent model; `Recipient` and `title` will be used to filter the associated `Gift` model name. We then configured the `RecipientsController` to use the `Prg` component, as explained in our previous recipes.

Switch our `POST` request data into query string parameters, using the following code:

```
$this->Prg->commonProcess(null, array(
  'paramType' => 'querystring'
));
```

Parse the request parameters into conditions for the `Paginator` component, as shown in the following code:

```
$this->Paginator->settings = array(
  'Recipient' => array(
    'paramType' => 'querystring',
    'conditions' => $this->Recipient->parseCriteria($this->Prg->parsedParams())
  )
);
```

Then, run the `paginate()` method, as shown in the following code, to retrieve the fields from the recipients table, using the pagination request parameters to filter the number of rows retrieved:

```
$this->set('recipients', $this->Paginator->paginate());
```

We also configured the `Recipient` model to use the `Searchable` behavior. Note that we're using an associated model field to filter the query using `Gift.title`. Using this notation is how we use associated models in the `$filterArgs` property. In this case, `Recipient` belongs to `Gift`.

```
public $actsAs = array('Search.Searchable');

public $filterArgs = array(
  'name' => array(
    'field' => 'Recipient.name',
    'type' => 'like'
  ),
  'address' => array(
    'field' => 'Recipient.address',
    'type' => 'like'
  ),
  'title' => array(
    'field' => 'Gift.title',
    'type' => 'like'
  )
);
```

Once set up, if we navigate to `/recipients` and fill in the search form, setting `Gift Title` to `mug`, and `Name` to `1`, we'll generate the following URL:

`/recipients?name=1&address=&title=mug`

The SQL generated by this URL is as follows:

```
SELECT `Recipient`.`id`, `Recipient`.`name`, `Recipient`.`address`,
`Recipient`.`created`, `Recipient`.`modified`, `Recipient`.`gift_id`,
`Gift`.`id`, `Gift`.`title`, `Gift`.`created`, `Gift`.`modified`
FROM `book_25`.`recipients` AS `Recipient`
LEFT JOIN `book_25`.`gifts` AS `Gift` ON (`Recipient`.`gift_id` =
`Gift`.`id`)
WHERE `Recipient`.`name` LIKE '%1%' AND `Gift`.`title` LIKE '%mug%'
LIMIT 20
```

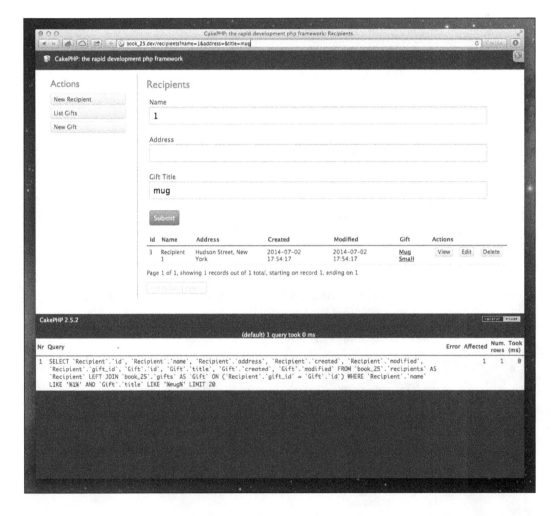

Note the LIKE conditions applied to both the Recipient and Gift models. From here, you can extend the scope of your search criteria to cover as much of your data set as needed.

See also

- ▶ PRG design pattern at `http://en.wikipedia.org/wiki/Post/Redirect/Get`
- ▶ The CakeDC Search plugin can be found at `https://github.com/CakeDC/search`
- ▶ The *Pagination* recipe

8
Events System

In this chapter, we will cover the following recipes:

- ▶ Listeners and subscribers
- ▶ Event-driven process
- ▶ Event stacking
- ▶ Managing event priorities

Introduction

Included in CakePHP is a powerful events system, which allows you to rapidly hook up callbacks through event objects within your application. This provides an event-driven model within your business logic; it can greatly improve the design and architecture of your application.

In this chapter, we'll look at the fundamentals of the events system, with a couple of recipes to get you handling events.

Listeners and subscribers

Listeners in the framework implement the observer pattern, as described at http://en.wikipedia.org/wiki/Observer_pattern. A listener object waits to be notified of a new event. If notified, it will then check if the event can be handled, and if so, it will run the event-handling method based on the event name.

In CakePHP, anything can be a listener; the only requirement is to implement the CakeEventListener interface and provide a public implementedEvents() method, which returns the names of the exposed events with their respective methods to process the event.

If you have significant processing logic in your event listeners for a live service, consider using a job queue. Refer to the *Event stacking* recipe later in this chapter.

In this recipe, we identified some e-mail sending logic in one of our models as a candidate to use events. Decoupling the e-mail processing logic from the model itself allows us to switch the event processing implementation in the future to something more complex, such as a process queue.

Getting ready

For this recipe, we'll work with packages. So, we'll reuse our existing `packages` table:

```
CREATE TABLE packages (
  id INT NOT NULL AUTO_INCREMENT,
  recipient VARCHAR(255) NOT NULL,
  address VARCHAR(255) NOT NULL,
  created DATETIME,
  modified DATETIME,
  PRIMARY KEY(id)
);
```

Update the file named `Package.php` in `app/Model/` with the following content (events-free code):

```php
<?php
App::uses('AppModel', 'Model');

class Package extends AppModel {

  public function afterSave($created, $options = array()) {
    parent::afterSave($created, $options);
    if ($created) {
      CakeEmail::deliver('admin@myapp.com',
        __('New Package was created id: %s', Hash::get($this->data,
'Package.id')),
        __('New package was created'),
        'default'
      );

    }
  }
}
```

How to do it...

Perform the following steps:

1. Create a new listener to process our e-mail alerts, in a file named app/Lib/Event/EmailAlert.php:

```php
<?php
App::uses('CakeEventListener', 'Event');
App::uses('CakeEmail', 'Network/Email');

class EmailAlert extends Object implements CakeEventListener {

  public function implementedEvents() {
    return array(
      'App.Model.Package.afterSave' => 'sendEmailAlert'
    );
  }

  public function sendEmailAlert($event) {
    $alias = $event->subject->alias;
    $id = $event->subject->data[$alias][$event->subject->primaryKey];
    CakeEmail::deliver('admin@myapp.com',
      __('New %s created id: %s', $alias, $id),
      __('New %s was created', $alias),
      'default'
    );
  }
}
```

2. Create a new configuration file named events.php to hold our events configuration in app/Config/ (note that we're using the common Package model's event manager):

```php
<?php
App::uses('ClassRegistry', 'Utility');
App::uses('EmailAlert', 'Lib/Event');

ClassRegistry::init('Package')->getEventManager()->attach(new EmailAlert());
```

3. Include your new events config file by adding this line at the end of the bootstrap.php file in app/Config/:

```php
config('events');
```

4. Modify the `afterSave()` method in the `Package` model class to emit a new event instead of handling the e-mail sending logic:

```
public function afterSave($created, $options = array()) {
  parent::afterSave($created, $options);
  if ($created) {
    // create a new event
    $event = new CakeEvent('App.Model.Package.afterSave',
$this);
    // dispatch the event to the Package event manager
    $this->getEventManager()->dispatch($event);
  }
}
```

How it works...

In this recipe, we created a new class that follows the CakePHP convention to store all listeners in `app/Lib/Event`. The listener implements the `CakeEventListener` interface and is composed of two main parts:

▶ The `implementedEvents()` method, which defines the event names processed by this listener, with the methods to be executed for each one

▶ The specific event processor methods themselves

The event processor method contains a simple `CakeEmail::deliver()` method to send a plain text e-mail to the sysadmin when a new e-mail alert is triggered.

We then created an `events.php` file in `app/Config/` to allow all event-related configuration to be stored separately from our other configurations and to allow it to be used by the framework's `Configure` utility class to include this file if it's present in the `app/Config/` directory. We'll update this file with new listeners later when we'll demonstrate how to add event-driven functionality without changes in the code of models.

We also refactored the `afterSave()` callback logic in the `Package` model to dispatch an event, instead of handling the e-mail instance creation and delivery directly. Here, we're dispatching an event named `App.Model.Product.afterSave` to be processed elsewhere.

Note that the event name dispatched and the `implementedEvents()` event name matches. This is required to detect if the event should be processed by this listener or not.

To dispatch an event, we first need to get an instance to the event manager as follows:

```
$this->getEventManager()->dispatch($event);
```

In this case, we're using the model's event manager. Note that there's a local event manager per model and also a local event manager shared between the controller and view. There is also a _global_ event manager available.

Once the event has been dispatched to the event manager, the event system will check all listeners attached to this event and run the listener logic to process the event.

Events have a name, subject, and an optional data array. Events usually get `$this` as the subject, and we also have the option to pass some related data, for example:

```
$event = new CakeEvent('event-name-here', $this, array(
    'key1' => $value1,
    'key2' => $value2
));
```

All the necessary context would be provided using the `$data` property of the `$event` that is retrieved from the listener code using the following code:

```
public function sendEmailAlert($event) {
    $data1 = $event->data['key1'];
    $data2 = $event->data['key2'];
}
```

As you can tell, working with and handling events in CakePHP is probably a lot simpler than you imagined and opens a whole world of possibilities in your applications.

See also

▶ A detailed description about the event system and its examples can be found at `http://book.cakephp.org/2.0/en/core-libraries/events.html`

Event-driven process

Events in CakePHP can also be used to define complex workflows in your application. In this recipe, we'll process a package, which was just created, to generate a PDF order and send the resulting file by e-mail (attachment) for further manual processing.

We'll chain the execution of two listeners for a specific event. The partial results of each listener will be stacked in our event, thus allowing listeners to use partial results from listeners that were executed earlier in the event manager queue.

Note that as discussed earlier, sending e-mails and generating PDF files are slow operations, so you should consider moving this logic to a job queue, instead of running them while the user waits.

Getting ready

For this recipe, we'll need to set up the CakePDF plugin and the related templates to generate a PDF file based on a `Package` model. We'll use git modules for the setup, but if you're not using git, you can simply download the ZIP file using the following command and place the contents of the plugin in a folder named `app/Plugin/CakePdf/`:

```
$ git submodule add git://github.com/ceeram/CakePdf.git app/Plugin/CakePdf
```

Then, edit your `bootstrap.php` file in `app/Config/`, and add the following code at the end of the file to load the plugin, process the plugin's bootstrap configuration file, and include the plugin's routes:

```
CakePlugin::load('CakePdf', array(
  'bootstrap' => true,
  'routes' => true
));
```

After this, we'll set up the PDF engine we want to use (as shown in the following code), as the plugin provides different options to render a PDF. For this example, we'll use `dompdf`, so we'll also add the following to the `bootstrap.php` file. Also, we'll configure the default e-mail recipient address here.

```
Configure::write('CakePdf', array(
  'engine' => 'CakePdf.DomPdf',
  'download' => true // forces PDF file download
));
Configure::write('App.defaultSender', 'app@example.com');
Configure::write('App.defaultRecipient', 'me@example.com');
```

We'll then need a PDF layout file named `order.ctp` in `app/View/Layouts/pdf/`, with the following content:

```
<div id="pdf">
  <h1><?php echo __('Order'); ?></h1>
  <?php echo $this->fetch('content'); ?>
</div>
```

This new layout will be used for all our orders to reuse headers, footers, and other common elements in our PDF orders.

Now, create a file named `package.ctp` in `app/View/Packages/pdf/` with the following content:

```
<h3><?php echo __('This is your new Package order'); ?>
<table>
```

```php
<?php
echo $this->Html->tableHeaders(array(
  'Id',
  'Address'
));
echo $this->Html->tableCells(array(
  array(
    $package['Package']['id'],
    $package['Package']['address']
  )
));
?>
</table>
```

We'll also reuse our `packages` table; currently, it could be recreated with the following SQL statement:

```sql
CREATE TABLE packages (
  id INT NOT NULL AUTO_INCREMENT,
  recipient VARCHAR(255) NOT NULL,
  address VARCHAR(255) NOT NULL,
  created DATETIME DEFAULT NULL,
  modified DATETIME DEFAULT NULL,
  fragile TINYINT(1) NOT NULL DEFAULT '0',
  category_id INT NOT NULL DEFAULT '0',
  active TINYINT(1) NOT NULL DEFAULT '1',
  PRIMARY KEY (id)
);
```

Finally, we will reuse the `Package` model, with the following `afterSave()` callback (and `EmailAlert` event listener) from the previous example:

```php
public function afterSave($created, $options = array()) {
  parent::afterSave($created, $options);
  if ($created) {
    // create a new event
    $event = new CakeEvent('App.Model.Package.afterSave',    $this);
    // dispatch the event to the Package event manager
    $this->getEventManager()->dispatch($event);
  }
}
```

How to do it...

Perform the following steps:

1. Dispatch a new event in the `afterSave()` method of our `Package` model:

```php
public function afterSave($created, $options = array()) {
  parent::afterSave($created, $options);
    if ($created) {
      // create a new event
      $event = new CakeEvent('App.Model.Package.afterSave',
$this);
      // dispatch the event to the local event manager
      $this->getEventManager()->dispatch($event);
    }
}
```

2. Create or update the file named `events.php` in `app/Config/` with the following content:

```php
<?php
App::uses('ClassRegistry', 'Utility');
App::uses('PDFGenerator', 'Lib/Event');
App::uses('EmailAlert', 'Lib/Event');

ClassRegistry::init('Package')->getEventManager()->attach(new
PDFGenerator());
ClassRegistry::init('Package')->getEventManager()->attach(new
EmailAlert());
```

3. Make sure that you have the following line at the end of your `bootstrap.php` in `app/Config/`:

```php
config('events');
```

4. Add a new `PDFGenerator` listener in a file named `PDFGenerator.php` in `app/Lib/Event/` with the following content:

```php
<?php
App::uses('CakeEventListener', 'Event');
App::uses('CakePdf', 'CakePdf.Pdf');

class PDFGenerator extends Object implements CakeEventListener {

  public function implementedEvents() {
    return array(
```

```
    'App.Model.Package.afterSave' => 'generatePDF'
  );
}

public function generatePDF($event) {
  $CakePdf = new CakePdf();
  $CakePdf->template('/Packages/pdf/package', 'order');
  $CakePdf->viewVars(array(
    'package' => $event->subject->data
  ));
  $filePath = APP . 'files' . DS . String::uuid() . '.pdf';
  if ($CakePdf->write($filePath)) {
    $results = (array)$event->result;
    $results['PDFGenerator']['generatedPDF'] = $filePath;
    return $results;
  }
  throw new CakeException(__('Unable to generate PDF File for
Package'));
  }
}
```

5. Update the `sendEmailAlert()` method of our existing `EmailAlert` listener in the file named `EmailAlert.php` in the same location with the following content:

```php
<?php
App::uses('CakeEventListener', 'Event');
App::uses('CakeEmail', 'Network/Email');

class EmailReport extends Object implements CakeEventListener {

  public function implementedEvents() {
    return array(
      'App.Model.Package.afterSave' => 'sendEmailAlert'
    );
  }

  public function sendEmailAlert($event) {
    $results = (array)$event->result;
    $filePath = Hash::get($results, 'PDFGenerator.generatedPDF');
    if (!empty($filePath)) {
      // send attachment
      $Email = new CakeEmail();
      $Email->template('attachment', 'default')
```

```
                        ->emailFormat('html')
                        ->from(Configure::read('App.defaultSender'))
                        ->to(Configure::read('App.defaultRecipient'))
                        ->subject(__('Your new package'))
                        ->attachments(array('Package.pdf' => $filePath))
                        ->send();
            }
        }
    }
```

6. Finally, create a file named `attachment.ctp` in `app/View/Emails/html/` with the following content:

```
<?php echo __('Please check the attached file'); ?>
```

This is how the generated PDF attachment appears:

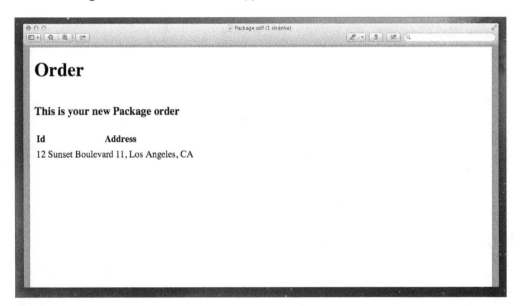

How it works...

In this recipe, we're setting up two chained listeners, waiting for any new `App.Model.Product.afterSave` events and working together to perform the following:

- Generate a PDF file, based on the new package contents
- Send an e-mail to the `Configure::read('App.defaultRecipient')` address, attaching the PDF file that was generated

Our first step was to check the following in our `Package` model:

```
public function afterSave($created, $options = array()) {
  parent::afterSave($created, $options);
  if ($created) {
    // create a new event
    $event = new CakeEvent('App.Model.Package.afterSave', $this);
    // dispatch the event to the local event manager
    $this->getEventManager()->dispatch($event);
  }
}
```

We then created a new `CakeEvent` with the name, `App.Model.Package.afterSave`, and set the subject as `$this`. As the current object reference is the `Package` model, we set the current package instance as the subject for this new event.

Next, we got an instance of the local event manager, tied to this model, and dispatched the event to the manager. The `dispatch($event)` method will check for any listener registered in this event manager and run the associated logic if the event name matches the listener events configured.

We then created a new configuration file to store our event-related settings (using the following code) and ensured that we attached the two listeners to the `Package` model's event manager:

```
ClassRegistry::init('Package')->getEventManager()->attach(new
PDFGenerator());
ClassRegistry::init('Package')->getEventManager()->attach(new
EmailAlert());
```

We also created a `PDFGenerator` event listener class that follows the CakePHP convention for listeners, which implemented the `CakeEventListener` interface and defined it in our `implementedEvents()` method (shown in the following code):

```
public function implementedEvents() {
  return array(
    'App.Model.Package.afterSave' => 'generatePDF'
  );
}
```

Note that we're matching the `App.Model.Package.afterSave` event name to the `generatePDF` method in the listener class we want to use when a new event is processed.

Following on, we implemented the event processing logic itself:

```
public function generatePDF($event) {
  $CakePdf = new CakePdf();
  $CakePdf->template('/Packages/pdf/package', 'order');
  $CakePdf->viewVars(array(
```

```
        'package' => $event->subject->data
    ));
    $filePath = APP . 'files' . DS . String::uuid() . '.pdf';
    if ($CakePdf->write($filePath)) {
        $results = (array)$event->result;
        $results['PDFGenerator']['generatedPDF'] = $filePath;
        return $results;
    }
    throw new CakeException(__('Unable to generate PDF File for
Package'));
}
```

Here, we created a new CakePDF instance, set the template view file to be used, and called the `viewVars()` method with the data array of the event subject:

```
$CakePdf->viewVars(array(
    'package' => $event->subject->data
));
```

This sends our event subject to the view and makes it available as a `$package` variable. Remember that the subject of the event will be the instance to the `Package` model, and the model data property will hold the array of the fields just saved for the `Package` model. So, we're passing the contents of the model we just saved to use them in the PDF view we're going to generate; this will allow us to use the address in our PDF.

We then created a new semirandom file in our `app/files/` path to write the PDF contents being generated. We append to the results array in `$filePath` if the `write()` method of the `$CakePdf` object runs without issues.

We return `$results` to let the event manager know that the listener logic is complete and that there are results to be attached to the event and passed to the next event listener. Here, the results will be passed along with the event to the `EmailAlert` listener, as it's attached to the same event manager and is also listening for events with the same name.

We changed the `EmailAlert` listener class the same way we did with the `PDFGenerator` listener. In this case, the implemented event processor will check and use the previous results attached to this event.

```
    $results = (array)$event->result;
    $filePath = Hash::get($results, 'PDFGenerator.generatedPDF');
```

This gets the generated file path with the PDF contents. The listener will then use this file to send a new e-mail.

```
$Email = new CakeEmail();
$Email->template('attachment', 'default')
    ->emailFormat('html')
    ->from(Configure::read('App.defaultSender'))
    ->to(Configure::read('App.defaultRecipient'))
```

```
    ->subject(__('Your new package'))
    ->attachments(array('Package.pdf' => $filePath))
    ->send();
```

Note that we're attaching the PDF file contents to the e-mail sent using `attachments(array('Package.pdf' => $filePath))`. Once the e-mail is sent to the configured user, which in our case is me@example.com, the latest attached listener finishes its execution, and the application flow continues after the following line:

`$this->getEventManager()->dispatch($event);`

See also

▶ The CakeEmail class is described in detail at `http://book.cakephp.org/2.0/en/core-utility-libraries/email.html`

▶ The *Listeners and subscribers* recipe

Event stacking

Once we have the events in place, we could start thinking about dispatching events to an event queue to let another one process, possibly in a different server, pick up the payload, and process the task. This is a useful technique to move your background processing away from the runtime process, thus giving faster response times and allowing resource-intensive jobs to be queued and executed by an optimized server.

In this recipe, we're going to use the CakeResque plugin to create a job queue, using Redis and a worker to process your tasks.

Getting ready

First, make sure you have Redis 2.2 or later installed. Check the detailed setup instructions in the Redis documentation at `http://redis.io/`.

Then, download and install the CakeResque plugin. We'll do the setup using git and Composer, but if you're not using git, you can simply download the ZIP file, using the following command, and place the contents of the plugin in a folder named app/Plugin/CakeResque/:

`$ git submodule add git://github.com/kamisama/Cake-Resque.git app/Plugin/CakeResque`

`$ cd app/Plugin/CakeResque`

`$ curl -s https://getcomposer.org/installer | php`

`$ php composer.phar install`

Afterwards, load the plugin in your `bootstrap.php` file located in `app/Config/` using the following code:

```
CakePlugin::load('CakeResque', array('bootstrap' => true));
// load CakeResque config overrides
Configure::load('cake_resque');
```

We'll reuse our database table named `packages`, shown in the following code, from the previous recipes:

```
CREATE TABLE packages (
    id INT NOT NULL AUTO_INCREMENT,
    recipient VARCHAR(255) NOT NULL,
    address VARCHAR(255) NOT NULL,
    created DATETIME,
    modified DATETIME,
    PRIMARY KEY(id)
);
```

Make sure that you also have a model named `Package.php` in `app/Model/`, with the following content:

```php
<?php
App::uses('AppModel', 'Model');

class Package extends AppModel {
}
```

You should also have a controller named `PackagesController.php` in `app/Controller/`, with the following content:

```php
<?php
App::uses('AppController', 'Controller');

class PackagesController extends AppController {
}
```

How to do it...

Perform the following steps:

1. Add your own config file to tweak the `CakeResque` parameters in a file named `cake_resque.php` in `app/Config/`. Note that we've copied the default config file provided in the `app/Plugin/CakeResque/Config/` directory:

   ```php
   <?php
   $config['CakeResque'] = array(
   ```

```
'Redis' => array(
  'host' => 'localhost', // Redis server hostname
  'port' => 6379, // Redis server port
  'database' => 0, // Redis database number
  'namespace' => 'resque' // Redis keys namespace
),
'Worker' => array(
  'queue' => 'default', // Name of the default queue
  'interval' => 5, // Number of second between each poll
  'workers' => 1, // Number of workers to create
  'log' => TMP . 'logs' . DS . 'resque-worker-error.log',
  'verbose' => false
),
'Job' => array(
  'track' => true
),
// NOTE: to restart, use
// echo "all" | Console/cake CakeResque.CakeResque stop &&
Console/cake CakeResque.CakeResque load
'Queues' => array(
  array(
    'queue' => 'pdf', // Use default values from above for
missing interval and count indexes
    'interval' => 1
  ),
),
'Resque' => array(
  'lib' => 'kamisama/php-resque-ex',
  'tmpdir' => App::pluginPath('CakeResque') . 'tmp' . DS
),
'Env' => array(),
'Log' => array(
  'handler' => 'RotatingFile',
  'target' => TMP . 'logs' . DS . 'resque.log'
),
'Scheduler' => array(
  'enabled' => false,
  'lib' => 'kamisama/php-resque-ex-scheduler',
  'log' => TMP . 'logs' . DS . 'resque-scheduler-error.log',
  'Env' => array(),
  'Worker' => array(
    'interval' => 3
  ),
  'Log' => array(
```

```php
        'handler' => 'RotatingFile',
        'target' => TMP . 'logs' . DS . 'resque-scheduler.log'
      )
    ),
    'Status' => array(
      'lib' => 'kamisama/resque-status'
    )
);
```

2. Add a worker class to process jobs in the PDF queue by creating a file named `PdfShell.php` in app/Console/Command/ with the following content:

```php
<?php
App::uses('AppShell', 'Console/Command');

class PdfShell extends AppShell {

  public function main() {
    $this->out($this->getOptionParser()->help());
  }

  public function perform(){
    $this->initialize();
    $this->{array_shift($this->args)}();
  }

  public function processPdfJob() {
    list($modelName, $id) = $this->args;
    $Model = ClassRegistry::init($modelName);
    $Model->id = $id;
    if (!$Model->exists()) {
        throw new OutOfBoundsException(__('%s not found',
$modelName));
      }
    // process PDF generation
    $this->out('<info>Starting PDF Generation...</info>');
    // slow processing takes place here...
    // Save status of the pdf generation to the database
    }
}
```

3. Change your event dispatch logic by adding this code to your `events.php` file in app/Config/, creating it if it doesn't already exist:

```php
<?php
App::uses('ClassRegistry', 'Utility');
```

```
App::uses('CakeResque', 'CakeResque.Lib');

ClassRegistry::init('Package')->getEventManager()-
>attach(function($event) {
  CakeResque::enqueue('pdf', 'PdfShell', array(
    'processPdfJob',
    $event->subject->alias,
    $event->subject->id
  ));
}, 'App.Model.Package.afterSave');
```

4. Ensure that your events.php file is loaded in your bootstrap, by adding this line at the end of your bootstrap.php file in app/Config/:

    ```
    config('events');
    ```

5. Make sure that you dispatch a new event in the afterSave() method of the Package model class:

    ```
    public function afterSave($created, $options = array()) {
      parent::afterSave($created, $options);
      if ($created) {
        // create a new event
        $event = new CakeEvent('App.Model.Package.afterSave', $this);
        // dispatch the event to the Package event manager
        $this->getEventManager()->dispatch($event);
      }
    }
    ```

6. We'll also add a debug_queue() method to our PackagesController:

    ```
    public function debug_queue() {
      $result = $this->Package->save(array(
        'Package' => array(
          'recipient' => 'John Smith',
          'address' => 'Collins Ave., Dallas, TX'
        )
      ));
      debug('just saved a new package');
      debug($result);
      $this->_stop();
    }
    ```

7. Start your worker processes with the following command:

    ```
    $ Console/cake CakeResque.CakeResque load
    Loading predefined workers
    Starting worker ... Done
    ```

8. Check that the workers started alright with the following command:

```
$ Console/cake CakeResque.CakeResque stats
Resque Statistics
----------------------------------------------------------------

Jobs Stats
  Processed Jobs: 0
  Failed Jobs: 0

Queues Stats
  Queues count: 0

Workers Stats
  Workers count: 1
   REGULAR WORKERS
   * mirror-12:21545: pdf
       - Started on: Wed Jun 04 15:26:26 CEST 2014
       - Processed Jobs: 0
       - Failed Jobs: 0
```

How it works...

For this recipe, we downloaded the CakeResque plugin and loaded it in our `bootstrap.php` file, thus creating a specific file to override the plugin's default configuration.

The configuration in `app/Config/cake_resque.php` holds the Redis server instance information. You'll need to tweak this file if your application isn't able to connect to the Redis server located in your environment. The default values are provided, so you shouldn't have any issues connecting to Redis as long as it's listening to the connections on `localhost:6379`.

Note that you should have the Redis server process enabled. Check the Redis documentation (`http://redis.io/topics/quickstart`) to start the Redis server in your environment. Usually, this is done using the following command (in Linux):

```
$ sudo service redis-server start
```

Also, note that we defined a new queue in the `cake_resque.php` file using the following configuration key:

```
'Queues' => array(
  array(
```

```
        'queue' => 'pdf',
        'interval' => 1
    )
  )
```

Here, we're setting a default `pdf` queue, and setting one second as the polling time to detect if there are new jobs in the queue that are ready to be processed.

We then added our worker. The worker is a CakePHP console shell that will be executed by CakeResque when a new job is being processed. The new shell file located in `app/Console/Command/PdfShell.php` holds a method to process the PDF generation logic.

This worker also has a `perform()` method, which is required by the CakeResque plugin, to adapt the input parameters. This is something managed internally by the CakeResque plugin, so you only need to worry about configuring this method to be available to all the worker shells, as stated in the CakeResque setup documentation.

CakeResque will then pass the job parameters as arguments to the shell, so we first need to get these arguments in our processing logic.

```php
public function processPdfJob() {
   list($modelName, $id) = $this->args;
   $Model = ClassRegistry::init($modelName);
   $Model->id = $id;
   if (!$Model->exists()) {
     throw new OutOfBoundsException(__('%s not found', $modelName));
   }
   // process PDF generation
   $this->out('<info>Starting PDF Generation...</info>');
   // slow processing takes place here…
   // Save status of the pdf generation to the database
}
```

Here, we get an instance of the model, check if the model exists, and process the PDF generation logic. We're not dealing with this logic, as the main focus of this recipe is to learn how to manage a job queue, but you can use our previous PDF generation recipe if you're interested in generating a real PDF file and attaching it to an e-mail.

The next step then is to configure our event system to enqueue a new job into the Redis job queue every time an `App.Model.Package.afterSave` event is triggered. For this, we use the `CakeResque::enqueue()` method, passing the queue name, the shell to process the job, and an array of parameters for the job itself. The first parameter will be the name of the method in the shell class to process the job, and the rest of the parameters will be passed as arguments to the processing method. In this case, we're sending the model alias and model ID.

We're going to use the model instance as the subject of the event, so we will pass the following as parameters, using the `alias` and `id` properties of the model instance:

`$event->subject->alias,`

`$event->subject->id`

You may have noticed that we attached an anonymous function to the `Package` event manager. This function will be executed on the dispatch of any event named `App.Model.Package.afterSave` to the `Package` event manager. So, this code could be read as "Enqueue a new job into the `pdf` queue for every new event named `App.Model.Package.afterSave` dispatched to the `Package` event manager":

```
ClassRegistry::init('Package')->getEventManager()-
>attach(function($event) {
  CakeResque::enqueue('pdf', 'PdfShell', array(
    'processPdfJob',
    $event->subject->alias,
    $event->subject->id
  ));
}, 'App.Model.Package.afterSave');
```

The last action that we perform in this recipe is to configure the event dispatching in the `afterSave()` callback of the `Package` model class. Here, we get an instance of the local event manager and dispatch a new event to it. The event is configured to have the model instance as the subject (using `$this`) and the `App.Model.Package.afterSave` name.

If we start adding packages now, jobs will be enqueued to the `pdf` job queue, but we need to start at least one worker to listen to this queue and start processing jobs. This is done from the command line, using the CakeResque plugin tools:

`$ Console/cake CakeResque.CakeResque load`

This plugin shell will start one worker for every queue configured in the `app/Config/cake_resque.php` file. The worker will be listening for jobs, and as soon as the first job is enqueued in the `pdf` queue, it will be processed by the worker.

Now that we have our recipe's code in place, let's recap the application flow.

First, you'll save a new record in the `Package` model. Once saved, the `afterSave()` callback is triggered. We then dispatch a new event to the local event manager as follows:

`$event = new CakeEvent('App.Model.Package.afterSave', $this);`

Based on the `app/Config/events.php` configuration file, on dispatch, we enqueue a new job in the CakeResque `pdf` queue:

```
CakeResque::enqueue('pdf', 'PdfShell', array(
  'processPdfJob',
  $event->subject->alias,
  $event->subject->id
));
```

Here, we're using the following setup:

- Queue name = `pdf`
- Worker shell class name = `PdfShell`
- Parameters:

  - The first parameter, `processPdfJob`, is the name of the function to execute in our worker shell class
  - The remaining parameters will be passed as a `$this->args` array to the worker method

Once this new CakeResque job is enqueued, it's saved into the Redis `pdf` queue. Then, a new worker is assigned to process this task (in a separate process). The worker will create an instance of the `PdfShell` class and run the `processPdfJob` method. When the `pdf` generation is completed, we could then save the result into a `products` table to let the application know that the task is completed and conditionally display a download button based in the status value.

Testing how it works is simple—just point your browser to `/packages/debug_queue` and you'll get output similar to this:

Now, if you check the log, you'll see the following output from your new PdfShell there:

```
$ cat app/tmp/logs/resque-worker-error.log
Starting PDF Generation...
```

See also

▸ http://cakeresque.kamisama.me

▸ http://redis.io

▸ https://github.com/nicolasff/phpredis

▸ The *Generating a PDF* recipe from *Chapter 10, View Templates*

▸ The *Event-driven process* recipe

Managing event priorities

When a new event is dispatched in CakePHP, all the listeners which match the event name that are attached to the event manager where the event was dispatched will be triggered to process the event in order. Sometimes, we need to ensure that a specific order is followed when several listeners are triggered for a specific event. This can be done through the event manager API. We also have the ability to stop the event propagation and force the rest of the listeners to be ignored after the current listener finishes.

In this recipe, we look at how you can control the event dispatch process to keep your events executing accordingly.

Getting ready

We'll continue to use our `packages` table for this recipe. If you don't have it, create it with the following SQL statement:

```sql
CREATE TABLE packages (
    id INT NOT NULL AUTO_INCREMENT,
    recipient VARCHAR(255) NOT NULL,
    address VARCHAR(255) NOT NULL,
    created DATETIME,
    modified DATETIME,
    PRIMARY KEY(id)
);
```

Also, make sure that you have the related model file named `Package.php` in `app/Model/` with the following content:

```php
<?php
App::uses('AppModel', 'Model');

class Package extends AppModel {
```

```php
    public function afterSave($created, $options = array()) {
      parent::afterSave($created, $options);
      if ($created) {
        // create a new event
        $event = new CakeEvent('App.Model.Package.afterSave', $this);
        // dispatch the event to the local event manager
        $this->getEventManager()->dispatch($event);
      }
    }
  }
```

As we've done in the previous recipes, update the existing configuration file for our event named `events.php` in `app/Config/` with the following content (at least):

```php
<?php
App::uses('ClassRegistry', 'Utility');
App::uses('PDFGenerator', 'Lib/Event');
App::uses('EmailReport', 'Lib/Event');

ClassRegistry::init('Package')->getEventManager()->attach(new
PDFGenerator());
ClassRegistry::init('Package')->getEventManager()->attach(new
EmailAlert());
```

Then, load your configuration file in your `bootstrap.php` file, also in `app/Config/`, by adding the following to the end of the file:

```php
config('events');
```

Now, add a new `PDFGenerator` listener in a file named `PDFGenerator.php` in `app/Lib/Event/` with the following content:

```php
<?php
App::uses('CakeEventListener', 'Event');

class PDFGenerator extends Object implements CakeEventListener {

  public function implementedEvents() {
    return array(
      'App.Model.Package.afterSave' => 'generatePDF'
    );
  }

  public function generatePDF($event) {
    debug('we should be generating a PDF file now ...');
  }
}
```

Note that we're not generating a PDF file now; this is just a listener example to show you how to alter the priorities for the listeners attached to the same event.

Also, add a new `EmailAlert` listener in a file named `EmailAlert.php` in the same directory, with the following content:

```php
<?php
App::uses('CakeEventListener', 'Event');

class EmailAlert extends Object implements CakeEventListener {

  public function implementedEvents() {
    return array(
      'App.Model.Package.afterSave' => 'sendEmailAlert'
    );
  }

  public function sendEmailAlert($event) {
    debug('we should be sending an email here ...');
  }
}
```

We'll also create a file named `PackagesController.php` in `app/Controller/` with the following content:

```php
<?php
App::uses('AppController', 'Controller');

class PackagesController extends AppController {

  public function debug_events() {
    $result = $this->Package->save(array(
      'Package' => array(
        'recipient' => 'John Smith',
        'address' => 'Collins Ave., Dallas, TX'
      )
    ));
    debug('just saved a new package');
    debug($result);
    $this->_stop();
  }
}
```

How to do it...

Perform the following steps:

1. Alter the listener priority for the `EmailAlert` listener in `app/Lib/Event/EmailAlert.php`:

```php
public function implementedEvents() {
  return array(
    'App.Model.Package.afterSave' => array(
      'callable' => 'sendEmailAlert',
      'priority' => 5
    )
  );
}
```

2. Modify the `sendEmailAlert()` method to stop any other listener from triggering after this one:

```php
public function sendEmailAlert($event) {
  debug('we should be sending an email here ...');
  debug('and now we are not processing the PDF generation logic');
  $event->stopPropagation();
}
```

3. After dispatching the event, you might be interested in detecting if the event finished processing or it was stopped along the way. So, update the `afterSave()` method in the `Package` model class, as shown in the following code:

```php
public function afterSave($created, $options = array()) {
  parent::afterSave($created, $options);
  if ($created) {
    $event = new CakeEvent('App.Model.Product.afterSave', $this);
    $this->getEventManager()->dispatch($event);
    if ($event->isStopped()) {
      debug('event propagation stopped');
    }
  }
}
```

How it works...

The event managers in CakePHP assign a default priority of 10 to all listeners. You can tweak the priority to a lower value (higher priority) or a higher value (lesser priority) where required.

```
Priority = 0  1  2  3  4  5  6  7  8  9  10  11  12  13  14  15  16 +
     ← Higher Priority (run earlier)        Lower Priority (run later) →
```

In this recipe, we used two listeners attached to the same event named `App.Model.Package.afterSave` through the `Package` model's event manager. The listeners used are just for testing purposes, as they print a debug message when processing the event.

Saving a package at this point should display the following output:

```
book_25.dev/packages/debug_events

/app/Lib/Event/PDFGenerator.php (line 14)

'we should be generating a PDF file now ...'

/app/Lib/Event/EmailAlert.php (line 17)

'we should be sending an email here ...'

/app/Controller/PackagesController.php (line 35)

'just saved a new package'

/app/Controller/PackagesController.php (line 36)

array(
    'Package' => array(
        'recipient' => 'John Smith',
        'address' => 'Collins Ave., Dallas, TX',
        'modified' => '2014-07-03 19:10:09',
        'created' => '2014-07-03 19:10:09',
        'id' => '15'
    )
)
```

Here, we changed the priority of the e-mail listener using the following configuration setting in the `app/Lib/Event/EmailReport.php` file:

```php
public function implementedEvents() {
    return array(
        'App.Model.Package.afterSave' => array(
            'callable' => 'sendEmailAlert',
            'priority' => 5
        )
    );
}
```

Note that the array sets the priority and the callable public function, which is implemented in this listener class to process the event.

After this, we modified the called method for the event and stopped the event propagation using the `stopPropagation()` method:

```
public function sendEmailAlert($event) {
  debug('we should be sending an email here ...');
  debug('and now we are not processing the PDF generation logic');
  $event->stopPropagation();
}
```

After calling this method, any subsequent events would not be triggered.

We also added a detection in the `Package` model to check whether the dispatch method is running successfully or has been stopped along the way in the `afterSave()` callback method of our `Package` model:

```
$this->getEventManager()->dispatch($event);
if ($event->isStopped()) {
  debug('event propagation stopped');
}
```

Saving a new package will now display the following debug messages:

As you can see, the `PDFGenerator` listener was not processed, and we've detected that the event was stopped.

Defining priorities can sometimes be tricky, as the configuration is scattered throughout the listener classes. Another option is to have all of your event configuration in one file, using anonymous listeners and packing them into one single `events.php` file in `app/Config/`, for example:

```
<?php
App::uses('ClassRegistry', 'Utility');
```

```
App::uses('EmailAlert', 'Lib/Event');

//Attaching anonymous Listener, including priority
ClassRegistry::init('Product')->getEventManager()-
>attach(function($event) {
  $EmailAlert = new EmailAlert();
  return $EmailAlert->sendEmailAlert($event);
}, 'App.Model.Product.afterSave', array('priority' => 5));
```

See also

▶ The *Event-driven process* recipe

9

Creating Shells

In this chapter, we will cover the following topics:

- ► Console API
- ► Import parser
- ► Running cron shells
- ► Using the I18n shell

Introduction

While CakePHP is a framework aimed at developing web applications, it also exposes a feature-rich console API to build shell-based scripts. These can be used for anything, from filesystem tasks, to database- and process-intensive operations.

In this chapter, we'll outline some common use cases when using shell tasks, as well as some built-in shell commands that come with the framework.

Console API

CakePHP provides a rich console API to let you create and reuse specific project tasks that are more suited to being executed in a console environment. Keep in mind that when running commands from shell, you're not restricted by the same limitations the web server typically puts on server resources such as memory use and execution time. You can also have a less restrictive PHP configuration for your CLI environment, allow additional PHP extensions, and do more.

In this recipe, we'll create a new console shell and task to explore some of the features of the console shell API. Note that we'll be using a shell named PdfShell as an example, but no real PDF generation will happen.

How to do it...

Perform the following steps:

1. First, update our existing file named `PdfShell.php` in `app/Console/Command/` with the following content:

```php
<?php
App::uses('AppShell', 'Console/Command');

class PdfShell extends AppShell {

  public $tasks = array('Generate');

  public function main() {
    $this->out($this->getOptionParser()->help());
  }

  public function getOptionParser() {
    $parser = parent::getOptionParser();
    return $parser->description('My App PDF Shell')
      ->addSubcommand('generate', array(
        'help' => __('Generates a new PDF file'),
        'parser' => $this->Generate->getOptionParser()
      ));
  }
}
```

2. Then, create a new task in a file named `GenerateTask.php` in `app/Console/Command/Task/`:

```php
<?php
App::uses('AppShell', 'Console/Command');
App::uses('String', 'Utility');

class GenerateTask extends AppShell {

  public $tasks = array('Generate');

  public function execute() {
    $modelName = $this->args[0];
    $id = $this->args[1];
    $Model = ClassRegistry::init($modelName);
    $Model->id = $id;
    if (!$Model->exists()) {
```

```php
            throw new OutOfBoundsException(__('%s not found',
    $modelName));
        }
        // process PDF generation
        $this->out('<info>Starting PDF Generation...</info>');
    }

    public function getOptionParser() {
        $parser = parent::getOptionParser();
        return $parser->description('Generate a PDF file')
            ->addArgument('model', array(
                'required' => true,
                'help' => __('Model name, example: Package')))
            ->addArgument('id', array(
                'required' => true,
                'help' => __('ID of the model being generated')))
            ->addOption('output', array(
                'short' => 'o',
                'default' => APP . 'files' . DS . String::uuid() . '.pdf',
                'help' => __('Full path for the output PDF file to be
    generated')
            )
        );
    }
}
```

3. Now, show the help for your new console shell with the following command:

```
$ Console/cake pdf
Welcome to CakePHP v2.5.2 Console
---------------------------------------------------------------
App : myapp
Path: /home/user/myapp/
---------------------------------------------------------------
My App PDF Shell

Usage:
cake pdf [subcommand] [-h] [-v] [-q]

Subcommands:
```

```
generate  Generates a new PDF file

To see help on a subcommand use 'cake pdf [subcommand] --help'

Options:

--help, -h    Display this help.
--verbose, -v Enable verbose output.
--quiet, -q   Enable quiet output.
```

4. Also show help for your new PDF task:

```
$ Console/cake pdf generate -h
Welcome to CakePHP v2.5.2 Console
-------------------------------------------------------------
App : myapp
Path: /home/user/myapp/
-------------------------------------------------------------
Generate a PDF file

Usage:
cake pdf generate [-h] [-v] [-q] [-o /home/user/myapp/
files/538c7082-a578-4982-893d-24e3ebcde0a1.pdf] <model> <id>

Options:

--help, -h    Display this help.
--verbose, -v Enable verbose output.
--quiet, -q   Enable quiet output.
--output, -o  Full path for the output PDF file to be generated
              (default:
              /home/user/myapp/files/538c7082-a578-4982-893d-
24e3ebcde0a1.pdf)

Arguments:

model  Model name, example: Package
id     id of the model being generated
```

5. Finally, run your shell from the command line:

```
$ Console/cake pdf generate Package 1
Welcome to CakePHP v2.5.2 Console
------------------------------------------------------------
App : myapp
Path: /home/user/myapp/
------------------------------------------------------------
Starting PDF Generation...
```

How it works...

In this recipe, we've created a new `Shell` as well as a specific `Task` to generate PDF files from the command line.

Using `Tasks` to encapsulate shell logic allows you to keep your classes clean and focused, instead of writing a super-long file with all of the PDF-related features packed inside. The parent class, `PdfShell`, holds all of the logic related to PDF files, but we could also generate tasks and reuse them in other `Shell` classes.

Using the `out()` method is the correct way to send data to the console's standard output. The `out()` method allows formatting and is compatible with color terminals.

Here, we also overwrote the `getOptionParser()` method in our main `PdfShell` and `GenerateTask` classes to provide context-sensitive help and validate the console input parameters:

- At the `PdfShell` level, we're specifying one available subcommand
- At the `GenerateTask` level, we're providing validation for our two required arguments, `model` and `id`, and setting an `output` option with a default value

Command-line arguments are processed in order. We can access these arguments from the `$this->args` array, starting at position 0 for the first argument, `model`, and position 1 for `id`.

Options can also be set using long and short formats, for example:

```
$ Console/cake pdf generate --output ./out.pdf Package 1
$ Console/cake pdf generate Package 1 -o ./out.pdf
```

Additionally, options can have a default value. In our recipe, the `output` file is set as default. Of course, the default value can be overridden by the `--output` argument.

Shells in CakePHP use the `main()` method as the default entry point. In our case, we're printing the autogenerated help text to the standard output, as shown in the following code:

```
public function main() {
    $this->out($this->getOptionParser()->help());
}
```

You're also free to use models, third-party vendor libraries, or any other resource from our application. In our example, we used `ClassRegistry` to get a dynamic instance of a model alias passed as a console argument.

Remember that you can also output styled text to the console, using any of the predefined styles: `<error>`, `<warning>`, `<info>`, `<comment>`, or `<question>`. You can even define new styles to be used, for example:

```
$this->out('<info>Starting PDF Generation...</info>');
```

See also

▶ More info on the CakePHP console API can be found at `http://book.cakephp.org/2.0/en/console-and-shells.html`

Import parser

One benefit of using shells in CakePHP is to handle process-intensive tasks, which take a long time to run. In this recipe, we'll create a CakePHP console shell to deal with a mass CSV data import. We'll process a data file and import all rows, while logging import errors to another file.

Getting ready

As this is the only task in our shell, we're not using `Task` this time.

First, if you don't have it already, create the `packages` database table using the following SQL statement:

```
CREATE TABLE packages (
    id INT NOT NULL AUTO_INCREMENT,
    recipient VARCHAR(255) NOT NULL,
    address VARCHAR(255) NOT NULL,
    created DATETIME,
    modified DATETIME,
    PRIMARY KEY(id)
);
```

Then, create the associated model in a file named `Package.php` in app/Model/ with the following content:

```php
<?php
App::uses('AppModel', 'Model');

class Package extends AppModel {
}
```

How to do it...

Perform the following steps:

1. Create a file named `ImportShell.php` in app/Console/Command/ to import CSV files with the following code:

```php
<?php
App::uses('AppShell', 'Console/Command');

class ImportShell extends AppShell {

  public function main() {
    $this->out($this->getOptionParser()->help());
  }

  public function getOptionParser() {
    $parser = parent::getOptionParser();
    return $parser->description('Import shell')
      ->addArgument('inputFilePath', array(
        'required' => true,
        'help' => __('Full path for the input file')))
      ->addArgument('model', array(
        'required' => true,
        'help' => __('Model name')))
      ->addSubcommand('csv', array(
        'help' => __('Import a CSV file'),
      )
    );
  }

  public function csv() {
    list($inputFilePath, $modelName) = $this->args;
    $Model = ClassRegistry::init($modelName);
    $file = new File($inputFilePath);
```

```
      if (!$file->exists() || !$file->open()) {
        throw new OutOfBoundsException(__('File %s does not exist',
$inputFilePath));
      }
      $errorFile = new File($inputFilePath . '.error.log');
      $this->out(__('Start CSV import: %s', $inputFilePath));
      $db = $Model->getDataSource();
      $db->begin($Model);
      $headers = fgetcsv($file->handle);
      while (($row = fgetcsv($file->handle)) !== false) {
        $data = array();
        foreach ($row as $index => $fieldValue) {
          $header = $headers[$index];
          $data[$header] = $fieldValue;
        }
        $Model->create();
        $Model->set($data);
        if (!$Model->validates()) {
          $errorFile->append(__('error in line "%s", %s', $index,
print_r($Model->validationErrors, true)));
        } else {
          $Model->save($data);
        }
      }
      $db->commit($Model);
      $this->out(__('End import CSV'));
    }
}
```

2. Then, display the help for your new Console shell with the following command:

    $ Console/cake import

    Import shell

    Usage:

    cake import [subcommand] [-h] [-v] [-q] <inputFilePath> <model>

    Subcommands:

    csv   Import a CSV file

```
To see help on a subcommand use 'cake import [subcommand] --help'
```

```
Options:
```

```
--help, -h      Display this help.
--verbose, -v   Enable verbose output.
--quiet, -q     Enable quiet output.
```

```
Arguments:
```

```
inputFilePath   Full path for the input file
model           Model name
```

3. Now, edit a new CSV file named `newPackages.csv`, introducing the following content:

```
"recipient","address"
"recipient 91","address 91"
"recipient 92","address 92"
```

4. Finally, import the new file with the following command:

```
$ Console/cake import csv newPackages.csv Package
```

```
Welcome to CakePHP v2.5.2 Console
---------------------------------------------------------------
App : myapp
Path: /home/user/myapp/
---------------------------------------------------------------
Start import CSV: newPackages.csv
End import CSV
```

How it works...

In this recipe, we created an import shell to process valid records, reading them from a (potentially) large CSV file. In this `Shell`, there's only one subcommand available: `csv`. Both the file path and the model name are passed as required arguments to our console `Shell`, allowing us to use this shell with any model in our application.

If we look at the following code for the app/Console/Command/ImportShell.php file, we defined a main entry point, displaying the help for this shell if no task is defined:

```
public function main() {
    $this->out($this->getOptionParser()->help());
}
```

Then, we implemented the getOptionParser() method to provide context-sensitive help for our shell.

The main task implemented is the csv() method, which is divided into various blocks of logic, as seen in the following code:

```
list($inputFilePath, $modelName) = $this->args;
$Model = ClassRegistry::init($modelName);
$file = new File($inputFilePath);
if (!$file->exists() || !$file->open()) {
    throw new OutOfBoundsException(__('File %s does not exist',
$inputFilePath));
}
$errorFile = new File($inputFilePath . '.error.log');
$this->out(__('Start import CSV: %s', $inputFilePath));
```

Here, in this fist block, we use the arguments passed to the console task. The first argument passed will be the input file path and then the model name to import the data into. We then get an instance to the model using ClassRegistry::init($modelName), after which we check if the input file exists in the filesystem, and we throw an exception if it is not found.

We also prepare a new file handler to use in case of validation errors found while importing the CSV file.

```
$db = $Model->getDataSource();
$db->begin($Model);
$headers = fgetcsv($file->handle);
while (($row = fgetcsv($file->handle)) !== false) {
    $data = array();
    foreach ($row as $index => $fieldValue) {
        $header = $headers[$index];
        $data[$header] = $fieldValue;
    }
}
```

In this second block, we start a database transaction to ensure that the entire import operation, or nothing, will be executed. For this, we call `$db->begin($Model)` and prepare a `$data` array with the contents to be saved. Based on the headers present in the CSV file (the first line), we'll define the `$data` keys in the array (as shown in the following code), so it's important to match the CSV header line columns with the model fields to be saved, in this case, "address" and "recipient":

```
$Model->create();
$Model->set($data);
if (!$Model->validates()) {
    $errorFile->append(__('error in line "%s", %s', $index,
print_r($Model->validationErrors, true)));
} else {
    $Model->save($data);
}
}
$db->commit($Model);
$this->out(__('End import CSV'));
```

Then, in the last block, we call `$Model->set($data)` to prepare the model data for validation and check that the data is valid to be saved. If we find validation errors, we append the resulting errors in `$Model->validationErrors` to the error logfile, and if not, we save our model to the database.

Once all of the CSV rows are processed, we issue `$db->commit($Model)` to commit the transaction, and save only the valid models.

See also

▶ The *Using Transactions* recipe from *Chapter 6, Model Layer*

Running cron shells

Another typical scenario to use CakePHP console shells is to implement a data warehouse and a time-intensive and recurring task.

In this recipe, we'll create a recurring job to calculate our package ratings, based on some complex logic.

Getting ready

For this recipe, we'll assume that you have a `packages` table and the related model that we created in our previous recipe. However, we'll also add a new column to store our ratings per package with the following SQL statement:

```
ALTER TABLE packages ADD rating INT(20) UNSIGNED NOT NULL DEFAULT '0';
```

How to do it...

Perform the following steps:

1. First, create a file named `RatingShell.php` in `app/Console/Command/` with the following content:

```php
<?php
App::uses('AppShell', 'Console/Command');

class RatingShell extends AppShell {

  public function main() {
    $this->out($this->getOptionParser()->help());
  }

  public function getOptionParser() {
    $parser = parent::getOptionParser();
    return $parser->description('Rating Shell')
      ->addSubcommand('calculate', array(
        'help' => __('Calculate ratings'),
      )
    );
  }

  public function calculate() {
    $this->_checkLockFile();
    try {
      $Package = ClassRegistry::init('Package');
      // potentially slow operation, data intensive
      $status = $Package->calculateRatings();
    } catch (Exception $e) {
      $this->_removeLockFile();
      throw $e;
    }
```

```
      $this->_removeLockFile();
      return $status;
   }

   protected function _checkLockFile() {
      $lock = $this->_getLockFile();
      if ($lock->exists()) {
        $this->error('Job is already working, please wait until
calculate job finishes');
      }
      $lock->create();
   }

   protected function _getLockFile() {
      return new File(TMP . 'RatingShell.calculate.lock');
   }

   protected function _removeLockFile() {
      $lock = $this->_getLockFile();
      $lock->delete();
   }
}
```

2. Then, in the file named `Package.php` in `app/Model/`, add the following methods:

```
public function calculateRatings() {
   $totalPackages = $this->find('count');
   $index = 0;
   while ($index < $totalPackages) {
      $package = $this->find('first', array(
        'fields' => array(
          'id'
        ),
        'recursive' => -1,
        'limit' => $totalPackages,
        'page' => 0,
        'offset' => $index
      ));
      $this->calculateRating(Hash::get($package, 'Package.id'));
      $index++;
   }
   return true;
}

public function calculateRating($packageId) {
   // your complex rating calculation logic here...
}
```

3. Now, schedule a new `cronjob` to run your shell. For this, we'll use a standard Linux distribution as an example:

```
$ crontab -e

#add this line to the end of the file

0   *   *   *    * cd /home/user/myapp && Console/cake rating
calculate 2>> /home/user/myapp/tmp/myapp.cron.log > /dev/null
```

4. Finally, press *Ctrl + X* and then S to save changes, and apply the new `crontab`.

How it works...

Dealing with time-intensive tasks that need to run periodically in your system is always tricky. You need to ensure that your job keeps running and that you don't consume too many resources along the way.

In this recipe, we've created a `Shell` task with a `calculate()` method, as well as a couple of utility methods to take care of the following:

- `_checkLockFile()` will detect if a lock file exists and create a lock file if not
- `_removeLockFile()` will remove the current lock file
- `_getLockFile()` will get the name of the lock file

In this case, we've implemented a simple lock file check, to detect if there's another instance of this job running, so as to not overlap. Note that you could use environment-specific options for this too, such as the *Flock* tool in Linux. Here, we've used a CakePHP-specific solution, based on a lock file under the `tmp/` folder. It's not 100 percent perfect, but it will save the day.

In the `calculate()` method, we're using the related `Package` model, as it is a part of our business, to delegate the rating calculation logic. We're following the "fat models" mantra this time, by moving all of our business logic to our model layer. This will help us unit test our code and keep it reusable and organized.

By looking over the logic from the `calculateRatings()` method in `app/Model/Package.php`, even if it's slower, it's important that we process all of the packages one by one to prevent future *out of memory* errors when the packages table becomes (possibly) huge. If speed is important, which it almost always is, we could add an `is_rating_modified` field to our `packages` table to filter and process only the changed packages. Although this scenario has served to show how cron shells can work in CakePHP, the best approach here would be to use a worker queue and push a new job when the `Package` rating needs an update.

▶ The *Flock* tool for Linux and file-locking information can be found at `http://en.wikipedia.org/wiki/File_locking`

▶ The *Event stacking* recipe from *Chapter 8, Events System*

Using the I18n shell

CakePHP provides a powerful console shell to help you in the first steps of internationalizing your application. Addressing i18N is not an easy task, as there are many details to consider, such as dates and times, number and currency formats, dynamic content translation, and distinct dialects.

In this recipe, we're going to use the CakePHP I18n shell to prepare our application for translations with a simple flash message example.

Getting ready

First, we'll define a base language for our application. For this, we'll assume the base language will be English. All of your static content will then be displayed using any of the __() functions.

We'll assume you have the `gifts` and `recipients` tables created from our previous recipes, but also ensure that you create all of the CRUD-related classes using the `bake` shell as follows:

Console/cake bake all Gift

Console/cake bake all Recipient

Then, in your `app/Controller/RecipientsController.php` file, add the following method:

```
public function translations() {
  $defaultLang = Configure::read('Config.language');
  // switch to use English
  Configure::write('Config.language', 'eng');
  $message = __('This is my message') . ' in english';
  // switch to use Spanish
  Configure::write('Config.language', 'spa');
  $message .= '<br/>' . __('This is my message') . ' en español';
  $this->Session->setFlash($message);
  Configure::write('Config.language', $defaultLang);
  return $this->redirect(array('action' => 'index'));
}
```

Note that when running this action, initially, you'll get a flash message with incorrect content:

```
This is my message in english
This is my message en español
```

How to do it...

Perform the following steps:

1. Run the `i18n` shell to extract all the translation keys with the following command:

```
$ Console/cake i18n extract --exclude-plugins --merge no
--extract-core no


Welcome to CakePHP v2.5.2 Console
---------------------------------------------------------------
App : myapp
Path: /home/user/myapp
---------------------------------------------------------------
Current paths: None
What is the path you would like to extract?
[Q]uit [D]one
[/home/user/myapp/] >


Current paths: /home/user/myapp/
What is the path you would like to extract?
[Q]uit [D]one
[D] > d


What is the path you would like to output?
[Q]uit
[/home/user/myapp/Locale] >
```

```
Extracting...

----------------------------------------------------------------

Paths:

/home/user/myapp/

Output Directory: /home/user/myapp/Locale/

----------------------------------------------------------------

Processing /home/user/myapp/Controller/RecipientsController.php...

Processing /home/user/myapp/Model/AppModel.php...

...

...

...

Error: default.pot already exists in this location. Overwrite? [Y]
es, [N]o, [A]ll (y/n/a)

[y] > y


Done.
```

2. Now, create the following directories for your available languages:

   - ❑ app/Locale/eng/LC_MESSAGES

   - ❑ app/Locale/spa/LC_MESSAGES

3. Then, copy the .pot template file generated into the following available language directories as .po (notice the output file extension is .po and not .pot):

   - ❑ app/Locale/eng/LC_MESSAGES/default.po

   - ❑ app/Locale/spa/LC_MESSAGES/default.po

4. Edit the spa language file, and provide a translation to key for this message:

```
#: Controller/RecipientsController.php:124;127
msgid "This is my message"
msgstr "Este es mi mensaje"
```

5. Finally, navigate to `/recipients/translations` in your browser to check the translated messages, as shown in the following screenshots:

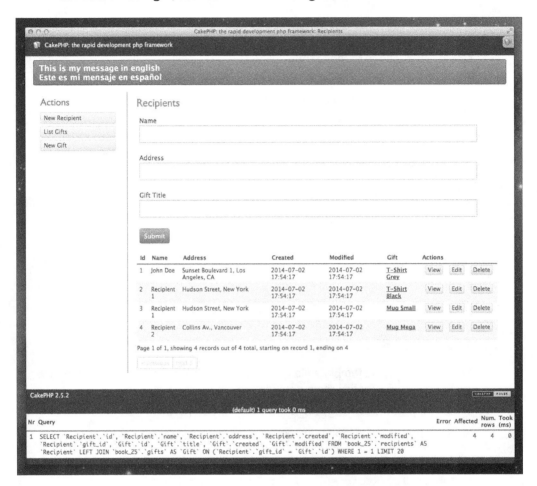

How it works...

Once your application is using the ___ () functions, it's easy to use the `i18n` console shell to extract the translation keys. The shell uses several options to restrict the folders to be parsed or to ignore translation keys from plugins or specific translation domains.

In this recipe, we used the following options:

- ▸   `--exclude-plugins` to ignore plugin translations
- ▸   `--merge no` to keep translation keys from different domains in separate files
- ▸   `--extract-core no` to ignore translation keys from the CakePHP core files

The shell will now parse each file under the selected directory and generate the `app/Locale/default.pot` file, with all of our translation keys ready to be processed.

Once we move the template `.pot` file to each of our available language directories, we can proceed to translate each key. As our default language is `English`, we can ignore the `/eng` directory, as the translation keys are the English translated values.

We then proceed to translate all our keys to Spanish, where we can use the *Poedit* tool, and benefit from automated fuzzy translations based on our previously translated keys. Please check the *Poedit* documentation to set up and use the tool in your system.

Once we finish editing the `.po` file per language, we then only need to set up or switch to a language, using the following configuration setting:

```
Configure::write('Config.language', 'spa');
```

If the language file is not found or the specific key is empty, the key will be used in its place. As we're using English as the base language to create our keys, the text will be displayed in English. For example, consider the following code:

```
echo __('this key does not exist in translation file or language not found');
```

This code would output the following:

```
this key does not exist in translation file or language not found
```

See also

▶ Learn more on internationalization of CakePHP applications at `http://book.cakephp.org/2.0/en/core-libraries/internationalization-and-localization.html`

▶ The *Poedit* tool (`http://poedit.net`)

▶ The *Translations* recipe from *Chapter 10, View Templates*

10
View Templates

In this chapter, we will cover the following topics:

- Using blocks
- Building an XML view
- Generating a PDF
- Writing some PDF content to a file
- Translations
- View caching
- The AssetCompress plugin

Introduction

Views are files that render the final output for a user to possibly be consumed by a service. They can be plain text, HTML, XML, JSON, or even a format that you define for your application. In CakePHP, these files are stored in a directory, which by convention is named after the controller it belongs to, with the `.ctp` extension in `app/View/`.

Using blocks

View blocks are snippets of content, which are captured at runtime, and then manipulated and rendered to a view.

In this recipe, we'll look at how to extend a view, and then use view blocks to populate certain areas of it.

Getting ready

For this recipe, we'll reuse the existing controller, which is `ProductsController`. If you don't have it, create a file named `ProductsController.php` in app/Controller/, and introduce the following content:

```php
<?php
App::uses('AppController', 'Controller');

class ProductsController extends AppController {
}
```

Then, we'll create a base view, which we'll extend with our view. Create a file named `base.ctp` in app/View/Common/, and add the following content:

```php
<h2><?php echo h($this->fetch('name')); ?></h2>
<div>
  <?php echo $this->fetch('content'); ?>
</div>
```

How to do it...

Perform the following steps:

1. First, add a `details()` method to `ProductsController` with the following content:

```php
public function details() {
  $this->set(array(
    'product' => 'Chocolate Cake',
    'details' => 'An awesome product!'
  ));
}
```

2. Then, create a file named `details.ctp` in app/View/Products/ with the following content:

```php
<?php
$this->extend('/Common/base');
$this->assign('name', $product);
?>
<p>
  <?php echo $this->get('details', __('No details found')); ?>
</p>
```

3. Navigate to `/products/details` in your browser to view the resulting output, as shown in the following screenshot:

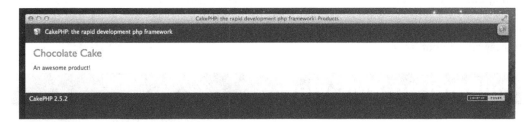

How it works...

Here, we first created an action in our `ProductsController` to define some view variables for use in our view. We then created a view for the action, following the conventions of file naming. It's worth noting that when using the `set()` method in a controller, you can pass two arguments: the first is the name of the view variable and the second is its value. Also, as we did here, we can pass an associative array, where the key is the variable name and the value is its corresponding value.

In our `details.ctp` view, the first thing we did was extend the `base.ctp` file in `app/View/Common/` using the `View::extend()` method. This informed the framework that we expect to build on the content of the view, populating the blocks it provides and contemplating the rest of our view as the content for the `content` block. Beware that there are certain block names that CakePHP handles by convention. For example, the `content` block is used to capture the view content for the layout and the content inherited through extended views. The `title`, `meta`, `css`, and `script` blocks are also used by the default layout to render the title of the page and the `<meta>`, `<link>`, and `<script>` HTML tags.

After extending the `base.ctp` view, we assigned a value to the `name` block. You'll notice that although we assigned this value from the `details.ctp` view by calling `View::assign()`, the resulting value populates in the extended view, as it extends a parent view that renders this block using `View::fetch()`.

We finally rendered some additional HTML in our view, also using the `$details` variable we set from our controller. In this case, we used the `View::get()` method instead of reading the variable directly, and thus we could define a second argument. This is used as a default value if the `$details` variable is not set. This will then allow us to handle the situation where a product exists, but it may not have any detail defined. This HTML content is then stored in the `content` block, which is rendered in the parent view via `View::fetch()`.

Extending views and using the block API is a powerful way to cut down on code in the view layer of your application, and it avoids repeating content elements unnecessarily. The ability to simply update content through blocks also allows you to easily create dynamic areas of your application, which reacts with the current being rendered. It's also good to know that there is no limit to extending views, so the complexity of your application can be assumed by the framework without issue.

Building an XML view

You may want to return your data at some point in a format other than HTML. For this, CakePHP comes with the ability to use data views. By default, the framework includes data view for XML, JSON, and RSS, but you can also build your own, handling content as required by your output format.

In this recipe, we'll use `XmlView` to generate an XML output of some records from a model.

Getting ready

We first need a table of data to work with. Create a table named `news` using the following SQL statement:

```
CREATE TABLE news (
  id INT NOT NULL AUTO_INCREMENT,
  title VARCHAR(50),
  summary TEXT,
  created DATETIME,
  PRIMARY KEY(id)
);
```

Then, run the following SQL statement to insert some news into our table:

```
INSERT INTO news (title, summary, created)
VALUES
('CakePHP on top', 'Nominated as the best framework!', NOW()),
('Facebook buys Twitter', 'Mark becomes the first zillionaire',
NOW()),
('The Larry peak', 'Founder of CakePHP admits beer helped his code',
NOW());
```

Before we start, we'll need to create a file named `NewsController.php` in `app/Controller/`, and then add the following content:

```php
<?php
App::uses('AppController', 'Controller');

class NewsController extends AppController {
}
```

How to do it...

Perform the following steps:

1. First, locate your `routes.php` file in `app/Config/`, and add the following line before any other code:

   ```
   Router::parseExtensions('xml');
   ```

2. Then, add a `$components` property and load the `RequestHandler` component in the `NewsController.php` file, as shown in the following code:

   ```
   public $components = array('RequestHandler');
   ```

3. In the same controller, add the following `latest()` method:

   ```
   public function latest() {
     $this->set(array(
       'news' => $this->News->find('all'),
       '_serialize' => 'news',
       '_rootNode' => 'latest'
     ));
   }
   ```

4. Now, navigate to `/news/latest.xml` in your browser to view the XML output, as shown in the following screenshot:

How it works...

In this recipe, we first set up our router to parse the `.xml` extension. This hooks up `XmlView` whenever a URL is called with this extension appended to it. We also added the `RequestHandler` component to `NewsController`, which is needed to handle the view.

We then created a `latest()` method on the controller to provide an action that returns the headlines. Here, we called the `find()` method on our `News` model (which we don't have actually, CakePHP created and configured an instance of `AppModel` for us), using the `all` find type to retrieve all records. We also defined a `_serialize` key with the value of `news`. This view variable determines if view variables are serialized for use with data views. The value of this variable can be a string with the name of another view variable, or an array of various view variables defined using the `set()` method in the controller.

Here, we also defined a `_rootNode` key with the value of `latest`. This is another special view variable, which allows you to specify the name of the root node used in the XML output. If this value is not specified, the framework will use `<response>` by default.

See also

▶ The *Parsing extensions* recipe from *Chapter 3, HTTP Negotiation*
▶ The *Generating a PDF* recipe

Generating a PDF

There comes a time when you'll want to create a PDF document in many applications. In this recipe, we'll look at how to output some content in a PDF document.

Getting ready

For this recipe, we'll use a plugin called `CakePdf`, which can be found at `https://github.com/ceeram/CakePdf`.

The contents of this plugin should be added to `app/Plugin/CakePdf/` and loaded by the application. To do so, add the following code to your `bootstrap.php` file located in `app/Config/`:

```
CakePlugin::load('CakePdf', array(
  'bootstrap' => true,
  'routes' => true
));
```

Then, we need a controller to generate a PDF document. Create a file named `ReportsController.php` in `app/Controller/`, and introduce the following content:

```php
<?php
App::uses('AppController', 'Controller');

class ReportsController extends AppController {
}
```

Then, we'll set up some configuration options for the plugin. The most important of all is the PDF engine we want to use, as the plugin provides a few. For this example, we'll use `dompdf`. So, we'll add the following code to `bootstrap.php`, where we previously loaded our plugin:

```php
Configure::write('CakePdf', array(
  'engine' => 'CakePdf.DomPdf',
  'download' => true // forces PDF file download
));
```

Finally, we'll also create a PDF layout file named `report.ctp` in `app/View/Layouts/pdf/`, and then create a view file named `download.ctp` in a directory named `app/View/Reports/pdf/` that we'll create.

How to do it...

Perform the following steps:

1. First, in `ReportsController`, add a `$components` property and load the `RequestHandler` component, as shown in the following code:

   ```php
   public $components = array('RequestHandler');
   ```

2. In the same controller, add a `$layout` property because we don't want to use a default one, as shown in the following code:

   ```php
   public $layout = 'report';
   ```

3. Also, in the same controller, add the following `download()` method:

   ```php
   public function download() {
     $this->pdfConfig = array(
       'filename' => 'report.pdf'
     );
     $this->set('report', array(
       array('Cake', 1337, 999),
       array('Cookie', 123, 0),
       array('Helper', 101, 69)
     ));
   }
   ```

4. Then, enter the following content into your `report.ctp` layout file in `app/View/Layouts/pdf/`:

```
<div id="pdf">
  <h1><?php echo __('Report'); ?></h1>
  <?php echo $this->fetch('content'); ?>
</div>
```

5. Finally, introduce the following code into your `download.ctp` view file in `app/View/Reports/pdf/`:

```
<table>
  <?php
  echo $this->Html->tableHeaders(array(
    __('Product'),
    __('Stock'),
    __('Sales')
  ));
  echo $this->Html->tableCells($report);
  ?>
</table>
```

6. Navigate to `/reports/download.pdf` in your browser to download the generated PDF, which will then look like the following screenshot:

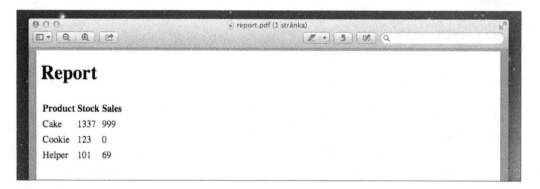

How it works...

The first thing we did in this recipe was to add the `RequestHandler` component, which is required by the `CakePdf` plugin. We then created a `download()` method to expose an action that allows a report to be downloaded. In this case, we set up some additional options for the plugin, specifically the filename of the generated content to download. There are numerous other options available, such as `pageSize`, `orientation`, and `margin`.

You can also overwrite the settings that we previously defined from our `bootstrap.php` file. The data we defined for the report was static in this example, but it could easily have been retrieved from a model, or even via an API to an external source (for example, when pulling data for the report from a third party).

We then added some HTML to our `report.ctp` layout file for the PDF. You'll notice that we used the `View::fetch()` method to load the `content` block. This contains the content from the view; in this case, the generated content from the PDF view. Our `download.ctp` view then created the HTML table for the report data. Here, the `Html` helper did the work of building the required HTML for the table rows and cells through the `tableHeaders()` and `tableCells()` methods.

For both the layout and the view, you saw that we placed these files in a `pdf/` directory. This is a convention used when dealing with extensions; in this case, `.pdf`. Additionally, remember that PDF documents expect to work with absolute URLs. You can also handle this by setting the full URL base for images and files, or you can use the `<base>` element in your HTML document.

Writing some PDF content to a file

You may want to create a PDF and save it to a file on your server. The `CakePdf` plugin can handle this with just the few following lines of code:

```
App::uses('CakePdf', 'CakePdf.Pdf');

$CakePdf = new CakePdf();
$CakePdf->template('example', 'report');
$CakePdf->write(WWW_ROOT . 'files' . DS . 'report.pdf');
```

First, we create an instance of the `CakePdf` class. The `template()` method then lets you define the view to use, followed by the optional layout. Note that the view, in this case, will be located in `app/View/Pdf/`.

If you wanted to handle the PDF output some other way, you can use the `output()` method on the `CakePdf` class to return the raw output that was generated.

See also

▸ The *Including a plugin* recipe from *Chapter 1, Lightning Introduction*
▸ The *Using blocks* recipe

Translations

Offering your content in various languages is an important step many applications face at some point in their life cycle. Fortunately for you, CakePHP comes well prepared for internationalized applications.

In this recipe, we'll look at how to handle translations in your views, showing the various functions available to deal with different scenarios, and provide a simple interface to the framework's I18n class.

Getting ready

For this recipe, we will create ArticlesController to display a list of articles. So, create a file named ArticlesController.php in app/Controller/ with the following content:

```php
<?php
App::uses('AppController', 'Controller');

class ArticlesController extends AppController {
}
```

We'll also need a table of articles, so create one with the following SQL statement:

```sql
CREATE TABLE articles (
    id INT NOT NULL AUTO_INCREMENT,
    title VARCHAR(100),
    content TEXT,
    created DATETIME,
    PRIMARY KEY(id)
);
```

Also, create some articles using the following SQL statement:

```sql
INSERT INTO articles (title, content, created)
VALUES
('Rapid application development', 'Article content ...', NOW()),
('How to upload files', 'Article content ...', NOW()),
('Creating a plugin', 'Article content ...', NOW());
```

Finally, create an index.ctp view file in app/View/Articles/.

How to do it...

Perform the following steps:

1. Create an `index()` method in your `ArticlesController.php` file with the following code:

```php
public function index() {
    $articles = $this->Article->find('all');
    $count = count($articles);
    $this->set(compact('articles', 'count'));
}
```

2. Then, open your `index.ctp` file in `app/View/Articles/`, and introduce the following content:

```php
<h2><?php echo __d('articles', 'Latest Articles'); ?></h2>
<p>
    <?php echo __dn('articles', 'There is %s article', 'There are %s articles', $count, $count); ?>
</p>
<?php echo $this->Html->nestedList(Hash::extract($articles, '{n}.Article')); ?>
```

3. Now, navigate to `/articles` in your controller to view the generated content, as shown in the following screenshot:

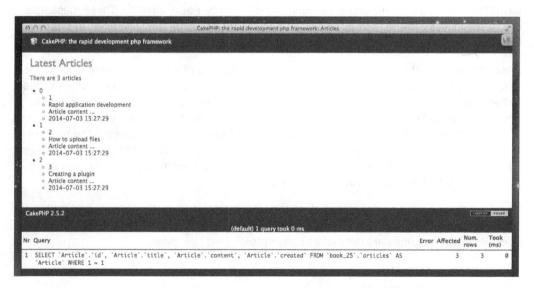

How it works

In this recipe, we set up a simple example that demonstrates the usage of the translation functions in CakePHP. We first created an `index()` method that reads the `all` records from our `articles` table through the `find()` method of the autogenerated `Article` model. We also used the `count()` function to give us the number of records returned. Also, there's a `count` find type, which we could call with `$this->Article->find('count')`; however, this would incur an additional hit to our database, which is unnecessary when we already have the results from the previous query.

We then created a view for our action, which first used the `__d()` function to print out the `Latest Articles` header. This is similar to the `__()` function you saw in other recipes, except that it allows the translated message to be defined under a domain. Here, the first argument is the domain, which in this case we called `articles`. This doesn't necessarily have to match with the controller or the model, but it should be a logical container for the message. When no domain is specified, the `default` domain is assumed. The message is then the second argument, which is the element that is translated. This is a *sprintf* formatted string, which can take additional arguments as an optional third argument.

For example, if you wanted to show a message that includes the user's name, you could run the following code:

```php
<?php echo __d('example', 'Hello, %s', 'Mark'); ?>
```

This results in **Hello, Mark** being printed to the view. All translation functions use a *sprintf* formatted string as their message, allowing any value to be easily injected. These messages are stored in files located in `app/Locale/`. See the recipe *Using the I18n shell*, in *Chapter 9, Creating Shells*, for details on how to generate translation files.

After this, we used the `__dn()` function to print the number of articles available. This is used to dynamically show a singular or plural message, based on a provided value. It works similar to the `__d()` function, except that it accepts five arguments. The first is the domain, which acts the same as before. The second and third arguments are the singular and plural versions of the message, which are displayed based upon the fourth argument, which is the number of records or items. The fifth argument is the values to use in the *sprintf* formatted messages. Finally, we made use of the `nestedList()` method of the `Html` helper to quickly render a list of our slightly reformatted array of articles.

There are three more translation functions to make a note of: `__c()`, `__dc()`, and `__dcn()`. These act similar to `__()`, `__d()`, and `__dn()`, except that they allow for a category to be specified. The categories are defined as constants of the `I18n` class.

- ▶ `I18n::LC_ALL`
- ▶ `I18n::LC_COLLATE`

- ▶ I18n::LC_CTYPE
- ▶ I18n::LC_MONETARY
- ▶ I18n::LC_NUMERIC
- ▶ I18n::LC_TIME
- ▶ I18n::LC_MESSAGES

The definition of the category to use should always be via the provided constants. For example, to call a translation for use with time, with the `Time` helper for instance, you should call one of the previous functions using `I18n::LC_TIME` as the category type.

There's more...

Models in CakePHP also allow translated validation messages. These use the `default` domain, unless a validation domain is set on the `$validationDomain` property of the model.

The translation messages set on validation rules can also use *sprintf* formatting as described for the previous translation functions. For example, if you have a rule that requires a minimum length, you can define your validation rule as follows:

```
public $validate = array(
  'title' => array(
    'size' => array(
      'rule' => array('minLength', 10),
      'message' => 'Your title must be at least %d characters long'
    )
  )
);
```

See also

- ▶ The *Using the I18n shell* recipe from *Chapter 9, Creating Shells*

View caching

Caching your views is an important step towards improving the loading time of your application as content is served faster. This can have a noticeable effect on users, as they get to content and features quicker, making them a bit happier.

In this recipe, we'll build an example scenario that shows off some of the base caching features of CakePHP.

Getting ready

First, open your `core.php` file in `app/Config/`, make sure the following line is *not* commented out, and set it to `true`:

```
Configure::write('Cache.check', true);
```

This configuration option enables and generates cached view files for requests.

Also, in your `bootstrap.php` file in `app/Config/`, make sure that `CacheDispatcher` is set in your `Dispatcher.filters` configuration. Take a look at the following example:

```
Configure::write('Dispatcher.filters', array(
  'AssetDispatcher',
  'CacheDispatcher'
));
```

We'll then need a controller to work with. So, create a `TimestampsController.php` file in `app/Controller/`, and add the following content:

```php
<?php
App::uses('AppController', 'Controller');

class TimestampsController extends AppController {

  public $components = array('Session');
}
```

We'll also need a view. So, create a file named `index.ctp` in `app/View/Timestamps/`.

How to do it...

Perform the following steps:

1. First, add the following `$helpers` property to the `TimestampsController` class:

    ```php
    public $helpers = array(
      'Session',
      'Cache'
    );
    ```

2. Then, in the same class, add the following `$cacheAction` property:

    ```php
    public $cacheAction = array(
      'index' => '+1 day'
    );
    ```

3. Now, define the following `index()` method:

    ```
    public function index() {
        $this->set('timestamp', date('Y-m-d H:i:s'));
    }
    ```

4. Also, define the following `change()` method:

    ```
    public function change($text) {
        $this->Session->write('text', $text);
        $this->redirect(array('action' => 'index'));
    }
    ```

5. Again, define the following `clear()` method:

    ```
    public function clear() {
        clearCache('timestamps');
        $this->redirect(array('action' => 'index'));
    }
    ```

6. Then, open the `index.ctp` file in `app/View/Timestamps/`, and add the following content:

    ```
    <h2>Caching example</h2>
    <p>
        Cache: <?php echo $timestamp; ?>
    </p>
    <p>
        <!--nocache-->
        <?php if ($this->Session->check('text')): ?>
            Text: <?php echo h($this->Session->read('text')); ?>
        <?php else: ?>
            <?php echo __('No text defined'); ?>
        <?php endif; ?>
        <!--/nocache-->
    </p>
    ```

How it works...

In this recipe, we set up an example that shows how the caching of views can be handled. So, let's quickly review how it works.

First, visit /timestamps in your browser. You will see something similar to the following screenshot, but with a different cache timestamp, which will be today's date and the current time of your server:

You'll notice that the view will state **No text defined**. So, now navigate to /timestamps/change/hello in your browser. It will show you the same view as before, but with the display **Text: hello**. However, you'll notice that the cache time has remained the same, as shown in the following screenshot:

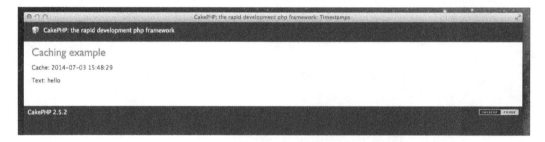

Now, if you navigate to /timestamps/clear, the same view will load again with **Text: hello** (as shown in the following screenshot), but with a newly updated cache timestamp. So what just happened?

In our `index()` method, we set the `$timestamp` view variable to the view that contains a formatted date and time, using the `date()` function. The `Y-m-d H:i:s` string provided uses the formatting options available for that function. Then, in the `change()` method, we first define a `$text` argument in the method's signature to receive a value. We use the `Session` component to store this value in the session associated with the `text` key. We then proceed to redirect the action back to `index()`. Finally, our `clear()` method contains a call to the `clearCache()` function, with the name of the controller to clear. This global function allows you to clear the view cache any time. If no argument is provided, the entire cache will be cleared.

In our view for the `index()` action, we first print the `$timestamp` variable to the view, which was previously set in our controller method. We have an `if` condition, which calls the `check()` method of the `Session` component to determine if the `text` key has been set. If it has been, it prints it out to the view; if not set, it simply prints **No text defined**.

So why is it that the timestamp does not update when we change the value of `text`? This is because in our `index.ctp` view file, we used the `<--nocache-->` and `<--/nocache-->` tags to define an area of our view that is not cached. The rest is being cached due to the settings we provided in the `$cacheAction` property of our controller. This array accepts the keys as the action names (methods), the value as a numeric value that represents the number of minutes, a string value that is compatible with `strtotime()`, an array that has a duration key for the previously mentioned values, and an additional `callbacks` key that defines if components and models should be set up on the controller to call the component's `initialize()` and `startup()` callback methods and the controller's `beforeFilter()` callback method. Bear in mind that setting `callbacks` to `true` (the default is `false`) means the caching of the view is less effective.

In this example, if `/timestamps/clear` was not called, the view for the `index()` action would be cached for 24 hours, as defined by the `+1 day` value of the `$cacheAction` setting.

See also

▸ More detail on caching in the framework can be found at `http://book.cakephp.org/2.0/en/core-libraries/caching.html`

The AssetCompress plugin

The handling of static assets, such as scripts and stylesheets, is an important aspect of applications that are expected to perform and deliver content quickly.

In this recipe, we'll look at how to include and set up the AssetCompress plugin to make sure we're serving content quickly and efficiently, without putting a burden on the server when the users are coming.

Getting ready

The `AssetCompress` plugin can be found at `https://github.com/markstory/asset_compress`.

The content of this plugin needs to be added in `app/Plugin/AssetCompress/` and then loaded in your application. To do so, add the following code in your `bootstrap.php` file located in `app/Config/`:

```
CakePlugin::load('AssetCompress', array('bootstrap' => true));
```

This should be added before the section of the file that calls the following:

```
Configure::write('Dispatcher.filters', array(
  'AssetDispatcher',
  'CacheDispatcher'
));
```

Now, create an `app.js` file in `app/webroot/js/`, and create an `app.css` file in `app/webroot/css/`. Also, create a cache directory in `app/webroot/`, and create the `js/` and `css/` directories in this directory. Make sure that all three directories are writable by your web server.

How to do it...

Perform the following steps:

1. First, create the folders `app/webroot/cache/css` and `app/webroot/cache/js`, and then add the following code to your `asset_compress.ini` file in `app/Config/`:

    ```
    [General]
    cacheConfig = false

    [js]
    cachePath = WEBROOT/cache/js/

    [all.js]
    files[] = app.js

    [css]
    cachePath = WEBROOT/cache/css/

    [all.css]
    files[] = app.css
    ```

2. Then, locate the `AppController.php` file in `app/Controller/`, and add the following code to the class:

```
public $helpers = array('AssetCompress.AssetCompress');
```

3. Now, edit your `default.ctp` layout file in `app/View/Layouts/`, and replace the line with the `$this->fetch('css')` echo, using the following content:

```
echo $this->AssetCompress->css('all.css', array(
  'raw' => (bool)Configure::read('debug')
));
echo $this->AssetCompress->includeCss();
```

4. Also, remove the line with the `$this->fetch('script')` echo, and add the following content before the `</body>` tag:

```
<?php
echo $this->AssetCompress->script('all.js', array(
  'raw' => (bool)Configure::read('debug')
));
echo $this->AssetCompress->includeJs();
echo $this->Js->writeBuffer();
?>
```

5. Finally, go to your console and execute the following commands:

```
$ Console/cake AssetCompress.AssetCompress clear
$ Console/cake AssetCompress.AssetCompress build --force
```

How it works...

In this recipe, we set up the AssetCompress plugin with an `asset_compress.ini` file, which outlines the configuration settings for the plugin. In this file, we first defined a `[general]` section. The `cacheConfig` option here states that we don't yet want to use our caching configuration to store our asset settings. If you use APC, Xcache, Memcached, or any other caching engine, you may want to take advantage of this feature to speed up access to the plugin settings. The next section, `[js]`, defined the `cachePath` option that configures the path where the compressed assets will be stored. After this, we defined an `[all.js]` file that holds the files defined in the `files[]` array. In this case, we currently only have `app.js`, but more scripts can be added here to compress them together. We then repeated the same for `[css]` and `[all.css]` for our stylesheets.

After setting up our .ini file, we included the AssetCompress helper in our AppController so that it's available across our whole application. We then used the helper in the default. ctp layout file to load our assets instead of including the files manually or via the css and script view blocks. The includeCss() and includeJs() methods of the helper handle the loading of the assets. In this case, we defined each of the files to load using the css() and script() methods, and we also set the raw setting with the Boolean value of our debug configuration. This is a useful check that forces the assets to be loaded separately when in debug mode (that is, during development) so that you can work against live CSS and JavaScript files as you update them. You'll also notice that we called the writeBuffer() method of the Js helper in case any script was previously buffered in the view.

We then proceeded to use the shell script included with the plugin to clear any previously compressed files using the clear command, the build command, and the --force option. This requests that the script run and generate the compressed files regardless of whether they have been changed. After running these commands, you will see the app/webroot/ cache/css/all.css and app/webroot/cache/js/all.js files. When debug is set to 0, you will see that your application loads these files instead of the raw files in your css/ and js/ directories.

See also

> ▶ The *Including a plugin* recipe from *Chapter 1, Lightning Introduction*

11
Unit Tests

In this chapter, we will cover the following topics:

- ▶ Dependency Injection
- ▶ Creating a fixture
- ▶ Mock objects
- ▶ Stub method configuration
- ▶ Model unit testing

Introduction

An application can become complex over time, and it can become difficult to introduce changes without affecting other areas of your code base. The concept of unit testing helps reduce this burden by allowing you to define tests that check and confirm the integrity of your application at any time.

In this chapter, we'll look at how CakePHP leverages the PHPUnit library to provide a solid base for unit testing, including handling dependencies, fixtures, and using the bake shell for testing.

Dependency Injection

The testing of tightly coupled objects is hard. You may end up testing code from other objects, and you'll also need to configure them to allow any testing at all. Tightly coupled objects are those that know too much information about each other, for example, their internals, or they know how to instantiate each other. In an object-oriented paradigm, this should be avoided, and all objects should only care about themselves. This follows the *single responsibility* principle, which says one class should have only one responsibility, and the related code should be encapsulated by the class.

Through the technique of injecting dependencies, objects can be provided with their dependencies by various means:

- ▶ **Constructor**: This passes the dependent object as a parameter to the constructor
- ▶ **Method** (setDependencyName(), for example): This passes the dependent object as a parameter and sets a protected or private property with the object, to be used later in other methods
- ▶ **Field**: This manipulates a public field to set the dependent object

In this recipe, we'll look at how dependency injection is handled in CakePHP and what you need to get it under control.

Getting ready

Let's first create a new database table named `tasks` using the following SQL code:

```sql
CREATE TABLE tasks (
    id INT NOT NULL AUTO_INCREMENT,
    name VARCHAR(255) NOT NULL,
    description TEXT NOT NULL,
    created DATETIME NOT NULL,
    modified DATETIME NOT NULL,
    priority TINYINT(4) NOT NULL DEFAULT '1',
    PRIMARY KEY (id)
);
```

We'll also create a `Task` model in a file named `app/Model/Task.php`, which sends an e-mail to the administrator upon every new task being created, using the `afterSave()` callback. This callback is executed by the framework every time the model is saved if it is present in the model class.

```php
<?php
App::uses('AppModel', 'Model');
App::uses('CakeEmail', 'Network/Email');

class Task extends AppModel {

  public function afterSave($created, $options = array()) {
    parent::afterSave($created, $options);
    if ($created) {
      $adminEmail = Configure::read('App.adminEmail');
      $replyEmail = Configure::read('App.replyEmail');
      $Email = new CakeEmail();
```

```
        $Email->from($replyEmail)
          ->to($adminEmail)
          ->subject(__('New Task created'))
          ->send(__('A new task was created'));
    }
  }
}
```

Note that there are two things wrong with this code:

► The code is tightly coupled with the `CakeEmail` class, because the `Task` model knows how to instantiate a new `CakeEmail` object. The model should not know this much about another object.

► The e-mail is being sent at runtime. This should be refactored to send e-mails through an e-mail queue, as users don't like to wait while we perform slow operations. We covered using a job queue in the *Event Stacking* recipe from *Chapter 8, Events System*.

So, we'll refactor the `afterSave()` method in our `Task` model to allow for dependency injection later on.

How to do it...

Perform the following steps:

1. First, add a protected `$_email` property, as shown in the following code, into the `Task` model class in `app/Model/Task.php`:

   ```
   protected $_email = null;
   ```

2. We'll also add the `getEmail()` and `setEmail()` methods:

   ```
   public function getEmail() {
     return $this->_email;
   }

   public function setEmail(CakeEmail $email) {
     $this->_email = $email;
   }
   ```

3. Now, we'll update the `afterSave()` callback method, as shown in the following code, to use the new `getEmail()` method instead of directly calling the constructor:

   ```
   public function afterSave($created, $options = array()) {
     parent::afterSave($created, $options);
     if ($created) {
       $adminEmail = Configure::read('App.adminEmail');
   ```

```
$replyEmail = Configure::read('App.replyEmail');
$Email = $this->getEmail(); // notice the new call here
$Email->from($replyEmail)
  ->to($adminEmail)
  ->subject(__('New Task created'))
  ->send(__('A new task was created'));
    }
}
```

How it works...

We first added a protected `$_email` property to our `Task` model class. The dependent `CakeEmail` object will be stored here to be used later on. We'll manage this protected property with a setter and getter method in the model class. For this, we then created two additional methods to set and retrieve the dependency. You'll notice here that we added a type hint in the signature of the `setEmail()` method. This is important, as it ensures that any dependency passed to the method is an instance of the `CakeEmail` class, thus allowing us to make assumptions about the functionality available on that object.

When testing this object, you would now call the `setEmail(CakeEmail $email)` method to pass an instance that is used for testing. The `Task` model is no longer aware of the `CakeEmail` object's instantiation logic, so we'll be able to create and configure the instance from outside the model or use a stub (we'll talk about stubs in a later recipe in this chapter). This would typically be an e-mail object that logs the message or sends it to an internal e-mail address.

See also

▸ The *Stub method configuration* recipe

Creating a fixture

When you're testing your code, it's important to have a static and defined state before you start every test to ensure that every test is isolated and does not impact further testing logic upon execution. Fixtures help you configure the database state before every unit test is executed. These are simply files that describe database tables and contents, and they are located by convention in `app/Test/Fixture/`.

CakePHP provides both a fixture generation tool using the `bake` console shell as well as a test database configuration (the test database is used automatically when you run your tests). This way, you can keep your real data and test data in two different databases to avoid any unwanted interactions.

In this recipe, we'll build a fixture using the `bake` shell for a given model.

Getting ready

We'll first need a table of data to work with. So, create a table named `blogs`, using the following SQL statement:

```sql
CREATE TABLE blogs (
    id INT NOT NULL AUTO_INCREMENT,
    title VARCHAR(255) NOT NULL,
    content TEXT,
    created DATETIME,
    modified DATETIME,
    PRIMARY KEY(id)
);
```

We'll also create a `Blog.php` file in `app/Model/`, with the following content:

```php
<?php
App::uses('AppModel', 'Model');

class Blog extends AppModel {
}
```

How to do it...

Perform the following steps:

1. First, bake a new fixture for the `Blog` model using the CakePHP console and the `bake` interactive shell. Using the `-t default` option will select the default template, in case we have multiple bake templates installed. Also note that Windows users will use `cake.bat` instead from the command prompt.

   ```
   $ Console/cake bake fixture -t default


   Welcome to CakePHP v2.5.2 Console
   ---------------------------------------------------------------
   App : app
   Path: /home/user/app/
   ---------------------------------------------------------------
   ---------------------------------------------------------------
   Bake Fixture
   Path: /home/user/app/Test/Fixture/
   ---------------------------------------------------------------
   ```

```
Possible Models based on your current database:
1. Blog
Enter a number from the list above,
type in the name of another model, or 'q' to exit
[q] >
```

2. Then, select the `Blog` model from the list of all available models in your application.

```
[q] > 1
Would you like to import schema for this fixture? (y/n)
[n] >
```

3. Answer no (n) to inspect the database and generate a static schema array, based on the `blogs` table. If the `blogs` table changes, we'll need to update this file to reflect those changes in the schema.

```
[n] > n
Would you like to use record importing for this fixture? (y/n)
[n] >
```

4. Also answer no (n) because we don't want to retrieve real data from the `blogs` table every time we run our tests, as we want static data that we can configure in this file to keep our database state consistent with our unit tests.

```
[n] > n
Would you like to build this fixture with data from Blog's table?
(y/n)
[n] >
```

5. Again, answer no (n) because we don't want data examples retrieved from the current data in the `blogs` table, as we're going to define the records manually for this fixture.

```
[n] > n


Baking test fixture for Blog...


Creating file /home/user/app/Test/Fixture/BlogFixture.php
Wrote '/home/user/app/Test/Fixture/BlogFixture.php'
$
```

6. Now, open the newly generated file in `app/Test/Fixture/BlogFixture.php`. You should see the following:

```
<?php
/**
```

```
 * BlogFixture
 *
 */
class BlogFixture extends CakeTestFixture {

/**
 * Fields
 *
 * @var array
 */
 public $fields = array(
    'id' => array('type' => 'integer', 'null' => false, 'default'
=> null, 'unsigned' => false, 'key' => 'primary'),
    'title' => array('type' => 'string', 'null' => false,
'default' => null, 'collate' => 'utf8_general_ci', 'charset' =>
'utf8'),
    'content' => array('type' => 'text', 'null' => false,
'default' => null, 'collate' => 'utf8_general_ci', 'charset' =>
'utf8'),
    'created' => array('type' => 'datetime', 'null' => false,
'default' => null),
    'modified' => array('type' => 'datetime', 'null' => false,
'default' => null),
    'indexes' => array(
      'PRIMARY' => array('column' => 'id', 'unique' => 1)
    ),
    'tableParameters' => array('charset' => 'utf8', 'collate' =>
'utf8_general_ci', 'engine' => 'InnoDB')
  );

/**
 * Records
 *
 * @var array
 */
 public $records = array(
    array(
      'id' => 1,
      'title' => 'Lorem ipsum dolor sit amet',
      'content' => 'Lorem ipsum dolor ...',
      'created' => '2014-05-20 12:06:40',
      'modified' => '2014-05-20 12:06:40'
    ),
    // there are 9 more generated records
  );
}
```

7. Finally, edit the `$records` property and set the array data that you want in the `blogs` table when you run your tests. For example, we'll create two records.

```
public $records = array(
  array(
    'id' => 1,
    'title' => 'Title of the first Blog',
    'content' => 'Contents for the first Blog',
    'created' => '2014-05-24 12:06:40',
    'modified' => '2014-05-24 12:06:40'
  ),
  array(
    'id' => 2,
    'title' => 'Title of the second Blog',
    'content' => 'Contents for the second Blog',
    'created' => '2014-05-24 12:06:40',
    'modified' => '2014-05-24 12:06:40'
  )
);
```

How it works...

In this recipe, we're using fixture data, instead of real data, when running our tests. You can tweak the fixture data to allow edge cases to be present in your database, model real-world data, check for valid contents, and so on.

Once we had our model and table in place, we started using the `bake` shell to generate the new fixture class. The `bake` shell has an interactive mode for fixture generation, and we're using it in this case to customize the way our fixture is being generated. In the interactive mode, `bake` will ask some questions along the way.

The `bake` shell can use several templates to generate the fixture files. Based on our currently installed plugins, there could be others apart from the default template, so we're using `-t default` to choose the default template.

The first question we need to answer is the model we want to use for fixture generation, `1. Blog`, in this case. Then, we were asked if we want to import schema for this fixture, and we answered no because we want to have the table schema written into our fixture file. The table schema is written into the `$fields` property array in the fixture, and it represents the structure of our table in the database in an array format. This array describes the columns and types present in our table.

If we had answered yes to this question, instead of having the table schema written to the fixture file every time we use this fixture, CakePHP would read the `blogs` table again and use the updated schema. If we want to keep our schema under control, it's better to say no and write it to the fixture file.

The next question is related to `record importing`. In this case, we've answered no because we don't want to use live data in our tests; we want to write the contents of the `blogs` table in the fixture file and be able to manipulate this file to configure the data. If we answered yes, when using this fixture, CakePHP would connect to the `blogs` table in the live database and retrieve those records.

The last question was whether we need to build this fixture with data from the `blogs` table. To this, we've answered no, because we don't want to copy rows from our live table. If we had answered yes, we'd be able to filter using a `WHERE` condition and retrieve real rows from our live table; then, that data would be copied into the fixture, so we'd be able to use those rows or modify them. Real data will not be used in any case; this is just a quick way to get some real data into our fixtures, so we don't need to write those record arrays with the table contents from scratch.

After we create our `Fixture` file, CakePHP will refresh the records in our `blogs` table (in the test database) *before* every test run, so the database state is fixed and consistent for every unit test. The `bake` console shell allows us to generate the fixture's main structure for all our fixtures, so we can then manually tweak the contents to allow specific data to be present.

Mock objects

Once you've used dependency injection to ensure you're only testing the code contained in your target object and don't test (again) the code from external dependencies, you can create and configure mock objects to replace a real object with a test double.

Test doubles are objects that behave exactly the same as other objects, but allow you to configure their methods to return any desired value (or simply return null), so you don't need to worry about their internal logic. You only need to define by `contract` the public interface of the `double` test object, the input method parameters, and their expected output results. You could even configure the behavior of the mock object to allow methods to call the original logic, while the rest of the methods return `null` by default.

Getting ready

For this recipe we'll first need to create a `Blog` model in a file named `app/Model/Blog.php`, with the following content:

```php
<?php
App::uses('AppModel', 'Model');

class Blog extends AppModel {
}
```

We'll also need to create an empty test file in `app/Test/Case/Model/AnotherTest.php`. This test file will use the `Blog` model class as a dependency, and we'll refactor this code to use a mock object instead of the real `Blog` model.

```php
<?php
App::uses('Blog', 'Model');

class AnotherTest extends CakeTestCase {

  public function testDummy() {
    App::uses('Blog', 'Model');
    // using the real Blog model now
    $Blog = ClassRegistry::init('Blog');
    // we use $Blog object as a dependency for other objects in this
test
    // $this->Another->setBlog($Blog);
    // run some test code in $this->Another object
  }
}
```

How to do it...

Perform the following step:

1. First, use the `getMockBuilder()` method to create a mock object. Replace the implementation of the `testDummy()` method in `app/Test/Case/Model/AnotherTest.php` file with the following code:

```php
public function testDummy() {
  App::uses('Blog', 'Model');
  // using the mock object now
  $Blog = $this->getMockBuilder('Blog')
    ->disableOriginalConstructor()
    ->setMethods(array('save', 'find'))
    ->setMockClassName('Blog')
    ->setConstructorArgs(array())
    ->getMock();
  // we use $Blog object as a dependency for other objects in this
test
  // $this->Another->setBlog($Blog);
  // run some test code in $this->Another object
}
```

Note that we further customized the way the mock object is created, using the following code:

```
// modify the class name of the new Mock Object
->setMockClassName($name)
// pass params to the constructor
->setConstructorArgs(array())
```

How it works...

We changed our unit test code to generate an instance of a mock object. Here, the mock object will behave as a test double of the `Blog` model. All of the methods in the `Blog` model will be available in the mock object instance.

The `getMockBuilder('Blog')` method is part of the PHPUnit framework itself, and it will inspect the `Blog` model class definition and create a fake object (extending `Blog`) to mimic all of the `Blog` methods. We're using the `MockBuilder` fluent interface to disable the call to the original constructor, because we don't really need to call the original `Blog` model's constructor, as we're going to use this model as a mock object.

We also called the `setMethods(array('save', 'find'))` method to configure our mock object and return `null` by default, if the `save()` or `find()` method is called. These two methods are referred to as *stub methods*.

If we were to call any other method in the `$Blog` object, we'd use their "real" logic, as the call will be passed to the real `Blog` model object. Only the `save()` and `find()` methods are faked and, therefore, will return `null` by default on every call. We can configure them to return anything we need in our tests. We'll delve into stub method configuration in the next recipe of this chapter.

Now, we can use the newly created "fake" instance of `$Blog` to inject this object into our real test target and ignore the original `Blog` model logic.

See also

▶ More details about test doubles can be found at `http://en.wikipedia.org/wiki/Test_double`

▶ The *Dependency injection* recipe

▶ The *Stub method configuration* recipe

Stub method configuration

Mock objects have the ability to customize the return values for specific methods. Instead of returning `null` by default, you can configure the mock object methods to return a specific value, something that you'll find useful in your unit tests to check for specific edge cases when calling other objects (dependencies).

These also have the ability to define expectations on the methods called, to check if the right methods were called with the expected parameters or if they were called in the right order, and so on. This way, we don't need to actually test an external dependent class, but we can define a `contract` between the tested object and the dependencies.

Mock object methods can be configured to act as stub methods:

Stub methods will return `null` by default, but you can configure the return value using the `will()` method. They are defined in the `setMethods()` array, or you don't call `setMethods()` or call it using `array()`.

Getting ready

In this recipe, we'll be using the previously defined `Blog` model in `app/Model/Blog.php`:

```php
<?php
App::uses('AppModel', 'Model');

class Blog extends AppModel {
}
```

We'll also use the following test file in `app/Test/Case/Model/AnotherTest.php` (this test file will use the `Blog` model class as a dependency):

```php
<?php
App::uses('Blog', 'Model');

class AnotherTest extends CakeTestCase {

  public function testDummy() {
    App::uses('Blog', 'Model');
    $Blog = $this->getMockBuilder('Blog')
      ->disableOriginalConstructor()
      ->setMethods(array('save', 'find'))
      ->getMock();
```

```
    // we use $Blog object as a dependency for other objects in
this test
    // $this->Another->setBlog($Blog);
    // run some test code in $this->Another object
  }
}
```

How to do it...

Perform the following steps:

1. First, configure the expectation for a stub method by calling `expects()` on the `Blog` model:

   ```
   $Blog->expects($this->once());
   ```

2. Extend that configuration by calling `method()` to set the method name:

   ```
   $Blog->expects($this->once())
     ->method('save');
   ```

3. Then, also configure the parameter's expectation by calling `with()`, as shown in the following code:

   ```
   $Blog->expects($this->once())
     ->method('save')
     ->with($this->equalTo(array(
       'Blog' => array(
         'title' => 'My Blog Title',
         'content' => 'Blog contents here...'
       )
   )));
   ```

4. Finally, we'll also define a return value:

   ```
   $Blog->expects($this->once()) // we expect to be called once
     ->method('save')
     ->with($this->equalTo(array(
       'Blog' => array(
         'title' => 'My Blog Title',
         'content' => 'Blog contents here...'
       )
   )))
     ->will($this->returnValue(array(
       'Blog' => array(
         'id' => 1,
   ```

```
            'title' => 'My Blog Title',
            'content' => 'Blog contents here...',
            'created' => '2015-01-01 10:00:00',
            'modified' => '2015-01-01 10:00:00',
        )
    )));
```

How it works...

Once the stub methods are configured and the test is executed, our `$Blog` mock object will call the original `Blog` model logic for all methods except `find()` and `save()`.

The first step was to configure the expectation of the number of calls to be made to this method. If, during the unit test, we didn't call this method once, we would detect this as an issue and mark the test as failed. We're using the `$this->once()` matcher function to detect if this method is called once. Depending on our test, we could use any other matcher function provided by the PHPUnit framework, such as `any()`, `at()`, `atLeastOnce()`, `never()`, or `once()`.

We then set the method name we're using for this expectation, in this case, `save`. Calls to the `save()` method on the `$Blog` mock object will instead return `null` by default, using this mock configuration.

After that, we set the parameter expectations for this method call to detect if the calls to the `save()` method are using the correct parameters. We're using `with($this->equalsTo(array( ... )))` to define this, specifying that it should pass one parameter, and that the parameter must be an array with the given values. There are many constraints available to define our expectations, for example, `anything()`, `equalTo()`, or `isTrue()`. If we were to call this method in our tested code and we didn't use exactly the same array as defined for the parameter, the test will be marked as failed, and we'll get a nice error message saying that the parameter expected was not used for the `$Blog->save()` method call.

The last option we defined was the desired return value we want to get from the method call, if the rest of the expectations are valid. The expectations are that the method is called once, the method's name is `save`, and only one parameter should be passed, which is expected to be an array, with a value equal to the following:

```
array(
  'Blog' => array(
    'title' => 'My Blog Title',
    'content' => 'Blog contents here...'
  )
)
```

Any calls to the `find()` method will return `null`, as this method's stub was not configured. If no calls are made to the `save()` method, an assertion error will be raised, as we're expecting this method to be called exactly once. If called using the expected parameters, the "fake" `Blog` array result will be returned, allowing us to mimic the `save` method even without saving anything to our test database!

See also

- More info on the matcher functions available in PHPUnit can be found at `http://phpunit.de/manual/3.7/en/test-doubles.html#test-doubles.` `mock objects.tables.matchers`
- The *Dependency injection* recipe
- The *Mock objects* recipe

Model unit testing

You might have already heard that using "fat models, skinny controllers" is a best practice. One of the main benefits of keeping all your business logic inside your model layer is the ability to develop simpler unit tests for your application. Model classes usually depend only on other models, behaviors, or utility classes (libs), allowing you to quickly start coding your unit tests without a ton of mock object configurations.

CakePHP integrates with PHPUnit and provides several tools to help you build your unit tests:

- Base classes
- CakeTestCase
- ControllerTestCase or you can use PHPUnit_Framework_TestCase
- Fixture integration
- Test datasource configuration
- Bake shell to build test files and fixtures

In this recipe, we'll go over most of these, and build a unit test for a CakePHP model.

Getting ready

First, we'll reuse the table named `tasks` from this chapter or create a new one using the following SQL statement:

```
CREATE TABLE tasks (
  id INT NOT NULL AUTO_INCREMENT,
```

```
    name VARCHAR(255) NOT NULL,
    description TEXT NOT NULL,
    created DATETIME NOT NULL,
    modified DATETIME NOT NULL,
    priority TINYINT(4) NOT NULL DEFAULT '0',
    PRIMARY KEY (id)
);
```

We'll also create a `Task` model in a file named `app/Model/Task.php`; this model sends an e-mail to the administrator upon every new high-priority task created using the `afterSave()` callback. This callback is executed by the framework every time the model is saved, if it is present in the model class, and is shown in the following code:

```php
<?php
App::uses('AppModel', 'Model');
App::uses('CakeEmail', 'Network/Email');

class Task extends AppModel {

  protected $_email = null;

  const PRIORITY_LOW = 0;

  const PRIORITY_HIGH = 1;

  public function getEmail() {
    return $this->_email;
  }

  public function setEmail(CakeEmail $email) {
    $this->_email = $email;
  }

  public function afterSave($created, $options = array()) {
    parent::afterSave($created, $options);
    if ($created) {
      $priority = (int)Hash::get($this->data, "{$this->alias}.
priority");
      if ($priority === self::PRIORITY_HIGH) {
        $this->_sendEmail();
      }
    }
  }
```

```php
  protected function _sendEmail() {
    $adminEmail = Configure::read('App.adminEmail');
    $replyEmail = Configure::read('App.replyEmail');
    $Email = $this->getEmail();
    $Email->from($replyEmail)
      ->to($adminEmail)
      ->subject(__('New Task created'))
      ->send(__('A new task was created'));
  }
}
```

Also, add the following configuration to your `bootstrap.php` file located in `app/Config/`:

```php
Configure::write('App.adminEmail', 'user@localhost.com');
Configure::write('App.replyEmail', 'user@localhost.com');
```

Note that CakePHP requires PHPUnit 3.7+ installed on your system. Follow the setup instructions for PHPUnit at `http://phpunit.de/manual/3.7/en/installation.html`.

How to do it...

Perform the following steps:

1. First, add the following new test case file named `TaskTest.php` in `app/Test/Case/Model/`:

```php
<?php
App::uses('Task', 'Model');

class TaskTest extends CakeTestCase {

  public function setUp() {
    parent::setUp();
    $this->Task = ClassRegistry::init('Task');
  }

  public function tearDown() {
    unset($this->Task);
    parent::tearDown();
  }

  /**
   * testAfterSaveShouldSendEmailForNewPriorityHighTask
   *
```

```
 * @covers Task::afterSave
 */
  public function
testAfterSaveShouldSendEmailForNewPriorityHighTask() {
    $this->Task = $this->getMockForModel('Task', array('_
sendEmail'));
    $this->Task->expects($this->once())
      ->method('_sendEmail')
      ->will($this->returnValue(true));
    $data = array(
      'Task' => array(
        'name' => 'priority task',
        'description' => 'description1',
        'priority' => Task::PRIORITY_HIGH,
      )
    );
    $this->Task->set($data);
    $this->Task->afterSave(true);
  }

/**
 * testAfterSaveShouldNotSendEmailForNewPriorityLowTask
 *
 * @covers Task::afterSave
 */
  public function
testAfterSaveShouldNotSendEmailForNewPriorityLowTask() {
    $this->Task = $this->getMockForModel('Task', array('_
sendEmail'));
    $this->Task->expects($this->never())
      ->method('_sendEmail');
    $data = array(
      'Task' => array(
        'name' => 'low priority task',
        'description' => 'description1',
        'priority' => Task::PRIORITY_LOW,
      )
    );
    $this->Task->set($data);
    $this->Task->afterSave(true);
  }
}
```

2. Then, run your test using the CakePHP console test runner with the following command:

```
$ Console/cake test app Model/Task --testdox

Welcome to CakePHP v2.5.2 Console
---------------------------------------------------------------
App : myapp
Path: /home/user/myapp/
---------------------------------------------------------------
CakePHP Test Shell
---------------------------------------------------------------
Task
   [x] After save should send email for new priority high task
   [x] After save should not send email for new priority low task
```

How it works...

In this recipe, we built a unit test for our `Task` model. The unit test class is placed in the file named `TaskTest.php` (by convention) in `app/Test/Case/Model/` and extends the `CakeTestCase` base class. This is the default base class used for unit testing all CakePHP classes except for controllers, as the framework provides a special `ControllerTestCase` class with specific features to make controller testing easier.

Our test class has a `setUp()` method, where we create a new instance of the `Task` model. It also has a `tearDown()` method, where all of our cleanup code will be placed, to ensure that there are no leftovers when the test finishes.

The `setUp()` method will be executed for all our test methods in this class before each test, and then, it will be followed by the `tearDown()` method. This will provide a clean environment for all of our test methods, without allowing for any undesired interactions between each test.

In the first test method named `testAfterSaveShouldSendEmailForNewPriorityHighTask()`, we check whether we're sending an e-mail only when a high priority task is created. To do so, we first generate a mock of our `Task` model and set the `_sendEmail()` method as a stub method:

```
$this->Task = $this->getMockForModel('Task', array('_sendEmail'));
```

Stub methods will allow us to configure expectations and hardcode output in our tests. In our test, we focus on covering the `afterSave()` model logic, so we don't really need to test the protected `_sendEmail()` method in this case.

The following code then defines an expectation for the `_sendEmail()` stub method:

```
$this->Task->expects($this->once())
  ->method('_sendEmail')
  ->will($this->returnValue(true));
```

We expect to call this method exactly once, and we'll force it to return `true` when called.

We then prepare the model data prior to executing the `afterSave()` callback. We don't really care to save the data to the database in our test, so we set the data to the model to simulate that it's being saved with the following code:

```
$data = array(
  'Task' => array(
    'name' => 'priority task',
    'description' => 'description1',
    'priority' => Task::PRIORITY_HIGH,
  )
);
$this->Task->set($data);
```

We finally run the method to be tested using the following code:

```
$this->Task->afterSave(true);
```

In this test, the only and most important assertion is the expectation of the `_sendEmail()` method only being called once. We also added a second test to ensure that we don't send an e-mail when the priority of the task is set to `Task::PRIORITY_LOW`.

We used the CakePHP console to run our tests, and using the `--testdox` output, we can retrieve a checklist of the passing tests. The reason for using those long names in the test methods is to get a human readable checklist of the expected behavior for our tests. It's good practice to always keep your tests short and focused, and cover specific edge cases with different tests. Using long names can help you quickly identify the expected behavior and why it's not working, for any test case you write.

It is also possible to run unit tests and examine their results in browser—navigate to `/test.php?case=Model/Task`, and you'll get following output:

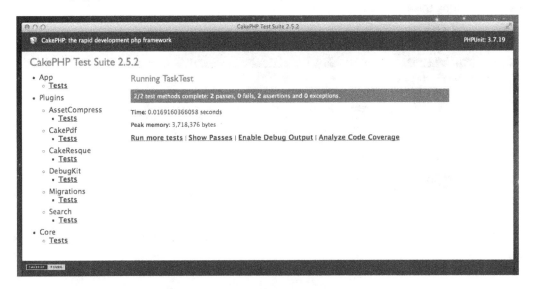

Now, click on **Show Passes**, and you'll get a list of all the passed tests:

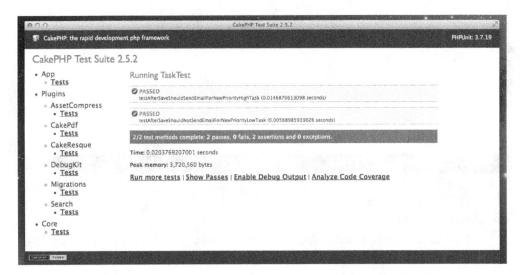

If you have xdebug installed and configured, you might even display the code coverage of your unit tests in the browser. Click on **Analyze Code Coverage**, and you'll see which lines were executed during this unit test:

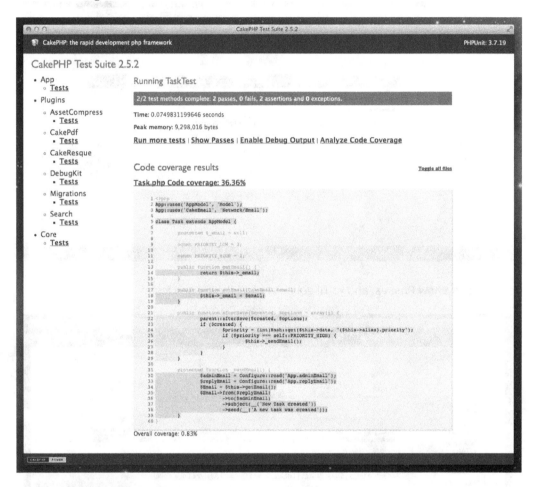

See also

▸ More details about test doubles can be found at http://en.wikipedia.org/wiki/Test_double

▸ The *Stub method configuration* recipe

12
Migrations

In this chapter, we will cover the following topics:

- ▶ Schema handling
- ▶ Syncing changes
- ▶ The Migrations plugin
- ▶ Injecting data

Introduction

Working with the database that powers your application can become a task in itself. Luckily, CakePHP provides a set of tools to easily handle your database schema and migrations.

In this chapter, we'll look at how simple it is to build and maintain your database while keeping your schema changes up to date with your code base.

Note that even if you use the schema and migrations plugin tool, *you should take regular and automated backups of your live databases* and store the backups on another host to avoid any loss in case of a server crash. The tools described in this chapter will help you save the changes you perform on your database schema, but you'll need to provide additional backup and recovery procedures, just in case of any issues.

Schema handling

CakePHP is packed with a console shell for schema management, which gives you the ability to keep your database structure defined in a schema file in your version control system. This schema file keeps track of the changes made to your database and applies schema changes without touching your current data.

A schema file is a regular PHP file, located by convention in `app/Config/Schema/schema.php`. This file describes your database tables using properties as one property per table. Each property holds an array with all the columns in your table, their type, and other metadata required to fully describe the table.

Getting ready

You'll need to create at least one table in your database and its associated model. The `shell` schema processes models defined in your application, not the actual tables in your database.

So, create a `profiles` table in your database, using the following SQL statement:

```
CREATE TABLE profiles (
    id INT NOT NULL AUTO_INCREMENT,
    title VARCHAR(100) NOT NULL,
    content TEXT,
    created DATETIME,
    modified DATETIME,
    PRIMARY KEY(id)
);
```

Then, we'll also create the `app/Model/Profile.php` file, with the following content:

```php
<?php
App::uses('AppModel', 'Model');

class Profile extends AppModel {
}
```

How to do it...

Perform the following steps:

1. Use the CakePHP console schema shell to generate a schema of your application model as follows:

   ```
   $ Console/cake schema generate

   Welcome to CakePHP v2.5.2 Console
   ```

```
-----------------------------------------------------------
App : myapp
Path: /home/user/myapp/
-----------------------------------------------------------
Cake Schema Shell
-----------------------------------------------------------
Generating Schema...
Schema file: schema.php generated
```

2. Inspect the newly generated schema:

```
$ Console/cake schema view
Welcome to CakePHP v2.5.2 Console
-----------------------------------------------------------
App : skelapp
Path: /home/user/html/skelapp/
-----------------------------------------------------------
Cake Schema Shell
-----------------------------------------------------------
<?php
class SkelappSchema extends CakeSchema {

  public function before($event = array()) {
    return true;
  }

  public function after($event = array()) {
  }

  public $profiles = array(
    'id' => array('type' => 'integer', 'null' => false, 'default'
=> null, 'unsigned' => false, 'key' => 'primary'),
    'title' => array('type' => 'string', 'null' => false,
'default' => null, 'collate' => 'utf8_general_ci', 'charset' =>
'utf8'),
    'content' => array('type' => 'text', 'null' => false,
'default' => null, 'collate' => 'utf8_general_ci', 'charset' =>
'utf8'),
```

```
    'created' => array('type' => 'datetime', 'null' => false,
'default' => null),
    'modified' => array('type' => 'datetime', 'null' => false,
'default' => null),
    'indexes' => array(
      'PRIMARY' => array('column' => 'id', 'unique' => 1)
    ),
    'tableParameters' => array('charset' => 'utf8', 'collate' =>
'utf8_general_ci', 'engine' => 'InnoDB')
  );
}
```

3. After generating the first schema, you may need to modify your database by adding new tables, columns, and so on. Once you're done with your changes, save your schema again to keep the schema file consistent with your database structure.

```
$ Console/cake schema generate

Welcome to CakePHP v2.5.2 Console
-------------------------------------------------------------
App : myapp
Path: /home/user/myapp/
-------------------------------------------------------------
Cake Schema Shell
-------------------------------------------------------------
Generating Schema...
Schema file exists.
[O]verwrite
[S]napshot
[Q]uit
Would you like to do? (o/s/q)
[s] >
```

4. Pick o (Overwrite) if you're using a source versioning system such as git (best practice), or keep several file snapshots on disk if you want to use files to track schema changes.

```
[s] > o

Schema file: schema.php generated
```

How it works...

The CakePHP schema shell first checks for models defined in your application. It then extracts the associated table description from the database, reading all of the tables using the model file configuration. In this case, there is only one model, `Profile`, so the cake schema shell will look for a table in your database named `profiles` and retrieve the metadata information about columns and properties for that table. This then writes all table metadata to a schema file by default in `app/Config/Schema/schema.php`.

This file contains an array per table, describing the table columns, indexes, and parameters in a database agnostic syntax, which is shown as follows:

```
public $profiles = array(
  'id' => array('type' => 'integer', 'null' => false, 'default' =>
null, 'unsigned' => false, 'key' => 'primary'),
  'title' => array('type' => 'string', 'null' => false, 'default' =>
null, 'collate' => 'utf8_general_ci', 'charset' => 'utf8'),
  'content' => array('type' => 'text', 'null' => false, 'default' =>
null, 'collate' => 'utf8_general_ci', 'charset' => 'utf8'),
  'created' => array('type' => 'datetime', 'null' => false, 'default'
=> null),
  'modified' => array('type' => 'datetime', 'null' => false, 'default'
=> null),
  'indexes' => array(
    'PRIMARY' => array('column' => 'id', 'unique' => 1)
  ),
```

This is a unique property, as we only have one table and model. Several properties would be generated if more tables and models were present in your application.

It's always important to first generate an initial schema to be used as a base state to compare against. Keeping the schema updated will help you detect only the latest changes when a new migration is generated.

See also

▸ More details on schemas and migrations can be found at `http://book.cakephp.org/2.0/en/console-and-shells/schema-management-and-migrations.html`

Syncing changes

Now that we have a base schema file from our previous recipe, let's do a few changes in our database and schema file and apply those changes.

Getting ready

Set up the `profiles` table and `Profile` model, as described in the previous recipe. Then generate a starting migration using the schema console:

```
$ Console/cake schema generate
```

You can check whether the schema was generated correctly using the following command:

```
$ Console/cake schema view
```

How to do it...

Perform the following steps:

1. Let's make some changes to our `profiles` table. Change the length of the `title` column to 100 characters, and add a new column to store the published date of our profiles with the following SQL statement:

   ```
   ALTER TABLE profiles CHANGE COLUMN title title VARCHAR(100) NOT
   NULL, ADD COLUMN date_published DATETIME NULL AFTER modified;
   ```

2. We'll update our schema file with those changes as follows:

   ```
   $ Console/cake schema generate

   Welcome to CakePHP v2.5.2 Console
   ---------------------------------------------------------------
   App : myapp
   Path: /home/user/myapp/
   ---------------------------------------------------------------
   Cake Schema Shell
   ---------------------------------------------------------------
   Generating Schema...
   Schema file exists.
   [O]verwrite
   [S]napshot
   [Q]uit
   ```

```
Would you like to do? (o/s/q)

[s] > o

Schema file: schema.php generated
```

3. We'll now do another manual modification to our database, dropping the date_published column:

```
ALTER TABLE profiles DROP COLUMN date_published;
```

4. We then want to revert this manual change and sync our database with our schema file:

```
$ Console/cake schema update

Welcome to CakePHP v2.5.2 Console

---------------------------------------------------------------

App : myapp

Path: /home/user/myapp/

---------------------------------------------------------------

Cake Schema Shell

---------------------------------------------------------------

Comparing Database to Schema...

The following statements will run.

ALTER TABLE `myapp`.`profiles`

    ADD `date_published` datetime DEFAULT NULL AFTER `modified`;

Are you sure you want to alter the tables? (y/n)

[n] >
```

5. Enter y to apply changes and sync your database with your schema file:

```
Are you sure you want to alter the tables? (y/n)

[n] > y

Updating Database...

profiles updated.

End update.
```

How it works...

Once we had our first schema generated, we made some changes to our database structure, adding a new date_published field and modifying the title column in the profiles table. We then dropped the date_published field as an example change done in your development cycle.

Running `cake schema update` will read your last schema status (in your schema file) and compare it with your current database schema, providing the list of changes to be done in your database (via SQL). If you approve those changes, your database will be modified to match your schema file.

Adding the schema file to your source code repository (such as git, for example) will allow you to share the right database schema with your team and let them update it with no manual intervention or data loss. You can even edit this file manually and then update the changes to modify your database tables without using any SQL code at all.

See also

▸   The *Schema Handling* recipe

The Migrations plugin

The CakePHP `schema` shell provides basic database change management, but when your project complexity grows and you need more control over database changes, the CakeDC Migrations plugin is the way to go. Distributed under the MIT License, it's open source and totally free to use in your commercial projects.

Getting ready

We'll assume that you have a `profiles` table created in the database and the `Profile` model file in `app/Model/Profile.php` from our previous recipes.

First, install the CakeDC Migrations plugin either as a git submodule or by downloading the ZIP file and dropping the file contents under the `app/Plugin/Migrations` folder. Refer to the *Including a plugin* recipe from *Chapter 1, Lightning Introduction*, for more details.

Remember to also load this plugin in your `app/Config/bootstrap.php` file, adding the following line at the end of the file:

```
CakePlugin::load('Migrations');
```

Once the plugin is loaded, you'll have a new CakePHP shell provided by the plugin. You can check whether the shell is available and the plugin is correctly installed by running the following command:

```
$ Console/cake Migrations.migration status
```

How to do it...

Perform the following steps:

1. Create your first migration with the following command:

```
$ Console/cake Migrations.migration generate
Cake Migration Shell
------------------------------------------------------------
Do you want generate a dump from current database? (y/n)
```

2. We'll generate a dump, so answer with y (yes):

```
[y] > y
------------------------------------------------------------
Generating dump from current database...
Do you want to preview the file before generation? (y/n)
```

3. We also want to check the contents of the migration file prior to its generation, so this also answer with y (yes):

```
[y] > y
<?php
class PreviewMigration extends CakeMigration {

/**
 * Migration description
 *
 * @var string
 */
  public $description = '';

/**
 * Actions to be performed
 *
 * @var array $migration
 */
  public $migration = array(
    'up' => array(
      'create_table' => array(
        'profiles' => array(
```

```
            'id' => array('type' => 'integer', 'null' => false,
    'default' => null, 'unsigned' => false, 'key' => 'primary'),
            'title' => array('type' => 'string', 'null' => false,
    'default' => null, 'length' => 255, 'collate' => 'utf8_general_
    ci', 'charset' => 'utf8'),
            'content' => array('type' => 'text', 'null' => false,
    'default' => null, 'collate' => 'utf8_general_ci', 'charset' =>
    'utf8'),
            'created' => array('type' => 'datetime', 'null' =>
    false, 'default' => null),
            'modified' => array('type' => 'datetime', 'null' =>
    false, 'default' => null),
            'indexes' => array(
               'PRIMARY' => array('column' => 'id', 'unique' => 1),
            ),
            'tableParameters' => array('charset' => 'utf8',
    'collate' => 'utf8_general_ci', 'engine' => 'InnoDB'),
        ),
      ),
    ),
    'down' => array(
      'drop_table' => array(
        'profiles'
      ),
    ),
  );


/**
 * Before migration callback
 *
 * @param string $direction, up or down direction of migration
process
 * @return boolean Should process continue
 */
  public function before($direction) {
    return true;
  }
```

```
/**
 * After migration callback
 *
 * @param string $direction, up or down direction of migration
process
 * @return boolean Should process continue
 */
  public function after($direction) {
    return true;
  }
}
```

`Please enter the descriptive name of the migration to generate:`

4. Enter a custom description for your migration step as follows:

    `> initial migration`

    `Generating Migration...`

    `Done.`

    `Do you want update the schema.php file? (y/n)`

5. The plugin will manage the schema file to keep it updated and use it to compare future changes done in your database, so again answer with y (yes):

    `[y] > y`

    `Welcome to CakePHP v2.5.2 Console`

    `---------------------------------------------------------------`

    `App : myapp`

    `Path: /home/user/myapp/`

    `---------------------------------------------------------------`

    `Cake Schema Shell`

    `---------------------------------------------------------------`

    `Generating Schema...`

    `Schema file: schema.php generated`

How it works...

Once the plugin was installed, we started by generating our first migration using the `Console/cake Migrations.migration.generate` command from the shell. In this step, the CakeDC Migrations plugin checked our database schema and created the following:

- ▶ A new `app/Config/Migrations` folder to store all migration files
- ▶ A new `app/Config/Migration/1400843285_initial_migration.php` file to hold the first migration
- ▶ A new `schema_migrations` database table to manage the migrations that have been successfully run

Note that you may use the `-f` parameter to generate a migration for all your database tables, ignoring the restriction to have a model associated.

The last step in the process is to update our schema file. The database `schema` file is placed by default in `app/Config/Schema/` and is generated using the CakePHP schema shell. Refer to the previous recipes in this chapter for details on schema generation.

From now on, you can manage specific changes to your database and allow other developers to work on their changes at the same time. The CakeDC Migrations plugin will take care of detecting pending migrations and running them the next time you use the `run all` option, because all migrations that are already executed are consistently stored in the new `schema_migrations` database table. This new table will allow several developers working on the same project to share their database changes safely.

See also

- ▶ The *Including a plugin* recipe from *Chapter 1, Lightning Introduction*
- ▶ The *Schema handling* recipe

Injecting data

Sometimes you need to save initial data for your newly created tables or ensure that old data is consistent with one of your migrations right after you applied it.

The CakeDC Migrations plugin provides a way to alter your database contents while running a migration, so you can execute custom logic before or after a given migration. This custom code can be used to insert or update data in your database to keep your changes consistent.

Getting ready

In this recipe, we'll add a new feature to our blog which involves setting up a unique group for our profiles. We'll want to allow groups to be dynamic, so a new groups table and Group model will be created and associated with our Profile model.

We'll first create a table for our groups using the following SQL statement:

```
CREATE TABLE groups (
  id INT NOT NULL AUTO_INCREMENT,
  name VARCHAR(255) NOT NULL,
  created DATETIME,
  modified DATETIME,
  PRIMARY KEY(id)
);
```

Now, we will use our profiles table created earlier (shown in the following code):

```
CREATE TABLE profiles (
  id INT NOT NULL AUTO_INCREMENT,
  title VARCHAR(100) NOT NULL,
  content TEXT,
  created DATETIME,
  modified DATETIME,
  PRIMARY KEY(id)
);
```

We will add a new group_id field to it:

```
ALTER TABLE profiles ADD COLUMN group_id INT NULL;
```

We will also add a new Group.php model file in app/Model/:

```php
<?php
App::uses('AppModel', 'Model');

class Group extends AppModel {
}
```

How to do it...

Perform the following steps:

1. Add a new migration to sync the new groups and profiles changes:

    ```
    $ Console/cake Migrations.migration generate
    :) ~/html/skelapp $ mig generate
    Cake Migration Shell
    ```

```
-----------------------------------------------------------------
Do you want compare the schema.php file to the database? (y/n)
[y] > y
-----------------------------------------------------------------
Comparing schema.php to the database...
Do you want to preview the file before generation? (y/n)
[y] > n
Please enter the descriptive name of the migration to generate:
> adding groups
Generating Migration...

Done.
Do you want update the schema.php file? (y/n)
[y] > y

Welcome to CakePHP v2.5.2 Console
-----------------------------------------------------------------
App : myapp
Path: /home/user/myapp/
-----------------------------------------------------------------
Cake Schema Shell
-----------------------------------------------------------------
Generating Schema...
Schema file exists.
 [O]verwrite
 [S]napshot
 [Q]uit
Would you like to do? (o/s/q)
[s] > o
Schema file: schema.php generated
```

2. Now we have a new migration file generated in the `app/Config/Migrations/` folder; edit this new migration file and locate the `after` method:

```
/**
 * After migration callback
 *
 * @param string $direction, up or down direction of migration
process
```

```
 * @return boolean Should process continue
 */
  public function after($direction) {
    return true;
  }
```

3. Introduce the following content into this method to insert data once the migration has been run (we'll be inserting four groups in our new `groups` table):

```
public function after($direction) {
  $groups = array(
    'CakePHP',
    'PHP',
    'Servers',
    'Personal'
  );
  $data = array();
  if ($direction === 'up') {
    //now adding all missing products
    foreach ($groups as $name) {
      $data[] = compact('name');
    }
    $Group = $this->generateModel('Group');
    $saveResult = $Group->saveMany($data);
    return $saveResult;
  }
  return true;
}
```

4. Test your migration by running the migrations down and up:

```
$ Console/cake Migrations.migration run down
Cake Migration Shell
----------------------------------------------------------------
Running migrations:
 [1400846198] 1400846198_adding_groups
     > Dropping table groups.
     > Dropping field group_id from profiles.
----------------------------------------------------------------
All migrations have completed.


$ Console/cake Migrations.migration run all
Cake Migration Shell
```

```
------------------------------------------------------------------
Running migrations:
 [1400846198] 1400846198_adding_groups
     > Creating table groups.
     > Adding field group_id to profiles.
------------------------------------------------------------------

All migrations have completed.
```

5. Finally, check the data in the `groups` table of your database using the following code:

```
mysql> select * from myapp.groups;
```

```
+----+----------+---------------------+---------------------+
| id | name     | created             | modified            |
+----+----------+---------------------+---------------------+
|  1 | CakePHP  | 2014-05-23 16:55:00 | 2014-05-23 16:55:00 |
|  2 | PHP      | 2014-05-23 16:55:00 | 2014-05-23 16:55:00 |
|  3 | Servers  | 2014-05-23 16:55:00 | 2014-05-23 16:55:00 |
|  4 | Personal | 2014-05-23 16:55:00 | 2014-05-23 16:55:00 |
+----+----------+---------------------+---------------------+
4 rows in set (0.00 sec)
```

How it works...

We first generated a new migration using the `Console/cake Migrations.migration generate` command. Once generated, we then used the `after()` callback method present in the migration file to run some custom logic as part of the migration process.

On every migration, you have the option to run custom code before and after the migration process. You can also execute different code depending on the direction of the migration ("up" or "down"). Going "up" means applying a migration you hadn't applied earlier in your database, while going "down" is the opposite.

This is the perfect place to update your legacy data or load default data based on a configuration file. In our case, for example:

```
foreach ($groups as $name) {
  $data[] = compact('name');
}
$Group = $this->generateModel('Group');
$saveResult = $Group->saveMany($data);
```

This code will return an instance of the $Group model, where you can then use the array of $groups previously defined with a list of names to save them all in one shot, by calling the saveMany() method:

```
$Group->saveMany($data)
```

Note that we're using the generateModel() method to get a new AppModel instance, instead of ClassRegistry::init(). This is useful to allow migrations to use a custom database configuration, if required by the project. For this, you can always use the --connection option to set the database configuration you want to use, for example:

```
$ Console/cake Migrations.migration run all --connection admin
```

The "default" database configuration will be used if no --connection option is set.

See also

▸ https://github.com/CakeDC/migrations
▸ The *The Migrations plugin* recipe

Index

Symbols

$findMethods property 179
$hasMany property 170
$layout property 269
$path variable 79
$priority property 63
$product variable 15
$recursive property 14, 174
$responseClass property 107
$searchQuery parameter 196
$settings property 191
$validate property 29
_checkLockFile() method 254
--connection option 321
__construct() method 74
__d() function 16, 274
__dn() function 274
--exclude-plugins option 260
--extract-core no option 260
_findSearch() method 194
--force option 282
-f parameter 316
_getLockFile() method 254
* key 146
--merge no option 260
__n() function 16
--output argument 245
_processFile() method 78
_removeLockFile() method 254
_serialize key 67, 268
_stop() method 74
-t default option 287

A

Access 112
Access Control Lists. *See* ACL
Access Control Objects (ACO) 156
Access Request Objects (ARO) 156
ACL
  working with 146-161
AclExtras plugin
  URL 148
aco_sync task 161
Actions authenticate class 161
add() action 23
addInputType() method 99
add() method 22
advanced search 205-211
afterDisptach() method 62
afterSave() callback 284, 298
Ajax requests
  processing 68-72
allow() method 29
API
  versioning 114-119
App::uses() 94
ARO tree 161
AssetCompress plugin
  setting up 279-282
  URL 280
association keys
  using, URL 167
associations
  defining, at runtime 180-183

Auth component
URL 32
AuthComponent::user() method 127
authentication API
setting up 108-113
authentication classes
BasicAuthenticate 122
DigestAuthenticate 122
FormAuthenticate 121
authorize() method 132, 145

B

bake shell
about 290
URL 206
BasicAuthenticate, authentication
classes 122
beforeDisptach() method 62
beforeFilter() callback
method 71, 82, 146, 160
beforeSave() callback method 79
bindModel() method 182
block option 71
blocks
using 263-266
body() method 74
build command 282

C

Cache::remember() 57
cacheConfig option 281
cachePath option 281
caching
URL 279
CakeDC Search plugin
about 198-203
URL 204, 211
CakeDC Users plugin
URL 30
CakeEmail::deliver() method 216
CakeEmail class
URL 225

CakePdf plugin
about 271
URL 268
CakePHP associations
URL 164
CakePHP File Storage plugin
about 80
URL 80
CakePHP Imagine plugin
about 80
URL 80
CakePHP model
model unit testing, building for 297-304
CakePHP Upload plugin
about 79
URL 79
CakeRequest::is() method 82
CakeRequest::$params array 57
CakeResponse::type() method 62
CakeResponse class 62
CakeResque::enqueue() method 231
CakeResque plugin
used, for creating job queue 225-233
calculate() method 254
callback detector 80
callback methods
URL 32
change() method 279
changes, schema file
applying 310, 311
check() method 86
checkNotModified() method 89
ClassRegistry::init() method 57, 58
ClassRegistry utility class 62
clear() method 279
commonProcess() method 203
compact() function 15, 57
components, CakePHP
URL 17
Composer
using 33
conditions option 50
console API
creating 241-246
URL 246

containable **171**

containable behavior
used, for configuring models 171-175

content block 265

controller 159

conventions, CakePHP
URL 17

cookie() method 86

cookie_remove() action 86

cookies
configuration options 86
working with 82-86

cookies, configuration options
domain 86
httpOnly 86
key 86
name 86
path 86
secure 86
time 86

counter() method 15, 192

count() function 274

create() method 22, 30, 78, 112

cron shells
implementing 251-254

CRUD (create/read/update/delete) 7

custom authorize class 127-133

custom finder
creating 176-179

custom RBAC 141-146

custom route class
creating 53-58

D

dashboard() action 139

data
deleting, URL 25
inserting, in database 316-321
reading, URL 17
saving, URL 23

database
data, inserting 316-321

data validation, CakePHP
URL 32

delegate() method 103, 104, 113

delete() method 25, 86

deny() method 29

Dependency Injection
about 283-286
constructor 284
field 284
method 284

detector
using 80, 81

detector types
callback detector 80
Environment Value Comparison detector 80
Options-based Comparison detector 80
Pattern Value Comparison detector 80

DigestAuthenticate, authentication
classes 122

disableCache() method 90

dispatch($event) method 223

dispatch filter
creating 59-63

download() method 270

E

edit() method 22

element() method 22

end() method 22

Environment Value Comparison detector 80

error handling
about 90-94
URL 94

error key 78

Etag 89

event-driven process
using 217-225

event priorities
managing 234-239

event stacking 225

event system
URL 217

exceptions, CakePHP
URL 94

expires() method 89

extensions
parsing 65-67

F

Facebook API
  URL 140
Facebook app
  URL 134
Facebook authentication 134-140
fields key 126
file-locking
  URL 255
file() method 79
files
  downloading 33
  PDF content, writing to 271
  uploading 74-80
filter option 193-197
findById() method 15, 22
find() method 62, 78, 268, 274
fixture
  creating 286-291
flash() method 30
FormAuthenticate, authentication
          classes 121
form helper, CakePHP
  URL 23

G

generateModel() method 321
getMockBuilder() method 292
getOptionParser() method 245, 250
Git clone
  using 32

H

HABTM 163
HABTM association
  about 164-169
  URL 164
Has and belongs to many. *See* **HABTM**
Hash::extract() method 57
Hash::get() function 132
Hash class usage
  examples, URL 67
hash() method 112

header() method 74
helpers, CakePHP
  URL 17
heredoc syntax
  URL 72
Html helper, CakePHP
  URL 23
HTTP authentication
  about 121-127
  URL 127
HTTP cache
  handling 87-90
HTTP header 74
HTTP socket class
  URL 107
hyper-text transfer protocol
  URL 104

I

I18n shell
  using 255-260
implementedEvents() method 213, 216
includeCss() method 282
includeJs() method 282
index() method 14, 50, 274
init() method 112
inputs() method 22
internationalization, CakePHP
  URL 261
inventory_update() action 71
is_rating_modified field 254
is_uploaded_file() function 79

J

JavaScript Object Notation
  URL 107
job queue
  creating, CakeResque plugin used 225-233
join through association type
  using 169, 170
Jsend spec
  URL 104
json_decode() function 106
json_encode() function 62

L

language() method 53
languages
  handling 51-53
Last-Modified header 88
last_modified() method 89
latest() method 268
link() method 16, 22, 79
listeners 213-217
listing() action 67
load() method 103
login
  adding 26-31
login() method 30
logout() method 30, 113

M

mapResources() method 98
matcher functions, PHPUnit
  URL 297
md5() function 79
Migrations plugin
  installing 312-316
mock objects
  configuring 291-293
models
  configuring, containable behavior
    used 171-175
model unit testing
  building, for CakePHP model 297-304
modified() action 89
move_uploaded_file() function 79

N

nestedList() method 57, 274
next() method 15, 193
numbers() method 15

O

OAuth 2.0 specification
  URL 113
OAuth protocol
  URL 140

object relational mapper (ORM) 170
observer pattern
  URL 213
on setting 63
Opauth
  URL 140
Opauth installation, CakePHP
  URL 140
Opauth strategies
  URL 140
Options-based Comparison detector 80
out() method 245
output() method 271

P

paginate() method 14, 209
pagination
  about 13, 187-193
  URL 193
pagination options
  URL 17
Paginator component 193
Paginator helper 192
paramType setting 191
parent::match() method 58
parent::parse() 57
parentNode() method 158
parseCriteria() method 203
parseExtensions() method 67, 99
parse() method 57
parser
  importing 246-251
parseResponse() method 106
Pattern Value Comparison detector 80
PDF content
  writing, to file 271
PDF document
  generating 268-271
perform() method 231
permissions.php file 146
PHP constants
  UPLOAD_ERR_CANT_WRITE 78
  UPLOAD_ERR_EXTENSION 78
  UPLOAD_ERR_FORM_SIZE 78
  UPLOAD_ERR_INI_SIZE 78

UPLOAD_ERR_NO_FILE 78
UPLOAD_ERR_NO_TMP_DIR 78
UPLOAD_ERR_PARTIAL 78
PHPUnit installation
   URL 299
plugins
   CakePHP File Storage plugin 80
   CakePHP Imagine plugin 80
   CakePHP Upload plugin 79
   Composer, using 33
   files, downloading 33
   Git clone, using 32
   using 32-39
plugins, CakePHP
   URL 39
Poedit tool
   URL 261
postLink() method 25
Post/Redirect/Get design pattern
   URL 198
prefix
   adding 41-51
prefix option 51
prev() method 15, 193
PRG design pattern
   URL 204, 211
processPdfJob parameter 233
ProductsController class 13

R

rapid application development (RAD) 7
RBAC definition
   URL 146, 162
realm parameter 126
records
   adding 17-22
   deleting 23-25
   editing 17-22
   listing 8-16
   viewing 8-16
redirect() method 30
Redis documentation
   URL 225, 230

register() method 30
request handling
   URL 67
resourceMap() method 98
respond() action 73
response
   building 72-74
REST
   URL 99
RESTful resources 95-99
Role Based Access Control (RBAC) 141
role field 145
routeClass 57
Router::connect() method 53
routing prefixes
   URL 134, 146
routing solutions
   custom route class, creating 53-58
   dispatch filter, creating 59-63
   languages, handling 51-53
   prefix, adding 41-51

S

saveAll() method 184
saveAssociated() method 184
saveMany() method 184, 321
save() method 22
saveTestUser() method 133
schema
   handling 306-309
schemas and migrations
   URL 309
scope key 126
scriptBlock() method 71
script() method 71
SearchableBehavior 202
search option 193-197
sendEmailAlert() method 237
sequential ID
   versus UUID 14
service
   consuming 104-107

session, CakePHP
  URL 23
Session component 279
setFlash() method 22, 25, 30, 78
set() method 15, 57, 67, 78, 86, 265, 268
setUp() method 301
sharable() method 89
SimplePasswordHasher class 29
sort() method 15, 192
statusCode() method 73
stopPropagation() method 62, 239
stub method
  configuring 294-297
submodule. *See* **Git clone**
subscribers 213-217
switch() statement 62

T

tag() method 127
tearDown() method 301
template() method 271
test doubles
  about 291
  URL 293, 304
transactions, MySQL
  URL 186
  using 184-186
translation functions
  __c() function 274
  __dc() function 274
  __dcn() function 274
translations
  handling 272-275
type() method 74

U

uniqid() function 113
Universally Unique Identifier. *See* **UUID**
upload() action 78
UPLOAD_ERR_CANT_WRITE 78
UPLOAD_ERR_EXTENSION 78
UPLOAD_ERR_FORM_SIZE 78
UPLOAD_ERR_INI_SIZE 78
UPLOAD_ERR_NO_FILE 78
UPLOAD_ERR_NO_TMP_DIR 78
UPLOAD_ERR_PARTIAL 78
userModel key 126
UUID
  versus sequential ID 14

V

validate() method 113
View::extend() method 265
View::fetch() method 271
view($id) method 14
view() method 50
views
  caching 275-279**

W

web service
  exposing 99-104
will() method 294

X

XML view
  building 266-268

Thank you for buying
CakePHP 2 Application Cookbook

About Packt Publishing

Packt, pronounced 'packed', published its first book "*Mastering phpMyAdmin for Effective MySQL Management*" in April 2004 and subsequently continued to specialize in publishing highly focused books on specific technologies and solutions.

Our books and publications share the experiences of your fellow IT professionals in adapting and customizing today's systems, applications, and frameworks. Our solution based books give you the knowledge and power to customize the software and technologies you're using to get the job done. Packt books are more specific and less general than the IT books you have seen in the past. Our unique business model allows us to bring you more focused information, giving you more of what you need to know, and less of what you don't.

Packt is a modern, yet unique publishing company, which focuses on producing quality, cutting-edge books for communities of developers, administrators, and newbies alike. For more information, please visit our website: www.packtpub.com.

About Packt Open Source

In 2010, Packt launched two new brands, Packt Open Source and Packt Enterprise, in order to continue its focus on specialization. This book is part of the Packt Open Source brand, home to books published on software built around Open Source licenses, and offering information to anybody from advanced developers to budding web designers. The Open Source brand also runs Packt's Open Source Royalty Scheme, by which Packt gives a royalty to each Open Source project about whose software a book is sold.

Writing for Packt

We welcome all inquiries from people who are interested in authoring. Book proposals should be sent to author@packtpub.com. If your book idea is still at an early stage and you would like to discuss it first before writing a formal book proposal, contact us; one of our commissioning editors will get in touch with you.

We're not just looking for published authors; if you have strong technical skills but no writing experience, our experienced editors can help you develop a writing career, or simply get some additional reward for your expertise.

Object-Oriented JavaScript
Second Edition

ISBN: 978-1-84969-312-7   Paperback: 382 pages

Learn everything you need to know about OOJS in this comprehensive guide

1. Think in JavaScript.

2. Make object-oriented programming accessible and understandable to web developers.

3. Apply design patterns to solve JavaScript coding problems.

4. Learn coding patterns that unleash the unique power of the language.

Instant CakePHP Starter

ISBN: 978-1-78216-260-5   Paperback: 76 pages

Learn everything you need to develop a feature-rich CakePHP app, from installation to deployment

1. Learn something new in an Instant! A short, fast, focused guide delivering immediate results.

2. Focus on an iterative practical approach to learn the myriad features of CakePHP.

3. Learn about Models, Views, and Controllers as well as scaffolding, themes, behaviors, and routing.

Please check **www.PacktPub.com** for information on our titles

HTML5 and CSS3 Transition, Transformation, and Animation

ISBN: 978-1-84951-994-6   Paperback: 136 pages

A handy guide to understanding Microdata, the new JavaScript APIs, and the form elements in HTML5 and CSS3 along with transition, transformation, and animation using lucid code samples

1. Discover the semantics of HTML5 and Microdata.

2. Understand the concept of the CSS3 Flexible Box model.

3. Explore the main features of HTML5 such as canvas, offline web application, geolocation, audio and video elements, and web storage.

PHPUnit Essentials

ISBN: 978-1-78328-343-9   Paperback: 314 pages

Get started with PHPUnit and learn how to write and test code using advanced technologies

1. Learn how to install PHPUnit as well as how to write and execute tests.

2. Understand the advanced concepts of testing using test doubles and the continuous integration process.

3. A hands-on, step-by-step guide full of real-life examples to help you learn quickly and effectively.

Please check **www.PacktPub.com** for information on our titles